JAPAN UNDER TAISHO TENNO
1912-1926

A. MORGAN YOUNG

Volume 53

Routledge
Taylor & Francis Group
LONDON AND NEW YORK

First published in English in 1928

This edition first published in 2011
by Routledge
2 Park Square, Milton Park, Abingdon, Oxon, OX14 4RN

Simultaneously published in the USA and Canada
by Routledge
711 Third Avenue, New York, NY 10017

Routledge is an imprint of the Taylor & Francis Group, an informa business

© 1928 George Allen & Unwin Ltd

First issued in paperback 2013

All rights reserved. No part of this book may be reprinted or reproduced or utilised in any form or by any electronic, mechanical, or other means, now known or hereafter invented, including photocopying and recording, or in any information storage or retrieval system, without permission in writing from the publishers.

British Library Cataloguing in Publication Data
A catalogue record for this book is available from the British Library

ISBN 13: 978-0-415-58795-2 (hbk)
ISBN 13: 978-0-415-8450-3 (pbk)

Publisher's Note
The publisher has gone to great lengths to ensure the quality of this reprint but points out that some imperfections in the original copies may be apparent.

Disclaimer
The publisher has made every effort to trace copyright holders and would welcome correspondence from those they have been unable to trace.

ROUTLEDGE LIBRARY EDITIONS:
JAPAN

JAPAN UNDER TAISHO TENNO 1912-1926

JAPAN

UNDER TAISHO TENNO
1912 ★ 1926

BY
A. MORGAN YOUNG

LONDON
GEORGE ALLEN & UNWIN LTD
MUSEUM STREET

All rights reserved

PRINTED IN GREAT BRITAIN BY
UNWIN BROTHERS, LTD., WOKING

FIRST PUBLISHED IN 1928

TO THE MEMORY OF
ROBERT YOUNG
FOUNDER AND FOR THIRTY-ONE YEARS

EDITOR OF THE

JAPAN CHRONICLE

PREFATORY NOTE

JAPANESE usage has been followed as regards names in this book: surname comes first and personal name after. As regards titles of nobility, the highest attained is used throughout, to avoid confusion. In such a case as that of Viscount Kato, however, the title by which he was actually known has been used rather than the death-bed or posthumous title.

CONTENTS

CHAPTER		PAGE
I.	AN END AND A BEGINNING	15
II.	KATSURA AND THE MOB	25
III.	THE KOREAN CONSPIRACY	31
IV.	YAMAMOTO AND THE NAVAL SCANDALS	39
V.	JAPAN ON THE EVE OF THE GREAT WAR	49
VI.	THE OUTBREAK OF THE GREAT WAR	70
VII.	THE MAKING OF EMPERORS	82
VIII.	JAPAN'S REACTIONS TO THE GREAT WAR	90
IX.	TERAUCHI AND HIS CHINA POLICY	97
X.	EFFECT OF AMERICA ENTERING THE WAR	104
XI.	WAR PROSPERITY IN JAPAN	110
XII.	THE HARA GOVERNMENT AND INTERVENTION IN SIBERIA	120
XIII.	THE KOLCHAK ADVENTURE	135
XIV.	SOCIAL DEVELOPMENTS AFTER THE WAR	143
XV.	THE INDEPENDENCE MOVEMENT IN KOREA	154
XVI.	JAPAN AND THE PEACE OF VERSAILLES	160
XVII.	STRIKES, TRADE UNIONS AND PATRIOTIC SOCIETIES	167
XVIII.	THE EMPEROR	176
XIX.	THE MASSACRE AT NIKOLAEVSK	177
XX.	SHANTUNG AND THE CONSORTIUM	188
XXI.	THE HUNCHUN RISING	200
XXII.	A STRANGE RELIGION	209
XXIII.	MORPHIA REPLACES OPIUM	215
XXIV.	THE ANGLO-JAPANESE ALLIANCE	218
XXV.	THE PATRIOTIC CULT	225
XXVI.	THE GREAT DOCKYARD STRIKES	230
XXVII.	A CROP OF SCANDALS	240
XXVIII.	THE MURDER OF THE PREMIER	248
XXIX.	THE WASHINGTON CONFERENCE	255
XXX.	SITTING TIGHT IN SIBERIA	261
XXXI.	THE END OF THE SIBERIAN ADVENTURE	269
XXXII.	DISSENSIONS IN ALL QUARTERS	279

CHAPTER		PAGE
XXXIII.	THE OLD AND THE NEW	287
XXXIV.	THE GREAT EARTHQUAKE	295
XXXV.	THE HIGHEST AND THE LOWEST IN THE LAND	307
XXXVI.	A BETTER CHINESE POLICY	316
XXXVII.	THREE REMARKABLE TRIALS	321
XXXVIII.	POLICIES AT HOME AND ABROAD	325
XXXIX.	A STORMY CLOSE TO A SHORT ERA	335
XL.	THE TAISHO TENNO	340
	INDEX	343

JAPAN UNDER TAISHO TENNO
1912–1926

I

AN END AND A BEGINNING

HISTORY, says Carlyle, is like one of those noble reliefs carved by Greek sculptors which show a section of the everlasting procession that has neither beginning nor end; yet, to understand the fragment seen, it is needful to know something of the past, however imperfectly, and of the future we may speculate as we choose. The speculations will often be as near the truth as the records; for the facets of life are so infinite in their variety that the most painstaking recorder can only observe a few; and while historians in the West disagree strongly as to what is important in the annals of their own countries, they are likely to be at a greater loss to determine the significance of such aspects of Japanese life as are accessible to them. So profound a scholar as the late James Murdoch, for instance, presented a reading of Japanese history almost entirely according to Western standards of value. A Japanese philosopher would probably assign to such matters as the Zen philosophy and the Tea Ceremony a degree of historic importance that would seem ridiculous to a European but less ridiculous in the eyes of any of his countrymen than an attempt to consider Japanese history without reference to such influences.[1] Japanese history written by an Occidental, therefore, can hardly be satisfactory unless the writer is one of unusual erudition.

The difficulties, however, which beset the presentation of Japanese history by Western scholars, and which were still present to the writers of the numerous histories of the Meiji period, are considerably lessened when we come to a consideration of the last reign, named Taisho. During a half-century in which public attention was concentrated on

[1] As recently as 1922 Dr. Fujishiro Tetsuke described the Zen discipline and the Tea Ceremony as constituting Japan's cultural mission to the world.

foreign intercourse much that had been specially characteristic of Japan was modified, and thought took new shapes. When the Emperor Meiji died in 1912, it seemed as though Japan's transformation was as complete as it could ever be; yet the developments of the next comparatively short reign could as little have been foreseen, and are almost as surprising as those of the long period of Meiji. During those fourteen years Japan became the third maritime Power of the world both in naval strength and commercial tonnage; her warships swept the Pacific and Indian Oceans and the Mediterranean; her arms penetrated three thousand miles into Siberia and controlled China; she lent money to Russia, France, and Britain; her representative at Versailles enforced her will on a reluctant Europe; her officers took part in determining Europe's new boundaries; her manufactures were in the most eager demand in every country in the world; and her growing power so alarmed the United States that the President called a Conference at Washington to try to limit it, while the Congress passed a bill to prevent Japanese immigration. She exchanged representatives with the Porte and the Vatican; so far did the Japanese flag fly that Britain found it convenient to ask her ships to carry succour to an Atlantic possession which no British line could reach; Japanese scientists took their place in the vanguard of research; and Japanese speculators had to be reckoned with in the world's markets.

These things were as little foreseen in Japan as elsewhere, and even less expected. When the last and greatest tumulus was piled over the remains of the Emperor in the imperial graveyard at Momoyama there was a general feeling that a great epoch had come to an end. Nearly half a century of intense activity had ended in a certain lassitude. Enthusiasm had spent itself and there was a reaction. Japan was settling down into a rut. It was true she had fought two great wars, and had almost doubled her territory, but she had become not much more than a second-rate European Power; she shared with Europe a growing difficulty with budgets and a load of public debt; and she feared the advent of the labour troubles which were making themselves a serious factor in European politics. Pessimism was increased by the fact that the cost of labour was increasing more rapidly than manual skill, so that, while the need for foreign goods increased, the demand for Japanese manufactures did not keep pace with it. More than all this, it was feared that a period of political and commercial corruption had set in; that the patriotic enthusiasm that had brought about the great achievements of Meiji had evaporated; and that it had been succeeded by a selfishness and cynicism inconsistent alike with the tradition of personal honour and the essentials of national progress. Events in China also engendered a vague uneasiness. That ancient Empire, Japan's source of learning and inspiration since she first emerged from barbarism, had been both beaten and plundered; but the unquestioned traditions of fifteen hundred years cannot be forgotten in a generation; and the sight of China, under European inspiration, becoming a republic, caused grave misgivings in Japan, which had adopted European tutelage for the firmer establishment of her empire.

It has never been questioned that it was the forebodings arising from these circumstances which inspired the decision to name the era of the new reign "Taisho," or "Great Righteousness." "Meiji," or "Enlightened Rule," had been the name given to the previous reign, which began with the momentous determination to adopt a polity of European pattern. It had been intended to impress the nation with a sense of the high endeavour to which it was committed; "Taisho," similarly, was intended, perhaps less as a trumpet-call than as an admonition, to carry home to all minds the most urgent need of the time. A dramatic occurrence of the day was interpreted in a similar spirit. Profoundly as the nation mourned the death of a great Emperor, its emotions were more deeply stirred by the suicide, on the eve of the imperial funeral, of General Nogi, the hero of Port Arthur. Nogi had always lived up to the highest military ideals of

Japan. Stern to others, and most of all to himself, he allowed no personal feelings, no thought of his own comfort or advantage to stand in the way of his entire devotion to his profession and his country. A tale was told of how he had refused to see his wife when he was on service, though she had come a great way to meet him. Their two sons fell in the bloody assault on the Russian fortress—themselves, it has been said, the most notable casualties of the war on account of their nobility of birth and their military eminence; and the General's wife, with little indeed to live for, cut her throat in the traditional manner at the same time that her husband, sitting on his heels, ripped his bowels across with a short sword. The idea still persisted in Japan, either handed down from the ancient practices of the Yamato race or transplanted as a piece of ready-made archaism from China, of the devoted servant accompanying his lord into the realm of death, and this, no doubt, was in part the inspiration of the act; but more than that, as explicitly stated in his testament, Nogi's object was to call attention by his death to the nation's growing slackness in its pursuit of patriotic duty. The idea is one well understood in Japan, to which it came from China; it may even be found in India; and it has not in Asia the fantastic and even immoral aspect which it inevitably assumes to the Western mind.

Thus the reign of the new Emperor began with the most impressive admonitions to pursue the path of duty; but there was a widespread feeling that in the way before them the people lacked tried and trusted leaders. At the beginning of Meiji some young men of extraordinary character and talent had played a notable part in the reforms. Some, like Marquis Inoué, were in their youth proscribed as rebels because of their journeying into foreign countries in defiance of the prohibitions. Of these leading minds, in later years, were formed the Genro, or Elder Statesmen, a body unknown to the constitution and possessing no official status, yet all-powerful in directing the course of policy and deciding on the personnel of government. Of these the greatest statesman, Prince Ito, was dead, killed at Harbin in 1909 by a Korean fanatic. Prince Matsukata and Marquis Inoué were weary and losing their interest in affairs. Prince Yamagata retained in age his full mental vigour, and, enjoying an unequalled personal prestige, became the unquestioned oracle of the State. Ito, Yamagata, and Matsukata had been Premiers in a succession of Governments, while Inoué had great diplomatic experience; they had first been called together in council on the assumption of the Premiership by Prince Katsura, in 1901. Katsura had already been several times Minister for War, but was regarded as one of the newer men, and, though undoubtedly able, he did not command the same degree of public confidence as the men who were now appointed as unofficial guardians to the still tender plant of constitutional government. Katsura was succeeded in the Premiership by Marquis (later Prince) Saionji, and these two, having established their position, seemed destined to hold the Premiership alternately until, in the fullness of time, they should become Elder Statesmen themselves.

At the time of the new Emperor's accession Marquis Saionji was at the helm of the State, the Premier's direction of affairs being—according to this conventional metaphor—rather like that of a pilot, subject to the sanction or overruling of the captain; and the captain, nominally the Genro as a body, was actually, by dint of force of character, Prince Yamagata. Saionji, who was to be a prominent figure throughout the reign, belonged to an ancient and noble family of Kuge peers: that is, of the nobility of old Japan, before the new peerage, on the British model, was created. The Kuge were associated more with that almost mythical Court at Kyoto than with the active rule of the Shoguns in Yedo. Their elegant and elaborate idleness might well have led straight to degeneracy, but art and religious philosophy saved them, and, on their emerging into the garish light of a new day they were somewhat contemptuous of the military swagger of the westernised Samurai.

To belong to an ancient family is not quite the same thing in Japan as it is in Europe. The custom of adoption is so extensively practised that a line need never fail. Every concubine may prove as barren as the legal wife; brothers, and even cousins, may be completely lacking; but there are always promising sons of respectable families glad enough to be advantageously adopted. In the case of the Saionji family there was a tradition that took the utmost advantage of the right of adoption. From generation to generation the heads of the house have been bachelors, each in turn adopting a suitable heir, though the actual difference between this and the normal run of succession was not so complete as a Western reader might suppose. Saionji was one of the three distinguished brothers, the others being Baron Sumitomo, head of a great and honourable banking and business firm, and Count Tokodaiji, a Court Chamberlain, who both died during the reign of the Taisho Tenno.

It was noticeable throughout the later and more distinguished phases of his career, especially those years which included the Taisho period, that Saionji took office only under protest. There is no reason to believe that he was other than sincere in his declarations that he would greatly prefer to spend the evening of his life in quiet seclusion and studious ease; but he was urged to take up important tasks with the assurance that there was nobody else who could possibly perform them.

Though the Elder Statesmen enjoyed such prestige, they were subject in later years to a good deal of criticism, and a point much dwelt upon, especially after the death of Ito, was their predominantly military character. Actually, of course, this was simply an admission that Yamagata was the only one left who retained energy and will-power. Like the military men of Japan as a class, however, Yamagata was always wise enough to be satisfied with the reality of power, and cared little for flaunting it. Nor was there any very strong objection to militarism itself; it was the cost which evoked criticism. It was the period when Sir Edward (later

Viscount) Grey uttered the warning that if things continued as they were, civilisation might be crushed under the weight of its armaments. Japan had to keep the place that she had won in the war with Russia, and successive Finance Ministers found the cost of such eminence increasingly serious. The farther the Empire extended, the lengthier became the borders to be defended. The theory was maintained that the territory of a weak neighbour was liable to be used as cover by a strong enemy; this naturally leads to absorption of the dangerous territory, until the borders of the strong Powers are coterminous. It is a process which is not only morally objectionable, but which is inevitably unpopular in the territories absorbed, as it leads not only to political subservience but to occupation by an alien garrison, and the native population regards the garrison, with much reason, as a means of suppressing their liberties rather than defending their frontiers. Thus it was in Korea, where the General Staff demanded two new army divisions for the adequate protection of this new extension of the Empire. Saionji was opposed to this idea. He disliked the vicious circle in which military ideas move, he was not to be impressed by alarmist tactics, and, above all, he objected to the cost of thus expanding the standing army. Most of his Cabinet were with him; but General Uehara, the Minister for War, insisted, and when the proposal was definitely rejected by a majority of the Cabinet he resigned. The constitution required that the Minister for War and the Minister of Marine should be respectively a general and an admiral on the active list, so the last word was always with the defence forces, for no officer would be bold enough to accept a portfolio in defiance of the General Staff and the Admiralty Board. There was no other course, therefore, but for the whole Cabinet to resign. Uehara's resignation was handed in on December 2, 1912, and that of the whole Cabinet immediately followed.

The Elder Statesmen met to discuss the situation. With them were associated Marshal Prince Oyama, a distinguished soldier but a passive statesman, and Prince Katsura,

Katsura, having been twice Premier already, seemed to be regarded as one of the Elder Statesmen. What passed at the conclaves was, of course, not reported, but it was evident that there was a good deal of doubt as to what was the wisest course to pursue. Amidst these doubts precedent prevailed over better judgment, and, in accordance with the Elder Statesmen's advice, the Emperor, on December 14th, summoned Prince Katsura once again and commanded him to assume office and form a Cabinet. Marquis Saionji, who made no secret of the fact that he was glad to lay down office, received an imperial message according him still the consideration due to a Premier, and commanding him to continue to hold himself in readiness to serve his Sovereign. This, confirming the precedent created by Katsura's association with the Elder Statesmen, was regarded as establishing a rule that to be twice Premier was to qualify for inclusion among the Elder Statesmen; but though the reign thus began with an act that was apparently intended to perpetuate the Council, it closed in the certainty that after Saionji the institution would be extinct.

Even where there is general suffrage and the elected body really rules, it is not always easy to discover what is undoubtedly the will of the people. It was much harder in Japan, where there were no more than three million voters, where the party favoured by the Government in power was always successful at the polls, where the Diet was almost impotent, and where the Press, though ubiquitous, had no object except circulation. Perhaps there was no characteristic of Taisho more outstanding than the growth of public opinion, expressing itself sometimes through the Press and sometimes in spite of it. At the moment when Prince Katsura assumed the Premiership for the third time there was no doubt that the Press, which was almost unanimously hostile, was in substantial agreement with public opinion. Katsura had never been a favourite. A soldier at the helm of the State during the Russo-Japanese War might have been expected to become a popular idol; but Katsura was ambitious and arrogant, and his being a soldier counted against him badly at a time when there was a widespread feeling that the army, caring nothing for public opinion or for the hardships of the poor, had seized the country by the throat in its determination to glorify itself and to add to the people's burdens.

The abolition of the feudal system and the substitution of a constitutional Government at the beginning of the Meiji era did not abolish the prestige or diminish the vigour of those who had been most powerful under the feudal system. The old divisions were gradually becoming blurred; but just as the names of the old provinces held their own against those of the new prefectures, so too provincial centres of power and influence remained in the midst of a reconstructed administration. It was recognised that as the inevitable result of two successful wars, which had greatly increased Japan's consideration among the Powers, the army and the navy were the most powerful bodies in Japan, and the mainstay of the army and the navy had from the beginning been the vigorous clans of Choshu and Satsuma respectively. Actually there were many exceptions to the rule, just as, in the Gempei wars, the two sides became less and less purely representative of the houses of Genji and Heike. The names of the two clans were often combined and their influence criticised as constituting a Sat-Cho Government. Often they were rivals rather than colleagues, but would come to an agreement between themselves regarding their respective pretensions rather than be so weak as to exhibit their jealousies in public. At a time when the army was so unpopular, the navy had an excellent opportunity to press its claims, and the first act of Prince Katsura was not to create the two new army divisions for Korea—that he did not even begin to do—but to accept Admiral Saito's plan for naval expansion to the tune of three hundred and fifty million *yen* (£35,000,000), only asking that the navy be satisfied with three or four millions as the first year's contribution, and to camouflage the enormity of the scheme by talking of a preliminary programme for the expenditure of ninety millions. Saito's plan was for the construction of eight super-dreadnoughts and four battle-cruisers, and it became in later years an object of considerable criticism both at home and abroad. The plan grew as time passed, but considering that its inception was in the period of the English naval enthusiasts' slogan, "We want eight, and we won't wait," it is not surprising that the more thoughtful minds in Japan, contemplating the comparative poverty of their country, were appalled at the vastness of the outlay demanded even in the programme's early form. In addition to securing the new Premier's adherence to the naval programme, the navy party also secured an imperial command to Admiral Saito to serve as Minister for the Navy under Prince Katsura, as he had served under Marquis Saionji. But while the navy gained these advantages, no progress at all was made with the plan for the expansion of the army.

II

KATSURA AND THE MOB

PRINCE KATSURA had no sooner formed his Cabinet than meetings began to be held to denounce it. The situation was all the more uncomfortable because the annual session of the Imperial Diet was due to begin shortly, and the new Government had all its programme, including the budget, to prepare in a few days. Even Saionji spoke vigorously in public against the new Government, and the Seiyukai leaders Ozaki and Motoda carried on a campaign for constitutionalism which created a degree of political excitement hitherto unknown. The Diet began with its customary false start. Summoned at Christmas, it performed the preliminary parliamentary exercises, and adjourned till Japan should recover from the annual paralysis of the new-year holidays. It was January 21, 1913, when excitement really began. In a joint interpellation in the Diet, Messrs. Ozaki and Motoda asked who, at a time when Prince Katsura himself was Lord Privy Seal and Grand Chamberlain of the Court, advised the Emperor to command Prince Katsura to form a Cabinet. Who, they asked, recommended the Emperor to order Admiral Saito to retain the navy portfolio? And would the Government, they also inquired, bring in a bill embodying the army expansion scheme?

The immediate reply to these and other awkward questions was an imperial decree proroguing the Diet for a fortnight. It was a weak move, but things were getting desperate. The Diet, it was true, had no power, and could be dissolved whenever the Premier liked to ask for an imperial decree for that purpose. But this had never given stability to Japanese Cabinets, which were generally short-lived. During the short time that he had been in power Prince Katsura had borne practical testimony to his belief in the importance of parties by endeavouring to organise one to support his own Government. His efforts resulted, too late for any useful purpose, in the creation of the Rikken Doshikai, of which Viscount Goto was a leading spirit. Goto, like Katsura, commanded far more popular respect for his abilities than for his personality. Associated with Katsura as Minister of Communications, he did not increase his chief's popularity. Of his own career more will be said in its proper place. Another effort on Katsura's part to put a better face on affairs was the creation of a Council of National Defence, by which he apparently hoped to camouflage the army and navy with an array of highly respectable gentlemen behind whom they could maintain their position without its being subject to continual attack.

Much more effectual work was done during the period of prorogation by the Opposition. The Diet met on February 5th, only to be immediately prorogued again till the 8th, and again till the 10th. Disorders immediately broke out. As they left the Diet, bodies of men surrounded the members' 'rikishas, pulled them open, and, when they recognised supporters of the Government they beat them. The Young Men's Constitutional Society, which had arranged a meeting on the 5th for anti-Government oratory, found that the hall they had engaged was taken over for another purpose. They proceeded to a temple, but were ordered away by the police; so they rushed, now a disorderly mob, to Hibiya Park, excitement intensified by every ill-advised measure of suppression. It was recalled that the last time that civil disturbances had been seen in the capital was in 1905, during an earlier Katsura administration, when the mob demonstrated against the terms of peace made with Russia.

It was on the 10th that the trouble culminated. A huge crowd assembled at the entrance to the Imperial Diet. Opposition members arriving, and distinguishable by their wearing a white flower, were cheered as friends of the people. Mr. Inukai, the leader of the Kokuminto, or Nationalist party, was specially cheered, though he had taken a less active part than Mr. Ozaki Yukio and other Seiyukai, or Constitutionalist, stalwarts. Presently the news came that there had been a further prorogation. This infuriated the crowd, which broke up into mobs who went raging round the streets, bent on mischief. That the mob was very keenly interested in the constitutional issues at stake it would be impossible to maintain, for it consisted largely of 'rikisha-men and coolies of all sorts; yet even so far as they were concerned they had become infected by the feeling that the nation was being trifled with. A target for their fury was found in the offices of those newspapers which had supported the Katsura administration—and some which had not. The *Miyako*, the *Kokumin*, the *Yamato*, the *Hochi*, the *Yomiuri*, and the *Niroku* were attacked, some merely having their windows broken and others being destroyed by incendiaries. A motor-car was captured and destroyed. Police-boxes (the wooden huts with which the Japanese system delights to disfigure the highways) were overthrown and burnt. The police drew their swords, and several citizens were killed and many injured without any restoration of order. From Hibiya Park to Ueno Park the battle raged, and the police station at Ueno was burnt down. By seven in the evening a couple of regiments had been hurried in to protect the more important places and people, but fighting and destruction went on in the darkness. Thousands of plain-clothes men mingled with the mob and effected the arrest of many of the most active of the rioters. The fire brigades were turned out, and in some cases the mob cut the hose and prevented them from saving the buildings which had been set on fire, while in others the firemen deluged the crowd with streams of icy water which quickly quenched their zeal. By midnight all was quiet again, with several hundred under arrest or in hospital, as well as some in the mortuary.

Simultaneously there were riots in Kobe, Osaka, Kyoto, Hiroshima, and other places. In Osaka there was some destruction of tramcars and police-boxes. In Kobe the target of the mob was the mansion of Mr. Kodera, member of the

Diet for Hyogo, but, beyond the destruction of the fence erected (*more Japonico*) before the front gate to prevent that elaborate structure from being used, little damage was done.

One of the last efforts made by the doomed Government was the extraordinary expedient of advising the Emperor to summon Marquis Saionji and command him to make a compromise with Prince Katsura. Saionji gave the necessary assurance of obedience to the imperial wishes; but the politicians at large had received no command, and it only made men with ten times the activity of Saionji more determined than ever that the Government should be overthrown.

At the meeting of the Diet on February 5th, Mr. Ozaki made a speech which caused the greatest excitement. Speaking on a "no confidence" resolution, he went straight to the root of an important constitutional matter. To his interpellation regarding the identity of the responsible Ministers who had advised the Emperor to call Katsura to the Premiers and Saito to the naval portfolio, and whose signatures should be attached to such commands, Katsura replied that the imperial summons in these cases had been, not a command, but a "message." Ozaki hotly denied that there was any distinction. To draw such a distinction, he said, was to throw on the Emperor personal responsibility for mistakes. This was greeted by a great uproar: "Blasphemy! Treason! How can an imperial message be mistaken?" Not a bit dismayed, Ozaki returned to the charge with some home truths about ministerial responsibility and the abuses of performing despotic acts under cover of imperial commands. There are people, he concluded, "who always mouth 'loyalty' and 'patriotism,' and who advertise themselves as the sole repositories of these qualities, but what they actually do is to hide themselves behind the Throne and shoot at their political enemies from this secure ambush. The Throne is their rampart. Rescripts are their missiles."

All this had badly needed saying for some time past, but Ozaki Yukio was the first man courageous enough to say it. His enemies were even more unscrupulous than he had declared, for immediately after this incident it was reported that Mr. Wakabayashi, the official stenographer of the House of Representatives, was put on the retired list because he refused to mutilate his record in such a way as to convict Ozaki of disrespect to the Throne. The League for the Protection of National Institutions—an entirely new body composed of adherents of the Katsura Ministry—issued a manifesto denouncing Ozaki, in the course of which they said: "Our Constitution definitely states that the Emperor is divine and superhuman, and the fact of his sanctity cannot in its nature depend on the responsibility of Ministers of State. . . . If such imprudent words and immoral actions be left unquestioned, the country will be shaken to its foundations. . . . We appeal with tears to all patriotic hearts and hope they will make earnest efforts for the sake of the country."

From all this it will be seen that patriotism in Japan, whether more or less intense than in other countries, bore the same stigmata. But it needed physical as well as moral courage on Mr. Ozaki's part to take the stand that he did, for patriotic assassination was held in extraordinary esteem in Japan. The manifesto declared that Mr. Ozaki had earned himself obloquy for his disloyal utterances when he was Minister of Education. One of his predecessors in that office, Viscount Mori, had fallen a martyr to patriotic fanaticism. Because with his walking-cane he had moved aside the curtain of an imperial shrine—behind which there was nothing to see—a young man assassinated him; and in a few years' time the Minister of Education was forgotten, though he had been an unusually able one, while his murderer, a perfectly useless young man, had a shrine erected to his memory.

The case of the Katsura Cabinet, however, was beyond the help of patriotic slogans. Immediately after the riots Katsura tendered his resignation, the Elder Statesmen met again, and Admiral Count Yamamoto was summoned and commanded to form a Cabinet. Thereafter, till his death on

October 11th, Prince Katsura was little heard of. As Lord Keeper of the Privy Seal he had been expected to become a second Shogun—perhaps the reviver of the system of delegated responsibility so closely woven with all Japanese tradition. But ill-health forbade what ambition coveted, and this possibility, much pondered over at the time, was averted.

III

THE KOREAN CONSPIRACY

WHILE at home a constitutional struggle was in progress, Japan was making, in her new overseas possessions, those mistakes which seem inevitable in the ungrateful task of ordering the affairs of alien peoples. The annexations of Formosa and Korea had gratified national pride, but the thoughts of the nation were by long ingrained habit insular, and little real interest was taken in the new territory, nor was any sense of responsibility apparent. Those things were for the officials to see to, and there was not even a Colonial Department for members of the Diet to badger with questions. In Korea the Japanese authorities had a particularly difficult task. During the last days of the Hermit Kingdom even the outward decencies of diplomatic intrigue were cast aside, and in 1895 the Queen had been murdered by a gang of Japanese and Korean bullies under direction of General Viscount Miura, the Japanese Minister, and with the complicity of General Kusunose, Commander of the Japanese troops. Miura thereafter became a national hero and a political oracle, and Kusunose lived to become Minister for War. For twenty years before the annexation Korea had been overrun by Japanese ruffians and adventurers, and when annexation came at last, General Terauchi, a good soldier and strict disciplinarian, but a man with all the typical shortcomings of the military mind, was put in as Governor-General. Of the great differences between restoring order and governing a people General Count Terauchi had little understanding.

The Koreans themselves seemed unlikely to give very much trouble. The recalcitrants of the "Righteous Army" were easily scattered, and many migrated, suffering great hardships in the passage and even in the subsequent settlement, to Chientao, across the northern border, in Manchuria. The people in general had been reduced to apathy by long misgovernment and extortion. They clung tenaciously to many customs and usages, but their spiritual outlook had become as hopeless as their worldly prospects. There was much superstition, but nothing left worthy of being called a religion. A new force, however, was coming into being. After a considerable struggle against prohibitory laws, Christian missions had established themselves in the peninsula and, together with theology, brought education. Pupils of the mission schools learnt English, and their minds were flooded with a new light. At the time of the annexation there were the beginnings of an intellectual renaissance. Men with ideas are naturally suspected by the police, and the result of these suspicions was the growth of a "conspiracy case" which deserves a prominent place among famous trials and preposterous mares' nests. The conspirators were supposed to have made their attempts on the life of the Governor-General, Count Terauchi, towards the end of 1910, a few months after the annexation, but the hearing in appeal, which took fifty-two days, practically coincided with the stormy career of the third Katsura Ministry. Neither the original trial, in the previous summer, nor this elaborate hearing in appeal, however, excited the least interest in Japan. The few Japanese newspapers which mentioned it assumed the guilt of the accused, and did not trouble themselves with the story.

The story, however, was an interesting one, especially from the judicial point of view. Some time in 1911 a couple of men were arrested for burglary. Under examination they hinted that they knew things of which the police would be glad to have information. What were they—the doings of disaffected Koreans? Yes, that was it. Was the Simmin Hoi, the New People's Society, involved? Most assuredly. And the Christians, were they in it? Of course! Then So-and-so and So-and-so were in it? To positive knowledge. Thus began the building up of an extraordinary story. On the strength of the confessions of the burglars 123 men were arrested, and they were all examined until they all confessed. The first arrests were made in the Syen Chuen mission school, an American Presbyterian institution of which the Rev. G. S. McCune was principal, and the majority of the accused were either Christian workers or men known to belong to patriotic societies, or to have shown other signs of not approving of the annexation. The confessions contained vastly more material than was used at the trial. In some of them Mr. McCune was said to have been the most active conspirator, and to have instructed the conspirators that, when they assembled on Syen Chuen station, he would go up to the Governor-General and shake hands with him: by this means they would know whom they had to assassinate. Other American missionaries were implicated, but, when they demanded to be put on trial with the Koreans, the procurator affirmed the right to accept or to reject the contents of the confessions at will.

According to the story pieced together from the confessions, there was a conspiracy the first object of which was to assassinate General Terauchi. Comings and goings of the conspirators were detailed, dates and places given for meetings, and on several occasions when the Governor-General had passed through the stations of Syen Chuen and Pyongyang, both in North Korea, crowds of conspirators were said to have assembled, with pistols concealed under their coats, to murder him. Attempts at other stations were also mentioned. Asked why they made no motion to carry out their intent, the confessing prisoners said either that their hearts failed them, that the Governor-General was too well guarded, or that they were so struck by the majesty of his countenance that they were powerless to strike. At the trial one and all repudiated their confessions. Nearly all declared that they confessed under torture, of which they gave details; the rest said that they were bullied and bamboozled into confessing. Asked how it was that they had made, in some cases, identical confessions, they declared that they had merely answered "yes" to leading questions. This the procurator indignantly denied, whereupon one of the conspirators said that the procurator was right, for in his case, at least, the police had made him repeat the statement after them.

As for corroborative evidence, there was none. An old swordstick, an antiquated pistol, some empty kerosene boxes said to have been used for storing ammunition, school essays of suspicious loyalty—such were the exhibits. Of the original burglars who had started the whole thing, one was banished and the other the police refused to produce. One witness testified to the holding of meetings on two days, the dates of which he remembered because they coincided with his own and his son's birthdays. It being proved that the birthdays were nowhere near the dates alleged, the prosecution swept this aside as an unimportant detail. It is naturally difficult, after a year, to prove alibis, but such as were offered were rejected. For one of the attempts thirty men had, according to the confessions, travelled from Chyongju to Syen Chuen one morning. It was shown that that day only nine railway tickets had been sold. Then they must have walked, the prosecution declared. "Twenty-eight miles during the morning in a snowstorm is rather a strenuous walk," objected counsel, whereupon the prosecution declared that the question of how they got there was irrelevant: it was sufficient that they were there, and this was proved by the confessions. The prosecution remained silent regarding the implication of the missionaries, but according to Mr. McCune's own account, on the great day when he was supposed to have played Judas, he turned out, with his whole school, by official order, but did not know whom they had to meet. The boys in line obediently bowed at the order of the police when the Governor-General alighted from the train, and Count Terauchi, whom Mr. McCune had not met before, came and shook him by the hand, saying how pleased he was at this spontaneous welcome.

Such was the evidence on which six men were sentenced

to ten years' penal servitude, eighteen to seven years, thirty-nine to six years, and forty-one to five years. Seventeen were discharged, and two were liberated without being brought to trial, because, though these two had made confessions identical with those of several others, it was proved that at the time when they should have been on a railway station assassinating the Governor-General, they were in the hands of the police being examined on a charge of theft, a few common rogues having, apparently, been swept up in the net. The only newspaper in Japan which reported the trial was an English daily, the *Japan Chronicle*, still edited at that time by its founder, the late Robert Young, whose thorough exposure of the weakness of the case compelled some notice both at home and abroad. At the hearing in appeal, which ended in March 1913, the procurator was like one at bay. With a brusqueness amounting to persiflage, he brushed aside every argument against the case and maintained, in spite of all, that a story so elaborate could not be other than true. But in the end Baron Yun Chi-ho, Yang Ki-tak, Im Chi-chung, An Tai-kuk, and Yi Seung-hun were sentenced to six years' penal servitude, and Ok Kwan-pin was sentenced to five years. The other ninety-nine were acquitted. If it be asked why these six were sentenced on evidence that was not good enough to convict the rest, the only reply is that "face" must be saved and that these six were under very strong suspicion of disaffection. That Baron Yun Chi-ho, who had been ennobled by the Japanese Government because of his eager willingness to persuade his countrymen to make the best of things, was in any way guilty, is very doubtful. He was a man who combined uncommon gifts with timidity and irresolution. He had travelled, was a fine linguist, and was an enthusiastic worker for the Young Men's Christian Association. But an obsequious tool is always suspected by his masters, and he was in constant touch with men tainted by "dangerous thought." As a scholar himself, he was conversant with the literature of the worship of liberty, and he confessedly would have preferred Korean independence if it had been obtainable. Lyu Tong-sol, formerly sentenced to ten years, and now the only one in that class acquitted, was probably the only formidable man in the whole company. A fine soldierly man, he had been trained for the profession of arms, and had been with the Japanese Army in Manchuria. Perhaps the regard felt for his soldierly qualities counted in his favour at the last. Yang Ki-tak was a scholar and a journalist of great ability. Ok Kwan-pin was a youthful and enthusiastic orator. The others do not appear to have been of any particular importance beyond being men of some local influence and disliking the new régime. All were eventually liberated on the occasion of a general amnesty at the time of the Coronation.

It is highly probable that a Japanese historian recording the events of the Taisho era would not consider this trial of sufficient importance to deserve mention. Not only has it some importance, however, in the story of Japan's imperial expansion, but it illustrates, in unusually high colours, some of the Japanese conceptions of the administration of justice and the manner in which Chinese tradition has affected the working of a code founded upon European jurisprudence. In his address to the court the procurator remarked on the frequency with which prisoners' confessions were repudiated by them at the trial—especially in Korea. Koreans, he said, did not understand court procedure, for until the annexation Korean practice had been based upon that of China, in which, generally speaking, confession must precede punishment; and there was probably not a man in the peninsula who understood that he could be convicted on the evidence, apart from any question of his own confession. The procurator's admission that the Japanese were not free from the same idea could hardly be avoided, for the Chinese tradition hung heavily over the Japanese courts in spite of a whole generation of the administration of justice on a system selected mainly from the practices of German and French courts. The idea of the necessity of confession is a direct incentive to torture, and there was no lack, throughout the

Taisho era, of bitter complaints of torture, sometimes with fatal results, in Japan. More often the methods of forcing a confession fell short of inflicting physical anguish, consisting rather of threats and cajolements, and of wearing down the resolution of the prisoner by questioning him in relays until he despaired from weariness. The police may do this for an unlimited time—having the power to extend the legal limit at will; and then the procurator has his turn. The Preliminary Judge (practically equivalent to the *juge d'instruction*) then takes it up, and it was only by a reform introduced near the close of the Taisho Tenno's reign that the accused was granted the right to have legal advice or the presence of, and communication with, a lawyer even at this stage.

Several undesirable results necessarily follow such a system. The finding of the Preliminary Judge is announced as though it were a verdict, which in practice it is. The public trial is an almost unnecessary formality, and little evidence is referred to, the whole charge resting upon the procurator's recital of the facts. There is very little development of detective ability among the police when it is so much easier to force a confession; while the pleas of counsel are mainly confined to prayers for leniency, endeavours to discover a good motive or extenuating circumstances, and juggling with points of law in order to show that the code does not demand punishment. In the Korean conspiracy case this last feature was particularly noticeable. Japanese counsel in plenty did their best for the prisoners, but not one took the line that the whole thing was a cock-and-bull story.

The conspiracy case was a striking example of the viciousness of forced confessions. The police, being full of vague fears, fostered by their spies and informers, were probably deceived themselves, and really believed the story that they had helped to manufacture. But they did not deceive the Koreans, who knew very well that whatever might be true, the conspiracy story was not. The formation of a military school at Chientao, across the Chinese border, with the intention of striking a blow for freedom whenever Japan might be engaged in war, was referred to in the course of the trial as one of the objects of the conspirators. It seemed the most absurd of the many allegations made, but, with all its fantastical hopelessness, the existence of such a project was perhaps the only grain of truth in the mountain of chaff.

The military character of the government of Korea was accentuated by this exhibition of the dangers existing. It was already the rule that none but an admiral or a general on the active list could be Governor-General; in the place of police, in the country districts, there was a large force of gendarmes; there was a considerable military garrison; judges and magistrates attended court in uniform, with swords girt by their sides; and even school teachers were similarly accoutred to instruct little boys in the Japanese syllabary. For the time being the military method became more salient than ever, and dire trouble followed before, later in the reign, these conditions were ameliorated and an endeavour made to introduce a more reasonable form of government.

IV

YAMAMOTO AND THE NAVAL SCANDALS

The replacing of Prince Katsura by Admiral Count Yamamoto did not completely restore confidence. This able and distinguished naval officer was not a popular hero, and the common use of his personal name Gombei (always regarded as a typically rustic name, like Hodge) was not by way of endearment. One of the Japanese papers went so far as to say, "Now Gombei is Premier we shall see some big naval contracts." So long as the Japanese Press refrained from mentioning subjects specifically prohibited and made no allusion in any way slighting to the Imperial House, it might exercise a great deal of licence. The attitude of the great was always that it was too contemptible to be regarded. But the impudent words about naval contracts were ominous, for the Yamamoto Ministry ultimately was driven out in a storm aroused by naval scandals, though the Ministry was quite innocent of them.

Little remained after the appointment of the Yamamoto Cabinet but to rush the budget through the Diet, and it got through by the smallest possible majority. With the close of the session immediately thereafter, a period of peace for the administration succeeded. Viscount Goto did some stumping in favour of the Katsura party, but the Prince himself soon fell into the mortal illness which was to dissipate the misgivings aroused by his ambitions, and foreign diversions arose such as are always rather a relief to statesmen who are embarrassed by domestic criticism and discontent. The anti-Japanese campaign in California took shape on a large scale, though it was to be ten years before its definite culmination; and, nearer home, the breach between Canton and the north brought about a civil war in China. It was no sudden outbreak, but was preceded by months of intrigue. A syndicate of bankers of six Powers joined together to monopolise the lending of money to China—a plan from which the United States withdrew, President Wilson expressing a distaste for advancing money which the lenders would expect to be collected by diplomatic pressure and even by force of arms if the instalments were not forthcoming. The other five advanced a large sum to President Yuan Shih-kai, nominally for the reorganisation of the Government, though actually it was used for the purposes of prosecuting the war. In March the Southern leader, Dr. Sun Yat-sen, came to Japan and made speeches on the beauties of peace, but as soon as he returned there were many complaints of Japanese participating in Chinese revolutionary movements, and of Japanese officers being among the Southern troops. Some of the loudest complaints were made against Mr. Inukai, the leader of the Kokuminto (the Nationalist party), but he was one of the most honest of Japanese politicians, and the charge was not taken seriously in his case, though it was true that China was overrun with Japanese adventurers, ready for any profitable enterprise, and few gangs of bandits were without a Japanese chief or so, while Japanese military science was at the disposal of those who cared to pay for instruction and leadership.

But the Southern troops fared ill, and there was the confusion of factions and the frequent change of allegiance which from that time onwards became recognised as the most baffling characteristic of Chinese internecine strife. By August the case was hopeless for the Southerners, and Sun Yat-sen again fled to Japan. Yuan Shih-kai's henchman, General Chang Hsun, a barbarous and illiterate soldier of the old school, marched on Nanking, which had been the stronghold of the Southern forces, and though the gates were opened without resistance, on a promise being given of peaceful entry, the city was taken according to the only method with which Chang Hsun was familiar, with murder, rapine, and loot as the reward of the conquering army. The Japanese in the city took refuge at the consulate, and among them three hawkers or petty shopkeepers, in spite of the warning of the consul, ventured out to save their belongings, if possible. On their way they fell in with some of the plundering soldiers and were murdered. This incident had effects out of all proportion to its intrinsic importance. There were meetings in Tokyo at which vengeance was demanded, and on September 5th, four days after the sack of Nanking, Mr. Abe, Director of Political Affairs in the Foreign Office and one of the most capable men engaged in the direction of Japan's foreign policy, was murdered by a young patriot, who afterwards spread a map of China on the floor, sat on it, and committed *harakiri* (literally belly-cutting, a privilege formerly granted to gentlemen as an alternative to the executioner's sword and even yet esteemed a highly honourable means of suicide). This crime was committed as a protest against the Government's weak policy towards China. The authorities were genuinely shocked, but, after all, they were not unwilling to make a demonstration in China, where their ambitions for the future lay, and in a few years the story of Viscount Mori was repeated: the man of character and ability, who had been basely murdered, was forgotten, while the memory of his murderer, because his crime was the outcome of patriotism, was sedulously cherished and honoured. That the man who breaks the law for a good motive should be honoured is natural enough, though the *motif* is one that is somewhat exaggerated in Japanese history. Combined with an unfeigned admiration for bloody deeds, it has often led youths, whose vanity was their most conspicuous quality, to commit the most deplorable crimes.

It was remarked that the Nanking affair gave Japan an opportunity for settling outstanding questions in China, but this was to be reserved for a still more suitable time. The chief measure taken at the time was to assemble marines and civilians before the Japanese consulate at Nanking, while the Chinese troops were marched up to salute the Japanese flag and hear the Kimigayo played three times. General Chang Hsun did not attend this ceremony, and though he nominally resigned thereafter, he did not relinquish his post and was soon promoted to honour. But solid consolation came to the Japanese in an indemnity of 800,000 *yen*. Trouble had arisen over clashes between Chinese and Japanese in other parts of China, but the "second revolution" was over and its leaders were abroad with a price on their heads. The Chinese Parliament met; the whips, by strenuous efforts, managed to get the large quorum required; and Yuan Shih-kai was formally confirmed in the presidential powers that he had been wielding for long past. In less than a month thereafter he dismissed the Kuomintang members of the Diet, and the rumours began about his ambitions of making himself Emperor. These ended ultimately in disaster, but for the time and for many months afterwards he was master of the situation, and the Japanese, who had long known him as a strong and arrogant man, who cared little for their feelings, bided their time.

Other excitements soon began to occupy public attention in Japan. Katsura was dead and Goto had dropped his new party, the Rikken Doshikai, but there was no lack of opposition to Count Yamamoto's Ministry, as he was suspected of lacking any sincere intention of carrying on the policy of Saionji. When the Diet met in January 1914, the Government was immediately attacked for its extravagance in respect of the defence forces. But more sensational matters soon eclipsed the ordinary parliamentary recriminations. Mr. Shimada Saburo, one of the original members of the Diet, introduced the question of the naval scandals, just then attracting attention owing to the telegrams from Berlin about the trial of one Richter on a charge of blackmail. Richter's attempt was based on the alleged bribery of Admiral Fujii and Captain Sawasaki by the firm of Siemens, Schuckert & Co., in connection with the supply and erection of plant for wireless telegraphy. Soon the stories of bribery extended to the English firm of Vickers & Co., in connection with the building, through the agency of Mitsui & Co., of the battle-cruiser *Kongo*, which had arrived in Japan some three months before. The greatest indignation was felt at the disclosures. A crowd of forty thousand assembled in Hibiya Park to demonstrate against this corruption in quarters which had pretended to a sacred purity. A couple of days later the troops had to be called out, owing to the violence of the demeanour of the crowds at countless meetings. The mob sought self-expression in the usual way, by oversetting and burning police-boxes, and similar incidents, on a less extensive scale, were witnessed in Osaka, Kobe, and elsewhere.

Mob meetings are ephemeral, but the feeling of responsible men increased in intensity as the disclosures proceeded. When the Diet session approached its real business of voting on the budget, the Lower House, with unusual inflexibility, cut 30,000,000 *yen* from the naval estimates. There was excellent reason for such a course, for the country was trying to keep pace with the gigantic naval expenditures of England and Germany, without possessing the means to do so; but there can be no doubt that the estimates would have been passed easily enough but for the indignation aroused by the very idea that a service which had been regarded as incorruptible was, after all, on not much higher a plane than the banks, municipalities, and business concerns whose "scandals" were the daily pabulum of the newspaper reader. The action of the Upper House was more remarkable still. The Peers showed their indignation by cutting the naval estimates to the extent of seventy millions. The Lower House, which was attached to the English precedent of claiming the sole voice in money matters and the voting of supplies, was indignant and refused to endorse the Peers' action. All attempts to settle the matter by a conference between the two Houses failed. The Diet was within a day or two of the normal end of its session, and on March 23rd Admiral Count Yamamoto and all his Cabinet handed in their resignations.

Amidst all this turmoil the Empress-Dowager passed away, and the national grief at this occurrence brought a moment's quiet. She had had a hard part to play, and was held in the highest regard by her subjects, who well understood her difficulties. Brought up in the old manner, she had to come out of seclusion to preside over a Court remodelled on a Prussian plan, to receive foreign dignitaries, speak at annual meetings of the Red Cross and other newfangled inventions, and generally to play the weary part of a European queen, rendered doubly wearisome by its utter difference in costume, ceremonial, and even physical attitudes, from all that was made pleasant and familiar by use and tradition. With the uncomplaining patience and simple devotion to duty characteristic of the women of her race, the Empress fulfilled her part to the end. She had not even the consolation of carrying on the imperial line. She bore children, who died young, but the Emperor Meiji's only son who survived infancy was the one borne to him by the Lady Yanagiwara, one of the Court Ladies. Even after her death the Empress was not entirely free from this foreign ceremonial, strangely crossed by an ancient Japanese custom. It was on April 9, 1914, that she died, at her favourite country villa, but the ancient Japanese laws precluded the immediate announcement of her death. Those laws were peculiar. A nobleman who died outside his own house was in danger of disgrace and forfeiture. In the case of members of the Imperial Family, the chief difficulty seems to have arisen from the more easily comprehensible necessity of beginning the funeral procession in a place where the difficulties and expense of the elaborate ceremonial would be greatly enhanced. So, though everybody knew what the announcements really meant, an elaborate pretence was kept up of the Empress being still alive, she was brought back to Tokyo by train, and all the ceremony of an ordinary arrival at the capital performed. A quarter of an hour after the carriage had crossed the moat into the Imperial Palace her death was announced as having just taken place. She was buried near her illustrious husband among the imperial tumuli at Momoyama, outside the old capital of Kyoto.

To find a successor for Count Yamamoto was no easy task, and the Elder Statesmen were by no means easy in their minds. Prince Tokugawa, who would, had Japanese history not gone off on such a strange tangent, have been Shogun, was invited to form a Cabinet, but declined. Viscount Kiyoura was discussed; he was a man with immense prestige but of little driving force. Mr. Hara's chances were also canvassed, but the Elder Statesmen were unwilling to propose a mere popular politician, however able. Finally, and not without much reluctance, Marquis Okuma was summoned and, after some preliminary discussion, consented to form a Cabinet. It was not the first time he had been Premier. Before the alternation between Katsura and Saionji there had been the Okuma-Itagaki Cabinet—a brief excursion into rule by democratic leaders. Okuma was already aged—sometimes being spoken of as Japan's Grand Old Man. He was no favourite of the Elder Statesmen, for whom he showed no reverence whatever. He was extremely versatile, and even learned, yet was hardly ever seen reading. He was not wealthy, yet lived in a lordly style. He founded the private University of Waseda, of which he was half jocularly known as the Sage. During the agitations at the close of the last century over the revision of the treaties, a young patriot, who thought him too complaisant towards foreign demands, threw a bomb at him, as a result of which he lost a leg. This man was almost as much glorified as the assassin of Viscount Mori, and so liberal was Okuma that he actually subscribed towards the memorial celebrations, saying that, though the would-be assassin was mistaken, he meant well, and was inspired by a patriotic motive.

There was a fund of cheerful persiflage in Okuma's manner, and when challenged over a point of policy he would say unblushingly that to advocate a policy in opposition and to pursue it in office were two different things. It was said that the failure of Kiyoura to form a Ministry was due to the demands of the navy. How Okuma made his bargain with the navy was never stated, but it is certain that before he took office he agreed with the army's demand for two new divisions in Korea. This eloquent hater of the "clans" bowed to practical necessity and purchased office at this price.

The naval scandal went on, unaffected by the change of Governments. The court-martial was naturally much more expeditious than the civil process, and passed sentence in May. While the trial by court-martial was proceeding, Admiral Count Yamamoto, lately Premier, and Admiral Saito, his Navy Minister, were both put on the reserve list —a removal from activity which was generally believed to be connected with the scandals, though the most emphatic official assurances were given that this was not the case. Vice-Admiral Matsumoto, who was implicated in the "squeeze" over the battle-cruiser *Kongo*, built by Vickers, was sentenced to three years' imprisonment and to pay 409,800 *yen*. Captain Sawasaki, who was mixed up in the placing of orders for wireless telegraphy with Messrs. Siemens, Schuckert & Co., was sentenced to one year's imprisonment, and ordered to pay 11,500 *yen*. The sums suggest a computation of the bribes taken.

A picturesque incident occurred a week or two before these convictions. A play was staged in a public theatre at Kure, the great naval port in the Inland Sea, in which the story of the naval scandals was told dramatically. It might be expected that, under a westernised judicial system, this would mean prosecutions for criminal libel and contempt of court. No such retribution, however, followed a course of action so thoroughly in line with tradition. In Old Japan, which did not altogether come to an end with the Meiji Restoration in 1868, not only were there no regular newspapers, but there was an absolute prohibition of the publication of news of any important event. The classical instance of the effect of this standing embargo is the creation of the play *Chiushingura* ("The Treasury of Loyal Retainers," as we rather clumsily translate it). In the early days of the eighteenth century two noblemen quarrelled in the Shogun's palace, and one drew his sword upon the other. The man who drew his sword had been most shamefully abused and insulted by his enemy, but no extenuation was allowed for such an offence. He was commanded to commit *harakiri*, his fief was forfeited, his castle razed to the ground, his family and retainers were scattered. Forty-seven of these retainers (popularly known as the Forty-seven Ronin, or masterless men) awaited their opportunity with terrible patience and fortitude, and at last, having consummated their revenge, placed their enemy's head on their lord's grave. The result was inevitable. They all died by the same honourable mode as their master. Such a story caused a thrill throughout a country which had had two centuries of peace with the inevitable talk of the degeneration of the qualities of loyalty and courage. Publication being prohibited, the story was represented on the stage. The great Chikamatsu wrote a play on the theme, but the one that gained acceptance, and which is played even to-day throughout Japan, especially at the new-year season, is the joint production of three authors—the *Chiushingura*, which transports the story centuries back into the Ashikaga period, and presents it against the background of a famous Montague and Capulet feud of that time.

The naval scandal drama at Kure did not survive to become famous, so this explanatory digression may seem impertinent; but Mr. Tokutomi, a great scholar and historian, in his history of Japan, devotes a great deal of attention to an incident around which has grown up a voluminous literature, and which has, as he rightly conceives, so coloured the whole thought of the nation that its story cannot be understood apart from it.

The civil courts, as was to be expected, did not act with the same dispatch as the naval court-martial, and it was not until the middle of July that the Tokyo District Court passed judgment on a number of men implicated, including sentences up to two years' imprisonment on directors and other important officials of the great Mitsui firm, who had bribed naval officers in order to get the order for the battle-cruiser *Kongo* placed with Vickers & Co., for whom they were the agents. The heaviest sentence of all fell upon Rear-Admiral Fujii Terugoro, whose trial did not end till September 14th, owing to delays in obtaining some of the evidence against him. He was sentenced to four years' imprisonment and to disgorge the sum of 368,306 *yen* and 5 *sen*—thus meticulously did the court-martial calculate his profits on the deal. Two British subjects and a German also received sentences of imprisonment "with stay of execution" in two cases, and, in the case of the third, with an opportunity for removing himself beyond the reach of the law. The whole business was felt to be a public disgrace, since directors of the greatest mercantile firm in Japan and high officers of the navy, Japan's special pride, were involved. Commercial morality, it was generally recognised, was at a very low stage, but that the navy should be thus venial was a great shock to national confidence.

V

JAPAN ON THE EVE OF THE GREAT WAR

Though Japan played a very small part in the Great War, the conflict affected profoundly both her economic position and her place among the Powers, and it may therefore be of interest to pass in review the condition of the country at the time when the Western Powers became so much afraid of one another that they rushed into war. To the eye of a discerning traveller it would probably seem that the wonderful transformation of Japan that had been so much talked about was a thing that affected only the ports and large towns, and the aristocratic and industrial part of the population. Japan as a whole would appear to be in much the same condition of rural simplicity as it had always been. In a country so mountainous that the hills are never out of sight, the great majority of the people lived in villages dotted over the narrow plains and winding valleys. Wooden houses with roofs of thick thatch huddled together. Country mansions were few, and private parks very rare. Rice was the most conspicuous crop, because of its cultivation requiring a skilful levelling and terracing of the land, and up every little valley the terraces rose in higher and narrower steps till the land became so steep that it was impracticable to carry the process any farther. The village, with its Buddhist temple, the Shinto shrines with the *torii* as an open gate indicating the way of approach, the terraced fields, and the hills above covered with spruce fir or bamboo, the higher mountains with their great temples and groves of cryptomeria, the lofty ridges crossed by narrow roads doubling and twisting to surmount passes which were little less in altitude than the main ridge itself—these were the features of a country unrivalled in its own type of beauty and unfailingly picturesque. The cultivators were frugal and laborious, the older ones reminding one of the "strange gnarled creatures" whom the Lady Murasaki had described in her *Tale of Genji* nearly a thousand years ago. The straw cape, like a porcupine, was still the only raincoat; a piece of leather with the edge turned up round the foot and a string run through was the primitive shoe for field work. The bullock dragged an inadequate plough and a not much more adequate cart. With hoe and spade the cultivator made the trimmest rows on which food crops were ever grown. Up to their knees in mud, both sexes tended the rice-plant—the most exacting of all cereals. They cut it with a tiny sickle, hung it up to dry, stripped it stalk by stalk, hulled it in stone basins or dragged it by bullock-cart up steep valleys, where it was hulled by little water-mills. Even more hardy and primitive, the fishermen all round Japan's innumerably indented coast plied their trade with no other apparatus than their fathers had used from time immemorial. These were the foundations upon which Japan had built all that made her a Great Power.

But even beneath this appearance of unchanged primitiveness, nothing was as it had been. Though the crude science of ancient methods of manuring still reeked to heaven, the cultivator was also spending enormous sums on chemical fertilisers brought from the ends of the earth. His coarse clothes were no longer the product of village looms, but of mills using Lancashire machinery and Indian cotton, and using up his superfluous daughters in the early excesses of industrialism. The farmer also came into touch with great organisations—the Government tobacco monopoly and the official body which wisely encouraged sericulture; and the mulberry and tobacco crops, both exhausting to the soil, added greatly to the contacts of this primitive person with the world's chemical industries.

No doubt there were also many aspects of the village of 1914 that would have struck the old inhabitant at once, had he come out of a period of seclusion and seen the changes wrought in recent years. Particularly outlandish would have seemed to him the bicycle, the convenience of which, as a commercial vehicle, the Japanese were quick to recognise. The old high bicycle had hardly appeared in Japan at all; but in the decade preceding Taisho the standardised bicycle as evolved in England in the early 'nineties flooded the country, and it was only a small or a remote village which did not have a bicycle shop. Still more astonishing would a Japanese Rip Van Winkle have found the electric light. Already at the beginning of Taisho there were hydro-electric generating plants all over the country, besides some steam plants in the ports, and from village to village the lighting system was spreading, hardly any place being reckoned too small or out of the way so long as there was a natural supply of power at hand that could be used, and in a mountainous country blessed with plentiful rain there were such supplies in abundance. The electrical industries had already absorbed a great deal of capital, and great amalgamation schemes for efficiency, economy, and the enrichment of the promoters were frequently brought forward. For their simple cooking and parsimonious heating the villages still used charcoal, and Japan to no small degree escaped the dreadful coal-and-gas phase of Western civilisation. The electric light was an unalloyed blessing: it decreased the dangers of fire, and it gave a bright and cheerful "night life" to villages which had hitherto turned out the lamps and gone to bed as soon as might be; since the illumination was not worth the oil or the danger of fire. Doubtless electricity played its part in the promotion of "luxurious tendencies," against which statesmen were for ever preaching, though this does not seem to have occurred to these amateur economists. It brought a great deal of cheerfulness into village life, and turned the barber's shop into a village club.

Japan also began to pass through an experience which had come to Western countries a century before. The introduction at the same time of manufacturing industries and of an improved knowledge of hygiene and medicine brought about a rapid increase in population with new opportunities of livelihood. The land was not deserted for the town; indeed, with increased numbers of farm workers and new methods of cultivation, more and more land was brought under the hoe, and not only did farming become much more diversified, but there was a great increase in the output of the staple crops. These were the stimuli that underlay Japan's rapid expansion. For the new army, navy, and civil service the disbanded samurai and the old officials were available, increased production supplied the means of feeding the increased population which began to flock into the towns, and a successful war with China, rewarded with the cession of Formosa and a huge indemnity in cash, had provided means for expanding industries. These, of course, were merely salient features of general trends; cotton-mills came into being long before the war with China, and the cities had always been the goal of adventurous sons and pretty daughters. With the war against Russia, resulting in the transfer of Southern Saghalien and of the leases of the Kwantung Peninsula and South Manchuria Railway zones, and leading directly to the annexation of Korea, a phase of self-conscious imperialism set in, together with a sense of the heavy burden of a foreign debt of some two hundred millions sterling.

These historical events belong to the Meiji era, but the position in the early days of Taisho cannot be described without reference to them. In 1914 it seemed that there was little creative work left to be done, and a sense of stress and incompleteness prevailed. What had been achieved, after all? The Empire had expanded, but they had a debt and a population problem; two successful wars had been fought, but even these successes suggested that some more formidable Power might be the next enemy. The cities were crowded with a new proletariat which was complaining of the price of rice and developing discontent. And these cities were nondescript places. Tokyo in spots was beginning to look something like a capital, but for the most part it was like an overgrown country town. It was no longer true, as it had been a few years before, that, seen from the neighbouring hills, any city in Japan was simply a sea of grey roofs, unrelieved by towers or high buildings, or even by chimneys; but it was still so far true as to emphasise the slowness of the change. It was still true that the Japanese had not begun to understand the desirability of a good road, or even to consider its possibility, though here and there a wide thoroughfare had been made; and even in a city of two million inhabitants the same sanitation was in vogue as in the smallest hamlet. Bitter experience of epidemics and newly acquired knowledge of their cause had, however, led to the creation of excellent water supplies for the great cities; while the convenience of railway traffic was so well appreciated that electric tramways followed, not only in the cities, but between city and city.

Inevitably there were many jeremiads over the decay of ancient virtues. No longer, mourned some, did children obey their parents as of old; but at least parents were as ready as ever to sacrifice children, and the licensed brothels, the tea-houses, and so forth, which increased with the growth of the cities, never lacked dutiful daughters, who could by this means earn more for parents than by more humdrum occupations.

Wages in Japan, though rising, were still on an Asiatic scale. There is still a good deal of misapprehension on this subject, it being commonly supposed that by some mysterious law of nature the Asiatic is able to live much more cheaply than the European. Actually it is largely a matter of gold and silver being mediums of exchange relatively more scarce among Asiatic peoples. The rapacity with which the precious metals were pursued, from the days of the *conquistadores* in Peru till the latest gold rush on the Yukon, supplied the Occident with an abundant currency which kept pace with its increased production and population; but it is obvious that neither the Italian peasant living on maize, nor the

English seamstress sewing desperately for the price of a diet of bread and tea could be described as being on a higher standard of comfort than the Asiatic. The poor in Japan had long been inured to a rigid economy somewhat resembling that of the Scotch peasantry, and it is probably no more than the truth to say that no people have ever managed to be clean and decent on so spare a scale of living; but the commercial contact with the West, though it brought new opportunities of earning, also began to press hard upon the wage-earners by raising the prices of the necessities of life. Among the official classes wages were particularly poor, and it was a matter for surprise, not that there should be so much petty corruption, but that there should be so much honesty. Among the police, largely recruited in the beginning from the disbanded samurai, the good effect of a tradition of honour was particularly striking, it being rarely that men living on a wage that barely supported life would take a bribe, or even a tip for services rendered.

The position of the policeman in the social organisation must be briefly described. From of old the Japanese people had been very much under the tutelage of their superiors. In Tokugawa times (the two and a half centuries that preceded the opening of Japan to foreign intercourse) the regulation of the people's lives was carried to a point of almost incredible minuteness. The same tendency constantly reasserted itself under the new order, and the police were the ultimate interpreters of the regulations to the people. House-to-house admonitory calls were received with due politeness, and to such a degree was it carried that even on occasions of loyal celebrations the citizens of each street would be instructed as to suitable decorations to be displayed. There were some exceptions to this submissiveness: the *Eta*, or pariahs, though no longer officially recognised as a distinct caste, except under the term *shin-heimin*, or "new commoners," still lived in their own villages or ghettos, and of them the police had a wholesome dread, as they were rough and intractable. But in general the police were the rather pernickety guides, philosophers, and friends of the people.

Nearly fifty years of an intensive cultivation of loyalty also left its mark on the people. The danger of the country being rent by the powerful aid of foreign countries being offered to warring factions had impressed the men of the Meiji Restoration, and they had sought unity in the inculcation of a devotion to the Emperor that amounted to worship. The policy was an effective one with a people so well trained to obedience and so little accustomed to independence of thought. The treaties with the foreign Powers had secured freedom for missionary work, and the constitution had guaranteed religious liberty; so that, in order to reconcile Emperor-worship with Christianity, a formal official declaration was made that State Shinto was not religious, but only consisted of signs of respect and loyalty.

The adoption of general education and of conscription had greatly facilitated this inculcation of loyalty. The earlier teachers were inspired with something of the idea of leadership in a great national advance, and lived a self-denying life on small wages. By the time the Taisho Tenno came to the throne the earlier impulse showed signs of exhaustion; poor pay could not attract ardent spirits for ever, and complaints were often heard of the high incidence of tuberculosis among the underfed teachers of the elementary schools, while in the secondary and higher schools the incompetence of the teachers frequently provoked demonstrations on the part of the students. However, though the teachers did not always succeed in themselves inspiring respect, they taught respect for the Imperial House. The photographs of the Emperor and Empress were the most sacred possession of the school, and when they were uncovered on national holidays all bowed with the utmost reverence, and listened to the reading of the Imperial Rescript on education in solemn silence. The pupils were also marched out from time to time to Shinto shrines, where flexions and prayers were also covered by the official declaration that these signs of respect were not religious. However, as religious exclusiveness never had any part in the make-up of Japanese Buddhism, it was easier for the small sprinkling of Christians to make the best of it. The charge of lack of patriotism was even more dreaded in Japan than in other countries, and there was no lack of patriots of that kind which depend for their reputation on the loud denunciation of any lack of patriotism in others. The wooden clapboard schools were very inflammable, and from time to time schoolmasters lost their lives in trying to rescue the imperial portraits from a burning school—such was the dread of patriotic sneers.

The inculcation of patriotism in the schools was continued in the army. But here too the enthusiastic impulse of the early years of Meiji had spent itself. In Old Japan the bearing of arms was the occupation of a gentleman; and though the samurai were often spoken of contemptuously as "rice-eaters" (or, as they would say in England, "non-producers"), it was nevertheless a matter of some pride to be enrolled in the army, especially an army of such unheard-of efficiency; but the novelty wore off, and while the memories of the victory over Russia were sufficiently glorious, the sense of economic hardship was more enduring. Obediently to instructions, friends and neighbours turned out with lanterns in joyful procession on the nights when the new recruits joined up, but conscription was dreaded and evaded. Of this there were many signs. General Kusunose, Katsura's Minister for War, for instance, denounced the continual evasions, and a priest of the Zen sect of Buddhism got into trouble in 1913 for selling prayers and charms against conscription. This became a rather common offence, but the more prosaic and economically sound method of taking out insurance policies against conscription was not objected to. All kinds of young men's societies and ex-soldiers' societies carried on the patriotic work, and later on, as will be described in its proper place, were taken under the official wing for their more efficient direction along the path of loyalty.

At the same time there were currents setting in directions contrary to all official approval. Japan had adopted European ideas and institutions on an eclectic basis, but it was impossible to exclude those which had no official approval. With the growth of industrialism there naturally came into being expressions of discontent similar to those which had accompanied its growth elsewhere. Before the Russo-Japanese War the Socialist movement consisted mainly of an intelligent inquiry into the principles of Marx as interpreted in England, and as long ago as 1898 a railway workers' union was organised and engineered a strike. Later some more extreme ideas came in from Russia, and in 1911 Kotoku Denjiro and eleven others were executed, after a secret trial. They are supposed to have been guilty of a plot against the life of the Emperor. The Russian extremists always thereafter hated the Japanese bureaucracy for these executions, exhibiting then that vendetta hatred which they adopted in their war against royalty. Royalty killed them when it could; they killed royalty when they could. Authority regarded the anarchist as a venomous reptile; the anarchist regarded authority as a bloodthirsty tyrant. This feeling made no further development in Japan, so far as could be discovered, and in 1914 there was little revolutionary activity. Osugi Sakae was the ablest and most extreme of the leaders at this time, and close after him came Katayama Sen and Sakai Toshihiko. Dr. Abe Iso, a professor at Waseda University, was perhaps more influential with the general public than any of these, as he was less doctrinaire and did not theorise in terms of high explosives. It was common enough already for the police to prohibit Socialist meetings: indeed, the very word "Socialist" could hardly be used, and Socialist papers had to change their name and their printer frequently in order to maintain their propaganda. It must be confessed that there was sufficient reason for these men to feel that they were initiating a very necessary crusade. The textile mills in particular had earned themselves a bad name. There were cases, it was frequently reported, where the girls employed in the mills, working two shifts in order to keep the machinery running twenty-two or twenty-three hours out of the twenty-four, also occupied the dormitories on the same plan, the girls coming off shift going to bed in the quilts from which those going on had just risen. One case reported early in 1914 was that of some girls in a silk-mill who went on strike, and who were locked up in their quarters and starved into submission. About this time, perhaps in connection with the same affair, Dr. Abe Iso published a powerful denunciation of the exploitation of women and children. Happily there were some bright exceptions to this rule among employers, a few of whom did their utmost to promote the health of their employees. Conditions in general were such, however, that it was complained that girls were sent back to their homes in an advanced state of tuberculosis, sometimes infecting the rest of the family; and the recruiters of labour, in spite of the increase in the population, found themselves compelled to go to the remoter provinces, and even to Korea, in order to find girls who were ready to accept their offers. Korean labourers about this time began to arrive in Japan in considerable numbers, and their advent was regarded with some apprehension, the possibilities of labour troubles being clearly foreseen. But strikes were still rare and labour unionism only in its earliest infancy.

Along with the expansion of industry, commercial houses of a modernised type came into being, and a modern banking system covered the country. To supply these and the official posts there were a large number of secondary and higher schools. In a period of expansion and of the adoption of methods not native to the country, the higher school certificates were more highly regarded in the commercial houses of Japan than in those of Western countries; but the type of young man who seemed to be rendered unfit by his education —a type so common in India—had appeared in Japan, and had taken to journalism. Many very able men also began their public careers in this profession. Of all Japan's new features none was more remarkable than the growth of the

Press. Technically it was a strange hybrid, the compositor having boys to run about and gather the three thousand characters used in their cumbrous system of writing, but the rest of the production was quite modern, with rotary printing machines and an elaborate system of news-gathering and newspaper distribution. The Press enjoyed considerable latitude, and the law of libel offered hardly any redress to any injured person. Police prohibitions had to be strictly observed, and the Imperial House had to be kept free from the slightest hint of irreverence; but otherwise the Press might say almost what it liked.

Naturally the Press was the chief organ for the expression of political opinion, but there was a singular lack of party papers. The political parties in Japan were gangs under personal leadership; they stood for nothing except their own advantage; and the bigger newspapers found it hardly worth their while to link their fortunes with such bodies. Not that the papers themselves had any more principle than the politicians. They seldom pursued a line of political policy consistently, but were devoted to one object only—the increase of their circulation—an aim in which they achieved astonishing successes. But as a penalty they sacrificed much of the influence that they might have acquired, and nobody ever confessed to taking the least notice of what the papers said. Their strong line was already "stunts," for they copied American models, but they had not yet reached the height of their development in 1914. The most popular page of every paper was the one specially devoted to scurrilous and sometimes witty quips.

Japan's contact with the powerful West, and the general feeling that there was leeway to make up, together with the lively curiosity natural to the people, led to tentative mimicries in social, æsthetic, and even religious matters, the results of which were not always happy. Utility naturally was a strong factor, and in merchants' offices both the building and the clothing of the employees had generally assumed a Western aspect at the period under discussion.

There were a few large structures, the most striking, perhaps, being the Akasaka Palace, in Tokyo, of which the architect was plainly inspired by Versailles. Fashions in clothes went by fits and starts, as fashions do everywhere. At Court, European clothes had long been the rule; though the Court ladies often retained their special dress of an archaic style suggestive nowadays rather of Korea than of Japan. Women in general, after the early experiments, had shown no inclination to abandon a dress in which they appeared to great advantage for one in which they looked awkward and ill at ease. Besides, a change in dress meant a change in domestic architecture and furnishings, a change even in the rules of deportment and courtesy. The revolution was too great for the time. The foreign character of the ports of Yokohama and Kobe therefore remained rather conspicuous, although the greater part of the foreign trade had already passed into Japanese hands, and this provided a text for patriotic diatribes to politicians who were at a loss for anything useful to say, notwithstanding the fact that, in comparison with her population, Japan had fewer foreigners than any other country in the world.

Besides the mercantile class there was another body of foreigners who were rather conspicuous. With the opening of Japan there had been a spreading thither of the missionary enterprises which accompanied nineteenth-century imperialism, and in 1914 there were about four hundred missionaries of the various English and American sects, and about fifty-three thousand converts. There was also a good deal of Roman Catholic propaganda, mainly in French hands; and there was even a Russian Orthodox cathedral in Tokyo. Except in so far as well-capitalised missions and educational establishments inevitably have a tinge of the "Kultur" of the country that sends them, the Christian missions had no political effect. Nor can their success reckoned in converts be regarded as in any way remarkable. But they had an important effect of a kind that their promoters could hardly have foreseen. It was long since Buddhism had produced any prominent scholars or reformers. Fukuzawa, the great educationist of New Japan, had declared that the Japanese were not a religious people. Superficially there was much to be said for his point of view. Religious zeal, as understood in the West, hardly existed, and the Buddhist foundations were inclined to be somnolent. Between Buddhism and Shinto there had never been much competition, and before the Shinto revival of the eighteenth century Buddhism had almost swallowed up and absorbed the older faith. But Christianity, with its key-note set by the First Commandment, brought the priests out of their sleep. There was no sudden outburst of new life, but a gradual keying up of the tone and aspiration of the colleges, so that by the beginning of Taisho not only had Shinto become important and conspicuous as the obligatory cult of patriotism, but Buddhism was also more alive and active than it had been for centuries. There were also popular religions of recent growth, which numbered their adherents by hundreds of thousands. These were commonly called Neo-Shinto, and we shall have occasion to make further reference to them. Notwithstanding Fukuzawa's criticism, there were plenty of evidences of religion in Japan. Temples of singular beauty existed in great number, and if the ordinary citizen was content with a little ceremonial observance and with giving his subscription, while he failed to make any study of sacred books or of religious philosophy, he was not very different from the ordinary citizen elsewhere.

In one respect it might be said that the Japanese were not religious. They, like Buddhists in general, were more interested in the philosophic content than in the historical dogma of religion; and missionaries were not infrequently exercised in mind over the fact that their congregations tended to be ethical societies rather than associations of militant dogmatists. So much was this the case that seldom to a Japanese, though frequently to Western Christians, did the repeated efforts of Mr. Tokonami, one of the most eminent statesmen of the era, to promote a combine of Shinto, Buddhism, and Christianity, appear ridiculous. Mr.

Tokonami was almost the ideal "superior man" of Confucius —a very able and conscientious bureaucrat, and his constant endeavour was to turn all popular energies into a patriotic channel. On no scheme was his heart more set than on this entirely hopeless one of combining the three religions. Some of his countrymen went far beyond him in their regard for religion purely as a handmaid to national advancement, for they suggested the official adoption of Christianity for purely diplomatic reasons, Christendom finding it difficult to deal with a non-Christian State on terms of perfect equality.

Those who regard an intolerant adhesion to exclusive dogma as the only firm foundation for ethical behaviour were inclined to see in the Japanese lack of aptitude for aggressive creeds the cause for a slackness which seems to be more reasonably ascribable to youthful inexperience—if there is really such a thing as a "young nation" with a "collective mind." Certain it is that, while the courts and the police enjoyed an enviable reputation for probity, corruption was rank throughout political and mercantile life, and had even, as we have seen, invaded the great defence services. In the first years of Taisho there was a remarkable crop of frauds and embezzlements, and some extraordinary judicial decisions concerning them. Just as the good motive would always sanctify a political assassination, so too the prevention of a financial panic was held to be a sufficient excuse for complicity and participation in widespread frauds. Justice, according to the standards of the countries whose codes Japan had adopted, miscarried very effectively in cases where a show of dishonour being rooted in honour could be made, but at the same time there were constant complaints about the torture of accused persons, and even of witnesses in judicial inquiries—the legacy of Chinese precedents. Mr. Takagi, a member of the Diet, introduced a bill on February 3, 1914, for the prevention of judicial torture. He cited cases of distinguished men who had been grievously tormented, and asked, if this were so where men of eminence were concerned, what was likely to be the state of affairs when the poor and humble were under examination. Official lectures on the need for a higher standard of commercial morality were as common as they were necessary, but only the gradual discovery of the superiority of honesty as a business policy really brought about any improvement. Like other virtues, it was of a slow growth.

Concerning a people so eminently artistic as the Japanese, something must needs be said on the subject of their arts in any attempt to view them comprehensively in this period of change. Japanese art was a part of the civilisation that they had borrowed from China, and while Japan contributed little that was entirely original, Chinese art in Japanese hands had been subject to a development and refinement that gave it an added and characteristically Japanese beauty. The great Tea Masters of the fifteenth and sixteenth centuries studied æsthetics and laid down rules which curbed all exuberance and vulgarity of taste, so that Japan came out of even the luxurious Genroku period (1688-1704) the richer rather than the poorer for having cultivated extravagance for a change. The æsthetic parsimony in ornament, which became a national characteristic, enabled a poor man to have a house as tasteful as a rich one, and the influence of the Tea Masters was even more usefully displayed in beautifying common household utensils, so that even the housewife's bucket or dustpan was a thing of comely proportion and elegant design.

The flood of new ideas that set in with Meiji made deep inroads into established canons. The cheapness and utility of articles stamped out by the thousand in mills commended them to the people, while their strangeness made their ugliness and vulgarity less apparent. Even among an æsthetic people it is comparatively few individuals who are blessed with a true genius for æsthetic discrimination, and foreigners were frequently astonished to see how Japanese, with a correct and discriminating taste in the artistic productions of their own country, seemed to lose all idea of beauty or refinement when they introduced Western objects into their houses. Japanese were equally astonished to see what examples of Oriental art were preferred by Europeans, and when, under the stress of the new industrialism, they found that commercial success lay chiefly in the mass production of articles which had no beauty whatever, some began to entertain a sort of contempt for the beautiful because there was no money in it.

Painting, literature, the drama and music, were all invading Japan from the West, but at this time they were not yet assimilated in any special degree. Foreign models were in the stage of study rather than of adaptation, though in fiction there were some interesting experiments in various European manners. Enthusiastic students had for many years been doing very useful work, and the time was coming for assimilation, but had hardly come yet. Generally speaking the classic models retained their hold. There was a new style of drama in which women played; but the old style, with all men, was still in full vigour and untouched by change: it seemed as though a *mélange* of homicide and loyalty would never pall. The Japanese mind was struggling through a thick jungle of translations, and new words were being created by the hundred.

The peculiar nature of the Japanese language had the effect of increasing the difficulties of translation the more progress was made. The original Japanese language had had a limited vocabulary, concerned, like most unwritten tongues, with concrete things. The Chinese ideographs were no more suitable for it than they would have been for Anglo-Saxon; but their use had become inseparable from the idea of scholarship, and the use of the Japanese syllabary without the Chinese ideographs was a sign of ignorance. Hence, for all the new words that had to express the new ideas learnt from Europe, fresh Chinese characters and combinations of Chinese characters were continually being introduced. The language became daily more cumbrous, and year by year demanded more and more energy from the

JAPAN ON THE EVE OF THE GREAT WAR 65

Japanese student who had to master modern knowledge through so ancient a medium. The early engineers and scientists of Meiji generally acquired their knowledge through the medium of English or German, but as time went on the student was provided with textbooks in his own language the reading of which was hardly less laborious than the acquirement of a foreign tongue; and in the end, if he desired to prosecute his researches further than the textbooks, he had to learn the foreign language after all. A great fault with the Chinese vocabulary was that it resulted in the creation of large numbers of homonyms, and conversationally scientific or technical language could be understood only by the help of a verbose context. Moreover, Japanese doing original work could only invade the republic of science by being their own translators. No Western scientist could learn Sino-Japanese in order to keep up to date in Oriental researches.

The progress of women may be mentioned here. China had long ago imposed her ideal of womanhood, always in subjection to the male; but this had never entirely overcome the freedom of the Japanese woman. At keeping a shop or managing an inn, the Japanese woman often supplied the brains and the direction, in the manner for which Frenchwomen are famous in similar occupations. And as was the case with Frenchwomen, the Japanese woman was always at liberty to appear beautifully dressed in public. In spite of there being a *hetairai* class whose business it was to entertain, and to some extent set the fashions, Japanese ladies also cultivated a personal elegance and ladylike accomplishments which went deeper than the meretricious tricks of the geisha. With the new knowledge women were beginning to take a larger part and play new rôles. Their appearance on the stage has already been mentioned. At this time there were the early beginnings of an adaptation of the European ballet and musical comedy in which women monopolised the stage. In the new fiction women were prominent, which was only natural in the descendants of **Murasaki Shikibu** and Sei Shonagon, the most elegant and original writers of Old Japan. In painting there were several women whose work was extremely popular; and in education there were several notable pioneers. It was in 1913 that women began to invade Japanese universities, the Imperial University at Sendai accepting four female undergraduates who attended lectures with the male students.

There is nothing incompatible between insular prejudice and imperial pride except the defect that was mentioned in regard to the conspiracy trial in Korea, that the combination results in a lack of any feeling of responsibility for the territories acquired. So much was left to the police in Japan that it is not surprising that in the colonies the police and the military between them did everything. A few voices of protest were raised against abuses, but always ineffectively and too tardily. Shimada Saburo, who insisted on the dragging into the light of the naval scandals of 1914, was one of the few politicians with a sense of imperial responsibility. He protested against the alienation of land in Korea, where grants of royal land had been made at nominal rents for loyal service, and where the tenants, who regarded these grants, some of them centuries old, as equivalent to ownership, were evicted in order to facilitate Japanese settlement on the transfer of the royal properties at the annexation. On the whole, Japanese agricultural settlement was never a success, in spite of the efforts of one of the many "semi-official" concerns, the Oriental Colonisation Company; but Japanese naturally monopolised a large part of the new trade and manufacture—a course in which they were greatly assisted by a law which provided that a limited company must have Japanese representation on the directorate. A certain amount of gold-mining in Korea had been carried on by foreign concessionaires; there had been extra-territorial rights; and the British-American Tobacco Company had developed a large trade. Although the annexation was not supposed to affect treaty rights, no more mining concessions were given, extraterritorial privileges were extinguished, and an extension of the Japanese Tobacco Monopoly froze out competition. Finally, the prosecution of so many Christians in the Conspiracy Case served as a demonstration that the missions afforded no protection to their flocks.

In Formosa similar troubles occurred under dissimilar conditions. Here was less room for any attempt at colonial expansion, nor did the Japanese show any inclination for manual labour in this hot climate. The population was mainly Chinese, so long settled as to have characteristics of its own. In the mountains and forests lived the aboriginal inhabitants, famous for the tradition among them that only by homicide could a man prove his virility—a theory which, if sufficiently extended, would render birth-control quite unnecessary. The Chinese by long patience had come to an understanding with the head-hunters, but the new Japanese authority took other methods. From time to time brief items of news appeared as to the progress of a grand battue of the aborigines, a report in August 1913 stating that ten thousand men were operating against a tribe numbering three hundred. In April 1914 General Viscount Sakuma announced that the execution of the plans for subjugating the aborigines in five years was almost completed; notwithstanding which the operations of an aerial bombing police and the annual contraction of a high-power electrical cordon were carried on for another decade.

Relations with the Chinese inhabitants were also unhappy. Japanese sovereignty in itself was not particularly resented, but the intense interference of an official body quite inexperienced in colonial administration caused great offence. Endeavours were made by large Japanese companies to handle the tea trade on monopolistic lines; the camphor trade was made a Government monopoly, and Japanese capital created a great sugar industry in Formosa, for which the cultivators were compelled to grow the cane and to sell it to the mills at a price officially fixed. Finally, the Press was very strictly controlled, and little but official news allowed to be published. The story of a mare's-nest conspiracy in Korea has already been related. In that case the procurator declared that if the police had followed out its ramifications the number of conspirators would have been too vast for any possibility of arrest and trial. Apparently in Formosa it was considered that the limits of amenable conspiracy could be considerably extended, for in December 1913 three hundred were arrested, of whom six were condemned to death and about 150 to terms of imprisonment, some for as long as thirteen years. No independent investigation of this and other alleged conspiracies was ever made; they hardly attracted any interest in Japan. The culminating point was reached in a conspiracy where the number of death sentences exceeded a thousand—a massacre which was stopped half-way by the amnesty that accompanied the Coronation.

Japan's most successful colonisation had been in California, where about 150,000 had settled, and the racial prejudice that their presence excited became serious in 1914, when Californian legislators began their campaign for exclusion by law. The Japanese authorities were not at this time so much interested as they became later. Colonisation within the empire and penetration into Manchuria would have been preferred, and its hopelessness was not yet realised. But the exclusiveness shown in California and some of the British colonies evoked an irritated racial consciousness. Not that there was anything in the abstract principle that was offensive; Chinese coming to Japan to share in the new opportunities for labour had been sent back many times; the Japanese claim to share with Europeans extraterritorial privileges in China had been conceded; it was noted with satisfaction that the Government of the Netherlands Indies counted the Japanese as a European; in British India he was an unquestionable "Sahib"; and the Anglo-Japanese Alliance placed Japan in the comity of Great Powers even more definitely than had two successful wars. The new sense of superiority, based on consciousness of achievement instead of on insular conceit, made the implication of inferiority galling, though the economic causes of exclusion were well enough understood.

It was at the beginning of the century that Japan had won full recognition among the Powers, with the liberty to make any commercial legislation consistent with the new treaties, and the Taisho Tenno came to the throne when the protectionist policy quickly adopted was making itself felt. The whole reign was a period of increasing protection, and there was a considerable amount of official aid extended to all sorts of enterprise. The Bank of Japan was entrusted with domestic finance and currency; the Yokohama Specie Bank with foreign trade and exchange; the Banks of Formosa and Korea with colonial development, and several other "semi-official" banks with various forms of economic development. The Government was itself a large manufacturer of steel, woollen cloth, and various other products; and it allowed nobody but itself to trade in salt, tobacco, camphor, and ginseng (a totally inert substance which the Chinese buy under the illusion that it is an aphrodisiac). Shipbuilding and shipping were encouraged by generous subsidies; and almost any new industry, so long as its promoters had some political friends, could secure exemption from taxation, even if no more direct form of subsidy could be obtained.

VI

THE OUTBREAK OF THE GREAT WAR

SINCE it was only in the last few days before the outbreak of war that the people of Europe realised the seriousness of the situation, it is not surprising that in Japan the coming and the nature of the struggle were even less apparent. Nevertheless, by the end of July 1914 developments on the other side of the world, perhaps for the first time in Japan's history, eclipsed more local interests. The question what Japan would do was an engrossing one, and it was known that its answer lay in the hands of the Elder Statesmen, among whom the deciding voice was that of Prince Yamagata. The Foreign Minister of the time was Viscount Kato (then Baron), who had been Ambassador in England and was friendly towards that country. The Anglo-Japanese Alliance made it extremely unlikely that Japan would take sides with Germany, though Italy's repudiation of the obligations of the Triple Alliance and her subsequent entry into the conflict against her allies were hailed in England and France as proofs of the highest nobility. But the Alliance only required Japan's armed assistance when British interests in India and Eastern Asia were threatened, so it was not to be expected that Japan should enter the conflict except in the circumstances indicated. On August 5th, after an extraordinary meeting of the Cabinet, a statement was published expressing the Government's hope that the trouble among the Powers would soon pass away and peace be restored. "Should the war unfortunately continue, the Government hopes at least that it will be localised within its present area. The Government trusts that Japan may be enabled to observe the strictest neutrality. The Government's most careful attention to its obligations is necessary, however. Should Great Britain be involved,

Japan may have to take such steps as are necessary to comply with the terms of the Anglo-Japanese Treaty of Alliance, but it has hopes that the contingencies calling for these steps will not arise."

On the 8th it was reported that a communication had been received from the German Government requesting Japan to observe a strict neutrality, and that Japan had replied that this depended upon Germany not committing any acts which would disturb the peace of the Far East, for such acts would make the maintenance of neutrality impossible.

It was probably impossible that, with a fortress and warships in the Far East, Germany should be able to avoid disturbing the peace, especially when Britain was similarly and even better equipped. But it is certain that in the first days of the war the German warships examined British ships and let them go. No special developments were seen till the 15th, when Japan sent an ultimatum to Germany. It was noticeable that in the ultimatum Japan did not accuse Germany of any of the acts against which she had warned her, but presented her demands "in accordance with her obligations under the Anglo-Japanese Alliance to maintain peace in the Far East." The demands were that all German warships should leave Chinese waters or proceed to Kiaochau Bay and be there dismantled; that the German forts at Kiaochau should be dismantled; that Kiaochau leased territory should be transferred to Japan before September 15th for retrocession to China; and that an unconditional reply be given by August 23rd.

No reply was ever received to this Note. Viscount Kato stated that a disturbance to the peace of the Far East had come about through "the capture and attempt at capture" of British ships, and that the ultimatum had been sent at Britain's request. Considering the terms of the previous statements, the demands might seem rather excessive, but guarantees of neutrality have before in history been demanded in exceedingly provocative terms.

An absurd invention of the time has become a legend; it was said that Japan, in her ultimatum to Germany, used words almost identical with those in which Germany had, after the war with China, advised Japan to evacuate the Liaotung Peninsula. There was no more resemblance than always exists between one diplomatic Note and another, and there would have been little point in any such exercise of ingenuity, since France and Russia were at least equally concerned in the "advice." One of the curiosities of the time was the statement of "a Japanese of high rank" in the Shanghai Press that a Japanese attack on Kiaochau was unthinkable, because to take advantage of Germany's embarrassment would be contrary to all the canons of *bushido*, or chivalry, and would, moreover, be ultimately unwise, as Germany was sure to win. Before five months had passed *bushido* was destined to develop an elasticity beyond the imaginings of this authority. Before the expiry of the period of the ultimatum, Viscount Kato, the Minister for Foreign Affairs, announced that the Government hoped that German merchants and others would remain in Japan and continue their business; Mr. Ozaki Yukio, the Minister of Justice, declared that German subjects would receive full protection of their persons and property; and these and other officials exhorted their countrymen not to allow hostility towards an enemy country to express itself towards civilian residents. On Sunday, August 23rd, no reply having been received from Germany, Japan made a formal declaration of war, and proceeded with her preparations for the taking of Kiaochau. Marquis Okuma, Premier and Minister of the Interior, in announcing the outbreak of hostilities, assured Germans that they might continue without fear or anxiety in all lawful occupations, with rights of travel and of redress at the courts unimpaired. The Imperial Rescript announcing the outbreak of hostilities stated that warlike preparations had proceeded in the German fortress at Kiaochau, and that German warships menaced the peace of the Far East by hovering near; but it included no declaration that any breach of the peace of the Far East had been committed. Generous regulations exempting German steamers from capture were promulgated.

Whatever preparations the Germans had made elsewhere, there is no sign of anything like a war policy in the Far East. The reasons that brought Japan into the war on August 23rd were equally valid on August 4th, but in the interval the German warships did nothing in the way of concerted action, and when the siege of Kiaochau began there were still some of them in harbour there. Germans resident in Japan were called to the colours with no better objective than to be sent to Tsingtau, whence in due time they were taken back to Japan to spend four years in internment camp.

On August 27th, four days after the expiration of the ultimatum, Vice-Admiral Kato Sadakichi, in command of the Second Squadron, announced the blockade of Kiaochau Bay. A British contingent was sent to take part, and the exchange of shots between British and German warships was reported. The landing of the investing troops began on September 2nd, well out of range of the German forts. The Chinese protested against the forces of nations which all professed friendship for China settling their quarrels on Chinese soil, and notified the belligerents that they were expected to confine their operations to the area which they had up to that date invaded—a notification to which not the least heed was paid. Time was no particular object, and the preparations for bombardment were carried out without incurring any unnecessary risk. Big naval guns were landed and placed in position. There was some hand-to-hand fighting with parties of Germans who came out to reconnoitre and to try to harass the besiegers; but the problem never at any time presented any difficulties for the Japanese. When, however, the operations had been proceeding for seven weeks, the Japanese forces suffered a disaster in the blowing up of an old cruiser, the *Takachiko*, which, on October 17th, struck a mine (or, according to some of the naval experts, was hit by a torpedo) and was completely destroyed. Of her crew, only four or five were picked up alive, 280 losing their lives.

When the preparations for the bombardment were complete, the German commandant was invited to send non-combatants to a place of safety, and then the final stage of the siege began. For a week the garrison endured a hail of destructive shell, and, after a totally unnecessary loss of life, capitulated, and were brought to Japan as prisoners, to the number of some eight thousand, of whom not much more than three thousand were really soldiers. Considering the unlimited time and resources which the Japanese had had, their own losses were sufficiently heavy. In the final assault, in which the Germans made some desperate sallies, two hundred were killed and 878 were wounded. The naval losses, besides the *Takachiko*, included a destroyer, a torpedo-boat, and three trawlers, and the total casualties, by land and sea, totalled 1,700. The Germans lost five gunboats, a cruiser, and a destroyer, the more important vessels of the Far Eastern Squadron having set out on other business, some of which came to an end as far away as Cocos and the Falkland Islands.

The Tsingtau garrison capitulated on November 7th, and the Japanese forces arranged a triumphal entry a week later. There were some jubilations in Japan, congratulatory speeches, lantern processions, and so forth. General Kamio, who had commanded the troops, arrived, and was duly interviewed. But with this exploit Japan's enthusiasm for the war petered out. Perhaps there was some kindly feeling for a foe that, so far as Japan was concerned, was already beaten. There was certainly an underlying fear that perhaps the wrong horse had been backed. Scientists and militarists had alike been in the habit of admiring German achievement and method. Japanese journalists were far too cynical to take propaganda with a childlike faith. It was impossible, after the capture of Tsingtau, to discern any enthusiasm for the cause of the Allies, and the further services rendered were on a strictly businesslike basis, some of the terms of which were not disclosed until the delegates met at Versailles to discuss the terms of peace. After all, there was no particular reason why Japan should like one side better than the other.

Militarism received a sufficient fillip, however, to enable Marquis Okuma to fulfil the conditions on which the War Office had allowed him to take office. Even Mr. Ozaki Yukio, Minister of Justice and one of Japan's most liberal statesmen, spoke fervently of the need of strengthening the defences, and the two new divisions were created immediately after the capture of Kiaochau, bringing Japan's total peace strength up to twenty-one divisions, totalling about 250,000 men.

In Europe there was a disposition to do everything possible to drag Japan right into the war, no matter at what cost. America was deeply suspicious of the results of such participation, and even in England there was a disinclination to invite Japan to take too free a hand. It was at Britain's urgent request that Japan put the interpretation that she did on the Anglo-Japanese Alliance, but it was for political purposes, and not in the least from military necessity, that a force was sent under General Barnardiston to participate in the siege. There was a vague assurance given in Parliament that Japan's operations would not extend south of the Equator, but if any such proposal was made Japan rejected it. While the siege of Kiaochau was proceeding, Japanese warships were scouring the Pacific on the look-out for the other vessels of the German Far Eastern Squadron, and more particularly to take possession of the Marshall and Caroline Islands, the Australian troops having already made a dash for German New Guinea, which vastly exceeded in area the tiny islands of these archipelagos.

But while there was an ill-defined uneasiness regarding Japan's participation in the war, there was little definite idea as to the manner in which she would endeavour to profit by the conflict. Yet there were indications of the line that her ambitions were taking. During the siege of Kiaochau a force was sent to take control of the railway to Tsinan.

This line was built largely with German capital, and there were some German interests throughout its length; but the Chinese protested vigorously against this seizure of the main artery of the province and against the maintenance under Japanese jurisdiction of the now unnecessary "war zone." They also observed with some trepidation that the Japanese forces did not go home again after the capture of the fortress, while Japanese civilians of dubious character began to arrive in considerable numbers.

It had been determined in Japan that there had never been an opportunity like the present, and that there was never likely to be one so favourable again, for bringing China under Japanese control. Mr. Hioki, the Japanese Minister in Peking, visited Tokyo, where, on December 4th, he was handed his instructions by Viscount Kato, the Minister for Foreign Affairs. On a suitable opportunity he was to present to the Chinese Government a series of demands which came to be known as the Twenty-one Demands, the Chinese and Japanese always referring particularly to the number of items in any agreement. The Chinese Government itself provided the opportunity. After several requests to Japan to abolish the military zone in Shantung, China herself announced its abolition on January 16, 1915. Mr. Hioki regarded this as the suitable time indicated, and on the 18th he sought an interview with the President, Yuan Shih-kai, and presented the demands to him. These demands were arranged in five groups. Group 1 provided that the Chinese Government should agree to Japan's arrangements with Germany for the disposition of the Shantung concessions, that China should not lease or cede any coast-land or islands of Shantung to any other Power, that China should consent to Japan making a railway from Chefoo to Tsinan, and that a number of new open ports should be created in Shantung. Group 2 provided for the extension of the Port Arthur and South Manchuria Railway leases to ninety-nine years, for Japanese land-ownership in South Manchuria and Eastern Inner Mongolia, and for Japanese mining rights in these regions, for foreign loans and railway enterprises in these regions to be unpermissible without Japan's consent, for the engagement of foreign advisers in the same area to be similarly subject to Japan's consent, and for the Kirin-Changchun Railway to be handed over to Japan for ninety-nine years. Group 3 gave Japan a stranglehold on the Han-yeh-ping Iron Company on the Yang-tse—a concern in which Japan was already financially interested. Group 4 provided that China should not cede to any third Power any harbour, island, or bay along the coast of China.

The fifth group was the most extraordinary. It provided that the Chinese Government should employ influential Japanese as political, financial, and military advisers; that Japanese hospitals, churches and schools in the interior should be given the right of owning land; that the police administration in important places in China should be jointly Japanese and Chinese; that China should purchase over 50 per cent. of her war material from Japan, and should employ Japanese experts for such as was made in China; that Japan should have the right to construct railways between Wuchang, Kiukiang and Nanchang, Nanchang and Hankow, and Nanchang and Chaochow; that if China needed foreign capital for railways, harbour-works, or mines in Fukien, Japan should be consulted, and that Japanese subjects should have the right of conducting missionary propaganda in China.

As regards the second and the last of these demands in the fifth group, subjects of other Powers had similar rights; but as no Japanese ever showed signs of missionary zeal, while teaching the Chinese Buddhism would be carrying coals to Newcastle, the demands looked all the more sinister.

Not the least unusual feature of these demands was that they were handed to the President instead of to the Minister for Foreign Affairs, and that he was enjoined to keep them strictly secret. It is difficult, however, to keep such things secret, and on the 21st Dr. Paul S. Reinsch, the American Minister, knew about the demands. The thing got whispered abroad. Reuter's agent in Japan, who was also head of the Japanese official news agency, telegraphed that there was absolutely no foundation for the rumours—by no means the only untruth published abroad as "Reuter" in the Japanese interest. The Powers were not so entirely wrapped up in war as to have no time for diplomatic inquiries, in reply to which the Japanese Government sent them a summary of the demands, but excluding Group 5. In the course of the negotiations Japan revised the demands, making them a little more gentle in phraseology, and at the same time sent thirty thousand men into Kiaochau and Manchuria—ostensibly reliefs, but for the time being, at least, reinforcements. On May 1st, in the course of a reply to the revised demands, the Chinese Government said that "although Japan did not indicate any difference between this group and the preceding four in the list which she presented to China in respect of their character, the Chinese Government, in view of their palpably objectionable features, persuaded itself that these could not have been intended by Japan as anything other than Japan's mere advice to China."

China went on to point out that the last set of demands infringed the treaty rights of other nations as well as her own sovereignty. The reply was considered highly unsatisfactory by Japan, who, on May 7th, sent China an ultimatum, giving forty-eight hours for compliance. In the course of the ultimatum she undertook "to detach Group 5 and discuss it separately in the future." Mobilisation by land and sea began, and China capitulated. Treaties and Notes embodying all except these temporarily withdrawn articles were signed on May 25th.

The passage quoted from the Chinese reply exhibited extraordinary astuteness; for, while it brought in all the Treaty Powers by an appeal to their interests, it pointed the way to the only course by which Japan could explain the omission of the terms of Group 5 from her communication to the Powers; and, while it offered a sort of complicity in that course, it politely gave the lie in advance to the explanation afterwards made by Japan that the demands in the fifth group were only desiderata. Diplomatically Japan's procedure seems to have been culpably awkward, for by her consent, in the ultimatum, to withhold the most obnoxious demands until another occasion, she showed that up till that point they had been demands and not merely desiderata or "advice." Japan had strength, which is of more avail than diplomatic nicety, but when the war came to an end, only for competition in armaments to be resumed on a larger scale than ever, she found that the opportunity had passed, and at Washington she surrendered much of what she had gained by this hectoring diplomacy. Her gains lay in other directions, as will be described in its place.

One of the features of the negotiations with China was the prohibition of their discussion in the Press in Japan. It was known that negotiations were proceeding, but even in the Chinese papers the matter was not thoroughly ventilated, and it was not until near the end of the negotiations that an Osaka paper issued an "extra" containing the text of the demands, which was promptly suppressed by the police. Meanwhile there were other things of topical interest, especially the general election which took place in March. The aged Premier was one of the most vigorous of the political orators of the day, and a new Diet was elected that was overwhelmingly pledged to his support. The Government members numbered 211 (Doshikai 152, Chuseikai 37, and Okuma Association 22), and the Opposition 138 (Seiyukai 110, Kokumin 28), besides which there were 31 Independents. Popular as was the vigorous policy which it was known was being pursued in China, the victory at the polls did not make the Government invulnerable to criticism, and when the new Diet met in May the extraordinary session opened with some very sharp questioning. On June 3rd, Hara Takashi, the leader of the Seiyukai and destined to figure as Japan's Great Commoner, brought in a bill of impeachment, in introducing which he attacked the Government particularly in regard to its foreign policy.

Its dealings with China, he said, had only destroyed that friendship which was so essential for Japan's prosperity; under pretence of relieving garrisons, the number of Japanese troops in China had been greatly increased, thus threatening a friendly neighbour; Japanese residents had had to withdraw because of the consequent Chinese hostility, and, finally, a general distrust of Japan had been created among the Powers by the withholding of information of the fifth group of the demands when the purport of the negotiations was communicated to the Powers. Mr. Inukai, the leader of the Kokuminto, or Nationalist party, seconded this attack, but naturally the motion was thrown out on a division.

The attack was mainly dictated by party considerations, but it was not altogether unjustified. There had been anti-Japanese riots in China and a boycott of Japanese goods, while Japan's most ardent admirers abroad had been so shocked by the procedure that Mr. Hioki's tenure of the legation in Peking, and even Mr. (later Marquis) Inoue's holding of the office of Ambassador in London, had become excessively uncomfortable. Later in the year, however, the Cabinet was to suffer a much greater shock. Constitutional politics in Japan had been from the beginning a notoriously venal business, as was only to be expected both from the mistakes made in the apportionment of authority and from the novelty and exotic character of the institutions. The wholesale bribery of members of the Diet was no new thing; yet when in June it was disclosed that Viscount Oura, a Katsura henchman forced into the Cabinet as Home Minister, had distributed 10,000 *yen* among members in order to make sure of the vote for the two new army divisions, there was real public indignation. Ozaki Yukio, whose independence had been suspect when he became an advocate for the demands of the army, was especially revolted; he was well known as a liberal statesman and one who had remained poor because he would not jeopardise his political integrity; and he now openly denounced his fellow-Minister. Oura resigned not only office but title, a career hitherto distinguished thus ending in inglorious eclipse. Such a storm was there, however, that on July 29th the whole Cabinet tendered their resignations. A compromise was come to, however, in the jettisoning of Kato, the Foreign Minister, in the vain hope of criticism being appeased by the offering of a scapegoat.

VII

THE MAKING OF EMPERORS

PREPARATIONS had already begun for the coronation of the Emperor, another matter that formed a popular diversion. As in the case of the coronation of King George the Fifth of England, there was an unprecedented study of ancient forms and usages, with a view to carrying out the ceremony upon a more magnificent scale than had ever been seen before. The Emperor Meiji had been buried among his ancestors near Kyoto, and his successor was to assume imperial state in the ancient capital. The preparations were elaborate, and while even to a Western eye they were not lacking in a strange grandeur, their prodigious cost was probably their most impressive feature. For long beforehand the details of the archaic robes and other paraphernalia of the coming ceremony afforded readers of the popular Press material for interest in imperial affairs, particularly when it was announced that Her Majesty the Empress, already the mother of three sons, would not be able to participate in the coronation or wear the garments prepared for her on account of the approach of the birth of another child, after a considerable interval of time.

The coronation, so called for lack of a more accurate term in English, was a strange blend of Western display and Oriental religious rites. When the Emperor left the Palace in Tokyo on November 6th, with a great procession, to travel down to Kyoto, he wore the uniform of *generalissimo* of the forces, and had a military escort; but in the procession was carried the family ark or shrine, the *kashikodokoro*, containing the Three Sacred Treasures—the Mirror, the Jewel, and the Sword, traditionally handed down from the times of Amaterasu, the Sun Goddess, ancestress of the Imperial House, to whom is dedicated the Grand Shrine at Ise, whither the Emperor resorts to report all important happenings to the spirits of the Imperial Ancestors. The household shrine, concealed from the vulgar gaze by a covering of rich silk, was carried by thirty-two specially selected young men, and accompanied by a large number of Shinto priests in bright robes and tall black head-dresses. A special car had been prepared for it and attached to the imperial train.

The public ceremony of an imperial procession through the city was held on the 10th, and never in history had there been so many people in the old capital. An imperial procession in Japan has special peculiarities. Much attention is paid to physical altitude as implying social elevation. It has become a part of the language itself. A thing is asked for as being lowered; when it is offered, it is "lifted up." To sit on the floor before a superior is more respectful than to stand. Hence, when majesty rides through the streets, all upper stories offer to the gaze only the blank stare of wooden shutters. Even a doorstep is an improper elevation; and tens of thousands of the Emperor's loyal subjects sat on their heels in respectful silence on the matting which had been spread on the roads, and even bowed their heads, hardly daring to look, when the Emperor passed, the high-priest of an ancient faith, in a modern closed carriage.

Before the Shunko-den and the Shishen-den, halls of ceremony in the grounds of the old Palace, were ranged numerous long banners, and these, with other decorations, made a brilliant scene. The Shunko-den, one of the specially constructed buildings, with a small annexe called the Giyo-den, where the Emperor changed his robes, was the repository of the Imperial Shrine, and here the monarch formally received and took possession of the Sacred Treasures.

The only part of the ceremonies which could be described as public were those performed at the Shishen-den, a permanent building, in which a gorgeous canopied throne had been installed. Here, in view of a large concourse of officials and notables, the Emperor read the Rescript announcing his accession, and Marquis Okuma, the Premier, received it from his hands and read a loyal address in reply. The contrast between the young Emperor in his archaic robes and the aged Premier in his European morning dress was one of those to which the Japanese eye appeared to have accustomed itself completely, but which, to an Occidental, never appear anything but incongruous.

But there were ceremonies of a deeper significance to follow. The Emperor of Japan is in a peculiar degree head of the Church. As descendant of the Sun Goddess, he is not only monarch, but high-priest of the cult. He officiated as high-priest in the prolonged rites held in three specially constructed buildings—the Yuki shrine and the Suki shrine, and the Daijo-kyu. These buildings were of the most simple possible character, denoting the primitiveness of the times from which the rite dated. Of plain, undressed wood, with the bark on whenever possible, and with a simple thatch of mere handfuls of straw, they yet had an impressiveness of their own. Within, at each of the shrines in turn, the Emperor performed the rites, which included the tasting of preparations of rice and millet and the sipping of "white" and "black" saké—the national drink brewed from rice. These rites and vigils lasted into the hours that precede the dawn.

The other most conspicuous part of the doings connected with the coronation was the banquet held in a vast hall built for the occasion, and, like the rest, afterwards dismantled. Here the diplomatic body were present, and there were the archaic "no" dances by way of entertainment. It was the 27th of the month before the Emperor returned to the capital from these strenuous ceremonials. It is doubtful whether he was ever quite well again. Even as a child his health had been precarious, and throughout his reign he was never able to take a very active part in affairs. Through physical weakness he was compelled almost to carry on the tradition of seclusion in which his House had lived for so many generations.

As in Japan, so too in China there were events which diverted popular attention from the grievances in connection with the Twenty-one Demands. During the summer rumours began to be circulated regarding the imperial ambitions of President Yuan Shih-kai. The government of China as a republic was proving a difficult task. There had been a "second revolution," and one of the hints thrown out during the conversations regarding the Twenty-one Demands was that there were many Chinese refugees in Japan who might organise a third revolution. Japanese warnings against a revival of the Empire were sharply resented in China, as much by those who were opposed to Yuan Shih-kai as by those who approved the project of his seizing the Throne. There was at least an arguable case for an Empire, and none stronger than the fact that the provinces refused to pay tribute to Peking, leaving the Central Government with little revenue to be depended on except that arising from the Imperial Maritime Customs, which was year by year becoming more and more completely hypothecated for the payment of interest on foreign loans. Nevertheless when, early in December 1915, Yuan Shih-kai announced that he had consented to assume the imperial sceptre, the Powers which had not long before advanced him a large sum warned him of the dangers of his course. Mr. Obata, the Japanese *chargé d'affaires*, was particularly minatory. Japan, indeed, was in a position rather different from that of the other Powers. Tsingtau was held in far greater force than the Germans had held it, and Japan controlled the railway to Tsinan, while Shantung province, and to a smaller extent every province in China, was penetrated by Japanese adventurers whose manners were very much those of conquerors. The war had already had important effects on the metal market, and Japanese agents went throughout the wealthy province of Shantung gathering in the brass coinage, which was shipped by hundreds of tons to Osaka, where it realised twice as much on the metal market as it had done in exchange. In vain Chinese local officials, and even the

Peking authorities, forbade this export: they had no power to prevent it.

This was typical of much that went on in those days, and there were frequent collisions. The opium trade had nominally come to an end, but in the circumstances there was nothing to prevent Japanese importers bringing in morphia, which in its turn became a serious problem and a source of quarrels. Chinese students in Mukden threw a bomb into a Japanese druggist's, a demonstration for which their Government had to pay 25,000 dollars indemnity, and "incidents" were numerous everywhere.

Yuan wished to become Emperor in as constitutional a way as possible, but the process proved to be difficult beyond all expectation. There were murmurs from the beginning, but after he had signified his consent and began to make arrangements for ensuring his election, disturbances broke out everywhere. Yunnan declared its independence; there was an upheaval in Szechuan. It was uncertain what Manchuria and Mongolia would do, and in any case they had too many of their own troubles and anxieties to help very much. Even that old-fashioned illiterate warrior Chang Hsun was strangely reluctant to come out in support of his chief. From Kansu to Kwangtung outbreaks were reported, and by the middle of January 1916 the factions opposed to Yuan Shih-kai seemed to be in the ascendant. A conspiracy to assassinate the would-be Emperor was discovered, and Yuan let it be known that the proclamation of his imperial state, which it had been intended to issue at the beginning of February, was postponed. At the end of March he formally cancelled the plans for a monarchy, and during the next two months there were frequent rumours of his pending retirement. It was mainly owing to the irresistible advice of Japan that he finally abandoned his ambitions. It was clear that this would not immediately calm the disturbances of China, and amidst the unquenchable turmoil Yuan broke down in health. He became seriously ill suddenly at the end of May, and died on June 6th.

His death was greeted with expressions of open satisfaction in Japan. One eminent professor began an article with the remark that it was the best thing that could have happened, and the ever-indiscreet Okuma spoke in a Press interview in terms very unusual for the head of one State talking of the head of a neighbouring State. He even gibed at Yuan for dying at the early age of sixty—twenty years less than his own age.

Yuan, in truth, had been a bold and implacable enemy of Japan, and it was his final defeat that really killed him. He had been Resident-General in Seoul in the days before Japan compelled Korea to declare its independence, and in 1894 he had crushed an attempted *coup d'état* engineered by a group of Japanese. He was said to have told Japan, in the negotiations over the Twenty-one Demands, that if she sent an ultimatum China must give way, but that without it she would not—a decision which had far-reaching consequences. Having endured the ignominy of the surrender to a threat of armed force, he offered to join the Allies in their war against Germany. The Japanese saw clearly enough the object of this move—it would bring China and the Kiaochau problem to the Peace Conference. All Japan's weight was therefore thrown into the balance, and her protest against involving four hundred millions more in the horrors of war was carried through. Finally, he was ordered to abdicate the Throne from which he had hoped to resist the further encroachments of China's vigorous and powerful neighbour. He was a determined and resourceful man, of the old school in his habits of thought, of the new in his conception of China as a nation.

It was this idea, after all, native rather to the enemy camp in the south than to his own, which was to hold China together in the years that followed more than the determination and sagacity of old soldiers like himself. After Yuan's death, it is true, things went from bad to worse. China was overrun with Japanese adventurers who abused their extra-territorial privileges without limit. There were Japanese leaders of bandit gangs, there were Japanese editors of Chinese papers—for it was in this troubled period that the Chinese popular Press came into being. There were countless "incidents," and the Chinese authorities were roundly told that for the purposes of settlement the Japanese version of such incidents had to be accepted. Liberal Japanese protested against this sowing of hatred among the Chinese as bad business. These protests, however, had no effect.

It is a common fault in the foreign estimation of Japanese policy to ascribe to it too deep a purpose, too pure a consistency. The Japanese, like every other nation, are liable to changes of mood and purpose. On some questions they fluctuate and wobble, but on one there was a consistency and steadiness of purpose which may have been due to the guiding hands of Ito and Yamagata, or, if there be such a thing as a collective mind, an example of the working of that phenomenon. That consistent purpose was a determination to be undisputed masters of Eastern Asia. Perhaps the "advice" of Russia, Germany and France to vacate the Liaotung Peninsula after the war with China served to root and anchor this determination in the national soul. When the Great War left Japan practically a free hand, the opportunity of turning China's military impotence to a profit was obvious to the meanest intelligence. More liberal minds were not only revolted at the idea of bullying, but pointed out that it would be more profitable to have China for a friend than for an enemy; that the war would come to an end sooner or later; and that the Chinese would then endeavour, with the aid of other Powers, to score off Japan. To this there was an effective reply: national friendships and hatreds are very ephemeral things, and when the Chinese realised that nothing was to be gained by appealing to other nations against Japan, they would throw themselves into Japan's arms, who would then be generous and friendly. Among the military men there seemed also to be a conception of China as another India. In a country where the chief difference between the empire and the republic was that the

THE MAKING OF EMPERORS

provinces, instead of being ruled by viceroys, had fallen into the hands of venal and rapacious chiefs, who had little sense either of honour or of solidarity, it seemed likely that a few Japanese would soon be able to bring the whole country under the sway of a well-organised and disciplined power that knew its purpose. Such an ambition does not seem to have been expressed in so many words, but that it existed and was an inspiring force can hardly be doubted. The chief obstacles to its fulfilment were not the stubborn determination and shrewd diplomacy of men like Yuan Shih-kai, the President, and Chang Tso-lin, the dictator of Manchuria, but the sense of nationality that was spreading among the Chinese. For centuries Japan had learnt from China; now it seemed that China was learning from Japan.

VIII

JAPAN'S REACTIONS TO THE GREAT WAR

WHEN the Great War first broke out, there was a grievous depression in Japan. Nobody knew what to expect, and nobody was willing to make any engagements. Perhaps the first sign of cheerfulness was the realisation on the part of Japanese importers that they had good stocks of German dyes on hand and that the dyers would have to pay whatever price they demanded for them. For some years the tendency of imports to exceed exports had been a source of anxiety to Japanese economists, and it was noted with satisfaction that in the first half of 1915 exports exceeded imports, though the satisfaction was somewhat damped by the fact that the change was even more due to the decline in imports than to the increase in exports. Raw silk, Japan's most valuable export, remained at a price that made sericulture hardly worth while, and with trade depressed and good crops the price of rice was also very low. In Japan so large a part of the population has always been interested in the cultivation and sale of rice that, even in days when exports have disappeared and given way to imports for the feeding of the increasing population, a low price for rice is regarded with more alarm than a high one. Marquis Okuma, in order to create stability, organised official companies which bought silk and rice. It seemed to be a very speculative and dangerous measure, but perhaps the talkative old Premier was shrewd enough to see that prices were certain to rise, and events amply justified his action. Prices of metals soon began to soar, and by the time the war had been in progress for a year there was a boom on the Japanese stock markets. The imports of Chinese coins have already been referred to. At the same time that these were attracting public attention the Premier was also congratulating the country on the steady inflow of gold, and economists were writing and lecturing in terms of the greatest enthusiasm regarding the unexampled opportunity which the war had afforded Japan both to get rich and to make good her position on the neighbouring continent. By May 1916 the Finance Minister, Mr. Taketomi, was almost lyrical in his congratulations to the country on the development of its foreign trade.

The prosperity resulting from the war, however, did not increase popular enthusiasm for the cause with which Japan was allied. The constant representations from British and French sources that Japan should send troops to the Western Front were irritating, and evoked some astonishing arguments against such a course. Viscount Kato, just after his resignation of the Foreign Office portfolio, was reported as stating in this connection that there was no *casus belli* between Japan and Germany, the hostilities that had already taken place being those provided for in the Anglo-Japanese Alliance. In large measure this was true, but it is difficult to be at war with a country in one part of the world and at peace with it in another, and as the conflict developed Japan did, as a matter of fact, perform notable services in the Mediterranean. Other eminent publicists advanced such arguments as the uselessness of sending less than half a million men and the impossibility of sending so many. A distinguished soldier was quoted as stating that if Japan sent troops she would insist upon their being under Japanese command and not at the direction of any Allied commander. In reality the question of cost was more than sufficient to keep Japan out of the war in Europe. There was a remarkable convention very strictly observed in the Great War regarding costs. Anything supplied to an ally was paid for, generally at an extortionate price; but everything pertaining to a nation's own participation in hostilities that nation paid for itself. Japan could not be blamed for declining to ruin herself in such an enterprise as sending troops to France.

However, the conciousness that perhaps something was being left undone had the strange reaction of creating a feeling of resentment, and there is always a popular field for writings derogatory of neighbouring nations, especially where national vanity has been deliberately cultivated. When the war had been in progress about a year, it was not uncommon to see in the papers libels on the Allied troops, especially the British. In December 1915 the *Mainichi*, with the biggest circulation, published a bitter article asking "When is Britain going to begin?" A sensational organ, the *Yamato*, took up the cry, and in its columns a millionaire politician, Kodera Kenkichi, demanded the abrogation of the Anglo-Japanese Alliance, on the ground that it obstructed Japan's claims to economic and political paramountcy in China. A general officer discoursed on the growth of pro-German sentiment. This proved to be such a popular line that the *Mainichi*, always working with a single eye to circulation, spoke contemptuously of the *Yamato*, and followed this up with an article declaring that Japan was sick of the alliance. It even came to questions in the Diet, when Viscount Ishii, the Foreign Minister, confining himself to the attacks on the alliance, was content to say that there were undesirable elements in both countries, and that it was advisable for all to avoid indiscreet utterances. The storm still swelled, however; it was noted as a curious coincidence that it became loud with the advent of the Grand Duke George Michaelovitch to Japan in January 1916; at its culmination it had involved a great part of the Press, without a single important or energetic utterance deprecating such a campaign; but after the signature of the Russo-Japanese convention at the end of March it dropped. The Grand Duke was given a magnificent and obsequious welcome; he travelled on a Japanese battleship, and the Elder Statesmen, as well as the Premier and Foreign Minister, gathered at the Palace to consult with him. The resulting convention did not seem particularly important, but when, in the fullness of time, the Bolsheviks published the secret clauses, it was seen that they rather strained the obligations of the alliance with Britain.

By this time the war was regarded only as a heaven-sent opportunity to make money. Red Cross units had, it is true, been despatched, and the naval policing of Eastern waters and the convoying of Australian troops became a regular programme, but the victorious "war against Germany" was commonly regarded as already belonging to history. The promised liberality to German residents soon began to present difficulties, but so long as these did not go beyond the adoption by German firms of their Japanese employees' names there was nothing disagreeable in the restrictions. When it came, however, to Japanese names appearing on the British "black list," there was not only great resentment on the part of those whose profits were affected, but also a feeling of soreness in higher circles at the implication of disloyalty, and this feeling, naturally enough, did nothing to increase the popularity of the war even among those concerned with honour and prestige. It was found impossible to permit the promised freedom to follow lawful avocations, and as time went on there was a very tight grip indeed. German activities were brought to a definite end by the Japanese Government itself, which closed the Deutsch-Asiatische Bank in September 1916. But this curtailment of activities had begun at the instance of Britain, and there was an undercurrent of resentment at the idea of Britain cutting off profitable avenues of trade. When in March 1916 Britain began a series of restrictions regarding imports, the hostility broke out anew. In May there were demonstrations in Yokohama against British limitations of silk imports. The Osaka brush trade was in a similar state of indignation. In August lacquer and glassware were added to the list. In October knitted goods were banned. The earlier items were not of very much importance, but the trade in knitted goods had grown rapidly and was exceedingly profitable. Articles appeared in the Press about Britain's war being one of trade, not of arms, and warning the public that after the trouble with Germany was settled Britain would carry on her economic trench warfare against Japan. Meetings were held in Osaka and Tokyo at the beginning of November, at which the most emphatic resolutions were passed denouncing the conduct of Britain as inconsistent with that of an ally, and these resolutions were forwarded to the Government with a request for transmission. Negotiations did, in fact, take place, and very liberal concessions were made. It was pointed out that Japanese vessels were engaged in the trade with Europe, and that they could not be loaded entirely with heavy goods, so that nothing was to be gained by an entire prohibition. Later in the war, when the shipping problem became more serious than the indignation of Japanese tradesmen, embargoes were imposed, and the agitators quietly informed that it was useless to fulminate.

Further evidence was given during the Okuma Ministry's direction of affairs that Japan meant to make the most of her opportunity in China. Wherever in China a considerable number of Japanese took up their residence, Japanese police-boxes would be set up and, in the more important places, Japanese troops would be stationed. Collisions often resulted, the most serious of these being at Chengchiatun, in Manchuria, where there was a military affray in which several Japanese soldiers were killed or wounded. Long discussions followed, and Japan was more punctilious than before about informing the Powers of her demands. A good deal of criticism began to be heard in America, where it was remarked that the terms of settlement were to all intents and purposes a revival of the fifth group of the Twenty-one Demands, so far at least as Manchuria and Mongolia were concerned. Indeed, in these regions the demands exceeded those of eighteen months before, as they included requirements that every military commander in Manchuria and Mongolia should have a Japanese adviser, and that Japanese instructors should be engaged in all military schools. A final settlement, with a considerable abatement of these demands, came much later.

But the Okuma Ministry was drawing to a close. It was bold, and even spectacular, in its acts. The old Marquis was at the helm at the important crisis of the outbreak of war; he had embarked on a policy of successful aggression in China which most of his countrymen frankly admired. He had made daring deals in rice and silk, and had proved them to be good business. Above all, he saw the country pass from a state of commercial depression to one of unprecedented prosperity. New industries were started on all sides, often with bountiful subsidies, a special and lasting effort being made in the manufacture of electrical apparatus. Ships were in such demand and the supply of shipbuilding materials was so scarce that the firm of Suzuki, ordering a new steamer in September 1916, had to pay the unprecedented price of 385 *yen* (then about £40) a ton. The scenes on the stock exchanges were described as fit only for a madhouse. In July it was announced that payments for the supply of war materials to Russia were over eighty million *yen* in arrears; but when in September the Russian Government placed seventy millions in treasury bills on the Japanese market, not only were they immediately subscribed, but there were bitter complaints because the money was not used for buying more stores, but for paying off liabilities already incurred. Ten million *yen's* worth of British treasury bills had already been taken up, and it was with no small satisfaction that Japanese found their country in a position to lend money to first-class Powers instead of being, as had been the case hitherto, a very poor relation.

Among the many acts by which Marquis Okuma pandered to the growing megalomania was the issue of decorations for the Kiaochau campaign to the number of 120,000, though not much more than 6,000 soldiers had taken part. One of the recipients, Mr. Takekoshi Yosaburo, a prominent member of the Seiyukai party, declined his decoration on the ground that he had done nothing to earn it. It was in no spirit of humility that Mr. Takekoshi made this renunciation, for almost simultaneously with it he wrote an article in a popular magazine—one of a symposium in which various eminent men expressed their views as to Japan's policy in these abnormal times—demanding that Japan take the utmost possible advantage of the preoccupation of the Powers and, at this moment when they could no longer hinder her, make a beginning in imperial expansion by seizing the Dutch Indies. With less extravagance, but far more force, Mr. Tokutomi, Japan's leading journalist and historian, developed the theme of a Japanese Monroe Doctrine in Asia.

Nevertheless, Okuma did not receive a very great deal of the credit for Japan's prosperity. It was too obviously a gift of fate. It was felt that he had had his fill of good fortune—even the most prominent rôle in the Enthronement ceremonies falling to him, as well as all these other opportunities. Mr. Hara, the leader of the Seiyukai, began a vigorous campaign of criticism, and at the beginning of August 1916 Okuma himself began to talk of his impending resignation. He held on for a couple of months longer, however, causing much indignation among his enemies by declaring with his usual impudence that he could find nobody to take his post, but at length, on October 3rd, placed his resignation, on the score of age, in the Emperor's hands. Count Terauchi was called from the governorship of Korea to succeed him—an appointment which was generally regarded as the direct work of Prince Yamagata, who was both weary of Okuma and afraid of him. Okuma received the imperial command to hold himself in readiness for service and retain the consideration due to a Minister of State; but this command, hitherto regarded as equivalent to appointment to the sacred ranks of the Elder Statesmen, was never so regarded by Okuma. He was one of the most uncompromising critics of the *genro* system, and never attended their councils.

IX

TERAUCHI AND HIS CHINA POLICY

By Terauchi's appointment, the bureaucratic element was supposed to be strengthened, and the Cabinet was certainly bureaucratic enough. Though without Foreign Office experience, Terauchi himself held the portfolio of Foreign Affairs, and he appointed Baron (afterwards Viscount) Goto Minister for Home Affairs and Baron Den Minister of Communications. Terauchi was a samurai of Yamaguchi. He had received his military education in France, and was Minister for War during the Russo-Japanese War. On the annexation of Korea he had been appointed Governor-General, and his military rule in the peninsula had, as has already been described, been open to criticism; but he was succeeded at Seoul by General Hasegawa, lately chief of the General Staff, whose little finger, as a disciplinarian, was thicker than Terauchi's loins. As in the case of Admiral Count Yamamoto's appointment to the Premiership, there was no lack of openly expressed belief that the placing of these high officers in power by no means contributed to the purity of the administration. Much talk at the outset was occasioned by an alleged offer on the part of a wealthy merchant, Mr. Takata, to finance the soldier-Premier. Takata was one of a syndicate known as the Taihei Kumiai, the other prominent members being Mitsui (whose victim, Admiral Fujii, had only just come out of prison) and Baron Okura (who had made a large fortune in the Russo-Japanese War, and was known as Baron Tinned-Gravel, because of the quality of the stores supplied). Prince Katsura was known to have made a large fortune in politics. Concerning Terauchi, it may be said that if his own fortune was more than he could well have saved out of his military pay, he was at least a stern repressor of corruption as a system.

The most marked effect of Terauchi's appointment was a relaxation of the practice, perfected under Okuma, of browbeating and humiliating China. A soldier has sometimes more freedom to be mild than a civilian, since it is taken for granted that he will do all that is necessary. Not long after the Terauchi Ministry came into being, Baron Hayashi, the Minister in Peking, reported a considerable improvement in Chinese feeling. The note had been sounded by Viscount Miura, whose organisation of the plot to murder the Queen of Korea, combined with his reputation for stern religiosity (he was an adherent of the Zen sect of Buddhism), made him a national oracle. At the time of Yuan Shih-kai's death Miura had summoned to his house Viscount Kato (leader of the Rikken Doshikai), Hara Takashi (leader of the Seiyukai), and Inukai (leader of the Kokuminto, the small but not unimportant Nationalist party), and had imposed upon them the dictum, as a rule of their political life, that there must be no diverse expression of opinion in diplomatic and military matters. Now, on the assumption of the Premiership by Count Terauchi, he said that China must be left alone, and that Okuma had been too meddlesome.

The main feature of the new policy was the lending of money to China. There was nothing sudden about the reform. China was still subject to dictation from time to time, and the lending of money had begun actively while Marquis Okuma was still in power. In July 1916 Mr. Chang Tsung-hsiang, the newly appointed Chinese Minister in Tokyo, complained that it was very easy for China to contract Japanese loans but very difficult to get any money. The borrowers were expected to take a large part of their loan in kind or in the form of credits. It was not a new idea, but had not formerly been pressed so hard. However, there were reports during August and September of loans by the Yokohama Specie Bank to Peking, by the Bank of Korea to Mukden, by the Bank of Formosa to the revolutionaries of the South; and there were other loans rumoured or discussed. A corporation unheard of before, the Asiatic

TERAUCHI AND HIS CHINA POLICY

Development Co., offered to lend money to the Chinese Government, but demanded as "collateral security" a licence for buying up copper cash throughout China. The total results of the purchases in Shantung and elsewhere, which the Chinese Government had at last succeeded in stopping, had shortly before been published, the figures given showing a total of 45,000 tons, and the estimated profits being 400 *yen* a ton.

The opportunities for enrichment only increased during Terauchi's administration, but there was a certain amount of reticence observed. One Nishihara went to China as a duly accredited, though not publicly acknowledged, agent of the Japanese Government, and many of the loans were carried through by his agency or with his assistance. There were also many private ventures in the way of lending and otherwise investing money in China.

The following list of loans made to China during the first eight months of 1918, but of which no particulars were given out, was subsequently published, and was never contradicted. It may be incomplete, and it is not clear which of these loans were negotiated by Mr. Nishihara, whose total exploits in this direction have sometimes been put at a lower total than these make:—

		Yen.
1.	Mitsui Bussan Kaisha to Central Government, for Bureau of Engraving and Printing	2,000,000
2.	Yokohama Specie Bank's share of Group Bank advance for flood relief	200,000
3.	Mitsui Bussan Kaisha to Military Governor of Chihli	1,000,000
4.	Second Advance on Second Reorganisation loan by Yokohama Specie Bank	10,000,000
5.	Japanese syndicate to rebel Government of Hunan	20,000,000
6.	Yokohama Specie Bank to Central Government, for plague work	1,000,000
7.	Loan to Fukien Province	1,000,000
8.	Mitsui Bussan Kaisha to Chihli Province, for flood relief	1,000,000
9.	Taihei Kumiai to Central Government, for arms	14,000,000
10.	Second loan to Bank of Communications by Bank of Korea, Bank of Formosa, and Industrial Bank	20,000,000
11.	Group of Banks in Korea to Telegraph Administration	20,000,000
12.	Bank of Korea to Mukden Province	3,000,000

		Yen.
13. Specie Bank loan to Shihpingkai-Chengchiatun Railway		2,000,000
14. Nanjin Railway loan.		100,000
15. Wireless loan		3,000,000
16. Bank of Korea to Chihli Province		1,000,000
17. Kirin-Huining Railway loan by Banks of Korea and Formosa and Industrial Bank		20,000,000
18. Loan to Shensi Province		2,000,000
19. Specie Bank to Hupeh Province		1,000,000
20. Okura Forestry loan		30,000,000
21. Kirin Forestry loan		30,000,000
22. Second Reorganisation loan (third advance)		10,000,000
23. Loan on Yu Kan iron-mines		3,000,000
24. Loan to Shantung Province		1,500,000
25. Peking Telephone loan		5,000,000
26. Manchurian and Mongolian Railway loan		40,000,000
27. Shantung Railway loan		26,000,000
28. Military Agreement loan		20,000,000
29. Peking-Suiyuan loan		4,000,000

Secrecy was not found so easy in the negotiation of these loans as was desirable. Count Terauchi was not the man to have much patience with the Imperial Diet, and members who had been elected during a period when Marquis Okuma was extremely popular were not likely to be congenial to Terauchi. Accordingly, the Diet was dissolved early in the year, with the consequence that the Government had a free hand with the budget. According to a rule copied from the Prussian Constitution, when a budget failed to pass the House, the previous year's budget had to be repeated, and this was the course nominally taken, though it was obviously impossible to follow a previous year's budget at all closely at a time when finance was in so abnormal a condition. As regards the general election that followed on the dissolution, Mr. Kodama, the Premier's son-in-law, who was Chief Secretary to the Cabinet, was reported as saying that if the newly elected Diet was also unsatisfactory, it would be dissolved, and the process repeated until one sufficiently amenable should be elected. Constitutionally this was quite feasible and had no lack of precedents, but the democratic idea had developed sufficiently to make such an utterance a very unwise one. However, there was but little public interest in party politics at this time, and even so provocative a remark failed to disturb the general apathy. A general election took place in April, and the amenable majority was duly secured.

But the amenable majority, though convenient enough for the purpose of voting Government measures and outvoting motions of censure, cannot prevent criticism, and when the new Diet met on June 25th the Nishihara business was the subject of some sharp interpellations. Mr. Shimada Saburo, the veteran politician, who had brought about the disclosures of corruption in the navy, began what soon became a bombardment of questions on the subject of Nishihara Kamezo, who, he stated, had gone to Peking on February 19th and had urged China to take part in the war, promising her tariff revision, on terms of reciprocity with Japan. These proposals, he said, were made to the President, and the uproar consequent upon them so embarrassed the Premier, General Tuan Chi-jui, that he was forced to resign. Baron Motono, the Foreign Minister, who had just described how Japan had deemed China's participation advisable, to the extent at least of breaking off relations with Germany, as the United States had already advised her to do (and which China actually did on March 14th, though she had not yet declared war), declared that Mr. Shimada's story was the product of an active imagination.

The subject was not so easily burked, however. Mr. Ozaki Yukio asked for a statement regarding the important mission on which such a person as Nishihara had been sent. The Premier replied that Nishihara was not such a disreputable character as some people declared, and that he had done very useful work for him in Korea in 1910. Shimada then returned to the charge, and demanded information about the loans that Nishihara was engineering, and about his connection with the Northern militarists.

After that, the Government took the extreme measure of stopping Press messages from China when they related to

Nishihara's activities—a mere foretaste of the rigidity with which it was soon to be stifling criticism of its China policy; but this flurry in the Diet was apparently enough to make Nishihara lie low for a little, as most of the loans that he engineered were not concluded till several months later.

Thus were some of Japan's earlier war profits invested—though in many cases, of course, it was in kind rather than in cash that the loans were made. Ministers of State (though not Mr. Nishihara) were decorated in consideration of their services in the negotiation of these loans. They turned out a sorry bargain.

The war poured money into both the United States and Japan, and the first recognition in America of the fact that Japan was becoming both wealthier and more aggressive was accompanied by a hostile reaction. There had already been trouble owing to racial prejudice aroused at the sight of a large and self-segregated Japanese community in California. The news of the capture of Tsingtau, of Japan's naval activities, and of the Twenty-one Demands made a hundred thousand Japanese look like a portent. All sorts of measures designed to make things difficult for the Japanese were introduced into the Californian Legislature. It was also clear that America would soon have to be looking abroad for opportunities for investing surplus capital, and Americans understood that Britain's world-wide influence was due as much to the investment of capital as to sea-power. An American writer in September 1916 said: "Only by investment in China shall we secure a position enabling us to exert an influence commensurate with our wealth and power." Mr. Elbert Gary, President of the Steel Trust, had just been on a visit to Japan, and on his return to America he spoke of the necessity of American investments abroad having diplomatic support, though it was a refusal as a matter of principle to give this support that had caused President Wilson to dissociate the American Government from participation with the six-Power group, known as the

Sextuple Syndicate, formed for the purpose of financing President Yuan Shih-kai's Government. But Mr. Gary also went on to deprecate the lending of money to China, declaring that it would be much safer to place it in Japanese hands in order to enable them to use it for developing China's resources. Marquis Okuma's gloss on this was that what China needed was American money and Japanese brains. But Okuma seemed to take a malicious delight in deliberate indiscretions.

X

EFFECT OF AMERICA ENTERING THE WAR

THE entry of the United States into the war in the spring of 1917 caused less stir than might have been expected. President Wilson's suggestions regarding possible terms of peace had been discussed academically, but Japan was a signatory to the Pact of London, agreeing that she would make no separate peace, and was not at all averse to the war continuing under the present profitable conditions. It was true, the participation of the United States threatened to bring the war to an earlier close, but on the other hand it ensured victory, which, with the secession of Russia, had become a little dubious. The Russian revolutionists had issued the reassuring proclamation that Russia would now be able to prosecute the war with undivided enthusiasm, but orders for war stores stopped completely, and it was obvious that the new rulers were in no condition to carry on the conflict. However, the disturbance of conditions in the United States incident to participating in the war promised greater demands for Japanese supplies and larger profits than ever. There was no inclination on Japan's part for direct participation, though it was diplomatically pressed, and when arm-chair enthusiasts for war suggested from editorial chairs in London or Paris that Japan should send a punitive expedition to Russia in the event of her making a separate peace, Japanese publicists dismissed the idea with contempt. War films had been sent to Japan by the British Government for the purpose of creating enthusiasm for the Allied cause, but they were exhibited to sparse and bored audiences, and did nothing to arouse an inclination for trench warfare in a distant continent.

There proved, however, to be several drawbacks to American participation. Embargoes on the export of steel quickly followed the declaration of war, and this caused great perturbations in Japan. It was no wonder, for Japan had by this time some sixty slips for shipbuilding, and all shipyards were tremendously busy with construction both for Japanese and for foreign customers. There were agitations and meetings of a more influential character than those which had demanded that the war be stopped if Britain refused to take knitted goods. Orders were in hand for ships for Britain and France, and even for America, so that the diplomatic machinery could be set in motion to secure a partial removal of the embargo. As soon as the shipbuilders saw that substantial concessions were to be obtained, their demands expanded, and by the beginning of December 1917 they put their requirements at 600,000 tons, or sufficient to build 1,800,000 tons of shipping. It was pointed out that the probabilities were against the war lasting so long as would be required for the consumption of all this material, but the existence of the war had become so much taken for granted in Japan that its cessation was incredible; there were many who, later on, had cause to regret having burdened themselves with so much material at war prices.

Almost as important as America's participation, in Japanese eyes, was that of China, which followed. Yuan Shih-kai was dead, but his wisdom in having offered to take part in the war was now better recognised than it had been during his lifetime. Just before the signing of the Sino-Japanese Treaty in May 1915, the United States had sent identical Notes to China and Japan declaring that America could not recognise any agreement between the two countries which impaired the political or territorial integrity of China or the policy of the "open door." America being then neutral, it was impossible to invite China to declare war, but the invitation followed immediately after her own declaration, and with the same object that had inspired Yuan Shih-kai's offer—the acquirement for China of a seat at the ultimate Peace Conference, when the Shantung question, and any other problems arising out of the war, would be settled with China's participation instead of without it.

Japan was still unwilling, but could find no valid reason for continuing her opposition. Besides, there were certain material gains. The organisation of a Labour Corps was under consideration, the equipment and convoying of which would be a very profitable task for Japan, and would carry still further the process of acquiring dominion by means of loans. On the other hand, China was demanding as conditions of participation the cancellation, or at least the suspension, of further payments of the Boxer Indemnity, the revision of the tariff, and the settlement on more favourable terms of various treaty disputes. These matters received some discussion at the hands of the representatives at Peking, who agreed to them "in principle," in July, and China declared war on Germany and Austria on August 14th.

Japan's acquiescence was the easier to obtain in view of the fact that she had, in February and March, before the United States came into the war, made secret agreements with Britain, France, Italy, and Russia, who undertook to support her claim at the Peace Conference to Germany's rights in Shantung and to the German islands north of the equator. It was certain that the United States would never agree, so some other means had to be adopted than that of merely keeping China away from the peace table.

Accordingly, immediately after China's declaration of war, Viscount Ishii was dispatched to America on what appeared to be merely a goodwill propaganda mission. This appearance was considerably intensified by the fact that he was accompanied by a gentleman of Irish origin and flamboyant manner, who was in the Japanese service in the capacity of expounder of Japanese news for the benefit of the foreign Press, and was also, unhappily, Reuter's agent in Japan. This gentleman's unfortunate style seemed to infect some of the Special Ambassador's speeches. There was comparatively little about the subjects in dispute between Japan and America with regard to China, on which there had been several exchanges of Notes since the sharp reminder of May 1915; the Californian immigration dispute was tactfully avoided; but America was warmly welcomed as a participant in the war for the upholding of civilisation, and the Senate and other audiences were informed that anything which they might hear that was derogatory to Japan's aims was the work of "half-informed critics and hired slanderers." It seemed rather odd language for an ambassador and previous Foreign Minister to use, but it was a time for enthusiasm, and it passed. Those in Japan at the time, however, remarked that, while such indignation was expressed at any adverse criticism of Japan, there was a fresh flood in Japan of contemptuous language regarding Japan's allies, and of discussion regarding the advantages that Japan was to win from the war. Dr. Nagase Hosuke, attached to the General Staff, for instance, declared in an article in *Shin Nihon* ("New Japan") that Britain's domination of the world was the real danger ahead. Captain Hosaka Hikotaro, of the Japanese Navy, went into raptures over the adoration in which Japan was held by the natives of Borneo and the South Seas. To counteract this sort of criticism a bilingual magazine had been started in Tokyo, called the *New East*, and Mr. Oba Kako, in *Japan and the Japanese*, demanded the deportation of its editor because he had dared to be critical. Mr. Tsukuda Kankaku published an attack on the British Indian Government, and an exaggerated sensitiveness was shown regarding any disapproval of such ambitions as Japan might evince. Such an outburst contrasted curiously with the warm unctuousness of the speeches that graced the Ishii mission and the mission which followed closely on its heels, whereof Baron Megata was the leader, whose business was to make satisfactory arrangements with regard to financial matters, the importance of which had greatly increased with the enrichment of the two countries as a result of the war.

The Ishii visit culminated, in November, in the exchange of Notes between Mr. Robert Lansing, the Secretary of State, and the Special Ambassador from Japan, in which the two Governments assured one another of their unalterable desires for the maintenance of the sovereignty and territorial integrity of China and of the principle of the open door, but in which the United States undertook to recognise that territorial propinquity created special interests. The degree of propinquity required and the nature of the special interests that Japan in this case acquired were left undefined. It suggested, however, that Japan must be consulted by any third Power in any matter affecting China. Though the Agreement was the subject of a good deal of criticism, it was not until the Peace Conference that its significance was disclosed.

It is noteworthy that there was at least one outspoken opponent of China's entry into the war. Mr. Ozaki Yukio, one of Japan's most liberal politicians, who, for the sake of being able to speak his mind, was already ploughing a lonely furrow, stood out to the last against the idea of Japan permitting China to participate. He demonstrated both his frankness and his perspicacity in declaring as his foremost objection the fact that China's participation in the war would give her a seat at the Allies' Peace Conference, when, as he well knew, the conditions upon which Japan had extended further help in the war would be disclosed, and perhaps jeopardised by this publicity, while the Chinese delegates would not neglect the opportunity of advertising to the world how Japan had taken advantage of the war to make encroachments which were not only inimical to the sovereignty of China, but hardly consistent with the equal rights of the other Powers. How little China was actually in a condition to go to war was illustrated only six weeks before her formal declaration by the incident of the old swashbuckler, General Chang Hsun, engineering a *coup d'état* by which, for a few days, the young Manchu Emperor was restored to the Throne, while President Li Yuan-hung took refuge in the Japanese Embassy. It was clearly for political purposes not entirely friendly to Japan that the United States invited China so pressingly to assist in preserving Western civilisation against the assaults of the Germans, and it was this very fact, together with a nice balancing of the probable advantages and losses attendant on her choice of policy, that decided Japan to endorse the American advice, and to try to prevent America from subsequently objecting to arrangements to which the other Allies had already secretly agreed.

XI

WAR PROSPERITY IN JAPAN

We may pause here in the chronicling of major events to consider some of the manifestations of war prosperity in Japan. Reference has already been made to the frenzied scenes on the stock exchanges, the progress of industry and shipbuilding, and other indications of prosperity. But while everybody was eager to make money, it was not realised what a revolutionary effect this prosperity was having. The war had not progressed very far when Japan found herself in the position of a monopolist supplier of a multitude of goods. In the Indian and Chinese markets she had hardly a competitor. The Dutch Indies and Australia depended increasingly on her factories for a number of their commodities; and before the war was ended South Africa and South America were offering almost any price for her manufactures. All this opportunity was not, of course, without vexatious vicissitudes. It was increasingly difficult to obtain the materials with which to supply the needs of other countries. The British Government required the whole clip of Australian wool, and there were strenuous diplomatic negotiations in order to obtain some modification of this demand. Often those who needed supplies were faced with the sheer impossibility of getting them. The cotton industry, for example, could have made much greater progress had it been possible to obtain machinery from Lancashire in the quantity desired. Japan was full of subsidised and protected industries, and these, after having been merely an expense, suddenly became a means of rapid enrichment; but at the same time Japan experienced rather poignantly the impossibility of a modern manufacturing country being "self-supplying." Attempts that were either far-sighted, or were based on the idea that the war must last for ever, were made to provide supplies. Numbers of Japanese, for example, took up land in the Malay States and Borneo, and planted rubber and coco-nuts. New companies for every kind of purpose were started in Japan. It hardly seemed possible to do any business without making money, though here and there, of course, there were sudden changes of fortune. Towards the end of 1916 a wealthy Osaka stockbroker named Iwamoto, who had not long before presented the city with a magnificent public hall, suddenly thought he was ruined, and committed suicide—a sort of rashness to which the Japanese appear to be specially prone.

Those who were anxious for the good name and enduring prosperity of Japan found much to criticise in the manner in which their countrymen encountered prosperity. Buyers abroad were so anxious to get their goods that rejecting shipments was out of the question; nevertheless, there were so many complaints that it was generally realised that in the hurry to get rich manufacturers and exporters were earning their country a very bad name. The inspection of exports in the endeavour to prevent goods below a reasonable standard from being exported was no new thing, and the system was extended in its scope. Unfortunately there were no experts available for such work, which was done with great inefficiency, while the effect of having inspectors was that exporters aimed only at getting the worst possible goods passed as standard. Complaints were many of matches that would not strike, pencils that would not write, soap that would not wash, and a hundred other articles that would not fulfil their proper functions; but orders were repeated at higher and higher prices.

In matters of business a custom came into vogue which, while it said something for the candour of promoters, illustrated with extraordinary force the recklessness of the times. New companies were frequently floated in which the vendors demanded premiums exceeding in amount the price of the shares subscribed for. It certainly minimised overcapitalisation, and the premiums were readily paid, only to be reinvested on similar terms in some other overweighted scheme.

Money easily won is easily spent, and the ostentation and extravagance of the newly rich attracted attention and condemnation. Even in the Genroku period (contemporary with William and Mary), famous for luxury and extravagance, life in Japan had been simple; and along with an elegance and refinement carried to a high pitch, there was always a sort of asceticism. Money might be spent on fine woods for the house, on porcelain and lacquer; but there was no equivalent of the "stately homes of England." Men who were rich did not own parks, packs of hounds, private yachts, picture-galleries, or even great mansions. Few of the opulences of the West had been learnt. Culture and refinement, moreover, were, in Japan, even more metropolitan in their habitat than in most countries. There were newly rich in cities like Osaka and Nagoya who could find no other outlet for their wealth than in the building of country villas in which they would install as chatelaine some complaisant geisha whose debts they had paid and who condescended to relieve them of the burden of their wealth.

Those professional entertainers, the geisha, naturally reaped a harvest. The Japanese restaurants were patronised as never before, and geisha were called in to entertain with unprecedented frequency. While the demand for workpeople had the gratifying effect of clearing off the streets the poor creatures whom penury drove into furtive prostitution, the generosity of the newly rich attracted to the profession of geisha a large number of young women utterly devoid of the proper accomplishments; but their patrons were as ignorant as themselves, so it mattered little. Some endeavoured to be spectacularly extravagant, one millionaire earning temporary fame by taking a score or more of geisha, with a hundred coolies to carry them, to some famous scenic mountain-top for a picnic. Nor was extravagance confined to a few; it came to a pitch where, especially on Sundays and holidays, it was easier to find room in a third-class railway carriage than in the superior classes. One new development of this time may be noted—a matter of fashion which was greatly stimulated by this unaccustomed wealth. Japanese building a new house, all of wood in the traditional manner, would attach a wing in stucco, in the European style, where they would entertain their guests, who had adopted European dress and learned to appreciate the ease of chairs and the flavour of whisky. Among many critics of contemporary manners we find Dr. Tsumura, of the Kobe Higher Commercial School, writing in 1917 in strong terms of the "double life" of his countrymen. To adopt European ways without breaking with Japanese tradition meant having not only two wardrobes, but two houses, so entirely different were the two manners of life and so little could they be comfortably combined. We have referred to penury and prostitution in some places disappearing together; but the mere gaining of wealth does not promote morality; and the fact that Oriental seaports all enjoyed in some degree their share of war prosperity soon caused the followers of the basest of all traffic to realise that there was money to be made by the export to the stews in all ports of their countrywomen, with the result that the increase in this traffic attracted the indignant attention of those who understood the shamefulness of the business.

The newly rich, however, had many acts to their credit. They became in many cases generous patrons of art, and while there is little to be grateful for in the creation of an inflated price for the comparatively recent antiques with which Japan abounds, the munificent encouragement of the artists of the day, many of them struggling with new art motives and sometimes with new media, was a boon of which the effects will be felt perhaps longer than the great buildings in which some of the millionaires indulged will last.

Though the plentifulness of work made indigence almost a thing of the past, high prices led to new forms of temptation and new kinds of theft. There were constant complaints of the grabbing of handfuls of cotton from bales, the snipping of telegraph and telephone wires, and, later on, even the stealing of iron drain-covers: for, under the influence of demands for iron for all purposes, its price rose almost to the level at which copper had stood at the outbreak of war. At this period small boys were to be seen with magnets, gathering the ferrous débris of stormwater drains by the roadside, an occupation at which they could often earn a few pence in a short time.

But the most important development of this period was not due to the wastefulness of wealth, but to the pinch of prosperity. For a long time prices rose much faster than wages, and the consequent discontent gave a great impetus to the development of socialistic ideas, which, up to that time, had been only a matter of academic study on the part of a few. The Yu-ai-kai, originally a friendly society among the Kawasaki Dockyard hands, developed into a trade union, with Mr. Suzuki Bunji, a lawyer and a keen student of the Socialist movement, at its head. The seamen also had a union, and so did the miners. But in these early days there were really no trade unions, as the term is understood in the West. They were not recognised by the authorities, and not to be recognised was to be illegal and to have no right to exist. Strikes were also illegal. When they happened, the police intervened, and if the strikers did not accept their decision, they were prosecuted and punished. "Victimisation" was the rule: the strike often resulted in a rise of wages, but the leaders were discharged. This, however, was no great hardship, because the demand for labour could never be satisfied.

The police in Japan are great statisticians, and in 1917 they recorded 398 strikes, in which 57,000 workmen were involved. It was clear that the situation was getting somewhat out of hand, and it is to the credit of Japanese publicists that they openly denounced the greed of the newly rich and showed sympathy with the hardships of the workers. The newly rich were called *narikin*, a term adopted from the chessboard, where it was applied to pawns which, on crossing the board, had been suddenly promoted. It was a word that soon became very familiar, and was used, more often than not, in a contemptuous manner. It was always a matter of some difficulty to get a rise in wages, but the prices of commodities were utterly capricious. In a fortnight in May 1917 rice rose 3 *yen* per koku, and speculators were buying "forward" for July at 3 *yen* higher still. By July 1918 prices reached over 50 *yen* per koku, or more than double that even of the reckless forward buying of a year before.

A high price for rice was not in itself a cause for complaint. In olden days the complaint was more often that prices were too low. When Japan was self-supporting and mainly agricultural, the farmer was very frugal—often to the extent of living on millet, while he sold his rice to the cities. A large landholding class who rented their lands to tenant-farmers were also interested in a high price for rice, and these being still the backbone of the Seiyukai, the largest political party, it was still customary to speak of cheap rice as a calamity.

But times had changed. There was a large working class in the towns, and people congregated together are always more effective than those dispersed. Yet it was among some of those who were comparatively dispersed that the trouble first took serious shape. After the farmers, the fishermen were always the most important class of food-winners. The price of fish, of course, rose considerably, but there was a complicated system of marketing under which commodities passed through several hands before reaching the consumer, so that the producers were the last to feel the benefit of a rise in market prices. In any case, even though the fishermen realised more for their catches, it was only the more annoying when the price of other commodities rose even more rapidly.

The Terauchi Government had never been squeamish in the suppression of news. On any occasion it would issue orders to the Press not to print or to comment upon whatever it thought would be better left unpublished, and among these prohibitions the news of strikes and of the spread of "dangerous thought" (by which Socialism was meant) was frequently included. Mr. Inukai, the leader of the Kokuminto, or Nationalist party, and reckoned one of Japan's more liberal politicians, protested vigorously against the attempt to mould the public mind with the hard hands of bureaucracy.

But the suppression of news was of no avail. When the storm broke, it was as though a call had been heard all over the land. It appears to have begun in fishing villages in the remote province of Toyama, where angry fishwives raided the rice-shops on August 4, 1918. During the next few days rice riots were witnessed all over the land. Alarmed authority endeavoured to keep the cities free by opening shops for the sale of cheap rice, but the measures taken were too late and too inadequate. On the 10th there were riots in Kyoto, on the 12th they began in Osaka and Kobe. It was in Kobe that they reached their most serious dimensions, and took a form more far-reaching than the mere mobbing of rice-shops. Crowds collected at Minato-gawa, the scene of a famous battle of old time and now become the popular amusement quarter. They were harangued by spokesmen whom the tide of excitement carried on its crest. The names of the principal profiteers were denounced. Presently the crowd began to move towards Suzuki's, a firm which had become very wealthy during the war and whose operations on the rice market particularly attracted the mob's hostile attention. Actually Suzuki's had been buying rice chiefly on the Government's behalf as commission agents, but it was believed that they were responsible for forcing up the price. Doors were battered in, kerosene poured over the furniture and the premises fired. The fire brigade—a branch of the police service—was driven away when it came up, and its hoses were cut. The firemen attempted to play on the flames from the windows of a Japanese newspaper office that stood opposite, whereupon the mob burnt the office as well. The same night the offices of a big house agency which had got the greater part of the dwellings in Kobe into its avaricious hands were burnt, besides the houses of a couple of unpopular money-lenders.

The next day troops were hurried into Kobe from Himeji, the nearest garrison town except Osaka, where they were needed for keeping order in their own city. The mob smashed all the windows in the principal shopping street, smashed a motor-car or two, and generally expended its energies in minor mischief, but came into no extensive collisions with the troops. In four or five days the disturbances were suppressed, but the soldiers had to be called out in twenty places, and demonstrators who were killed in the disturbances numbered something over a hundred: it was impossible to discover the real number even approximately. Indeed, the Government tried to keep the news out of the papers altogether, but could not withstand the united protests of the whole Press.

The riots were suppressed with no great difficulty. They had been spontaneous and unpremeditated. Without organisation the rioters faced disciplined troops, and although some of the boldest of them shouted to them not to fire on their fellow-workers, no trace of "dangerous thought" had yet infected the army, which had been brought up in the creed of the perfect obedience owing by the soldier to his officer. During the time of the riots the extensive organisation of plain-clothes police had mingled with the crowd, and many arrests were made. Very severe sentences, including some death penalties, were meted out, and it must be remembered in this connection that incendiarism was always one of the greatest of crimes in Japan. It was so easy, and the effects, in cities built entirely of flimsy wooden houses, were so terrible, that even the accidental burning of a house was regarded as a punishable offence. The incendiary under the old laws, still not entirely forgotten, might be punished by being himself burnt alive.

Notwithstanding the speedy restoration of order, the punishment of the riot leaders, and the measures taken to assuage popular discontent, the Terauchi Government found it inadvisable to continue in office, and resigned on September 17th. Its warmest supporters could hardly maintain that it had risen to the occasion. Its own minor servants were no better off than the poorest of the proletariat; their wages had been raised a little, but they suffered considerable hardships; indeed, many of the brightest among the lower officials left so penurious a service and devoted themselves to commerce; so that, with the work of the Government Departments increasing every day, its performance grew less and less efficient. The Department of Communications, with Baron Den at its head, seemed to give up almost without a struggle. Telegrams took days in transmission and were hopelessly mutilated; letters took weeks. In a smaller degree the same deterioration was observable in other departments as well, but these did not come so intimately in contact with the daily life of the public. The State railways, which were always well managed, did their best to cope with the immense increase in all kinds of traffic, but it was extremely difficult to obtain rails, engines, and materials for making rolling-stock. Even coal could only be obtained at fanciful prices. So there was deterioration here too. All public vehicles, both railway and tramway, were incredibly congested, and the municipalities were even less able than the railways to improve their plant, or even to keep it up to the normal standard of the days before the war. Even the handling of the overseas commerce, which was making the country so unprecedentedly wealthy, could not be managed, and from time to time there were bitter complaints of congested piers and customs-houses.

One notable piece of energy the Terauchi Government had manifested, and this it endeavoured to keep modestly hidden. Its policy of lending to China rather than threatening her has already been mentioned. It appears paradoxical, but is really quite natural, that a military Premier, at a time when there is a spirit of aggressive ambition abroad, can afford to be more moderate than a civilian. He has already proved himself, and is not liable to accusations of timidity or indecision. But the Terauchi Government was not merely sowing that others might reap: it wanted an early return for its money. In November 1917 there were sharp complaints in Japan that the American Minister in Peking, Dr. Paul Reinsch, was using his utmost influence with China to dissuade her from entering into a military alliance with Japan. There was much at the same time about the jealousy excited among those who thought the financing of China was their special province, when they saw Japan lending money, and the British Minister was mentioned as unfavourably as the American. A few weeks later there was news of a far-reaching contract pending for the supply of Japanese munitions to China. It was not till 1918, however, that the Japanese Press was forbidden for several weeks on end to mention anything about diplomatic questions pending between Japan and China. In the case of the Twenty-one Demands the President had been approached direct instead of the communication passing through the usual channel. Now, three years later, the Waichaiopu, or Foreign Office, was even more surprisingly ignored. The Japanese Government approached the Chinese War Office direct with proposals for a Military Agreement. The Foreign Office would, of course, have had to refer to the War Office on such a matter, and information would have been sure to leak out, as it had done in the negotiations of 1915. The War Office, therefore, was enjoined to secrecy, and the Military Agreement completed, the most important clauses of which, as it turned out, were those by which Japan undertook to assist China in case of her frontiers being threatened. The Chinese War Office was better disciplined than the other departments, and except for vague hints the Agreement remained secret. It was to be operated to prodigious effect in a short time, and nominally by a civilian Japanese Government, though actually the General Staff was the chief mover in such matters, the Chief having right of access to the Emperor and of receiving the imperial sanction to his advice.

XII

THE HARA GOVERNMENT AND INTERVENTION IN SIBERIA

MR. HARA TAKASHI, who succeeded General Terauchi as Premier, has sometimes been referred to as Japan's "Great Commoner," since he was the first untitled man to hold this important office. He was a man of great force of character, fighting his way through politics as a party man, attached to the Seiyukai, of which he had been the leader for some years before he succeeded in securing the highest constitutional office in the State. Exactly what political views he held it might not be easy to define: not that a great man must needs belong to a school—he sometimes shows his greatness by not attaching himself to any. Hara had a gift more useful in the circumstances in which he found himself—that of attaching men to himself in bonds of personal loyalty. He was a party man first and last—identifying himself with the Seiyukai, and the Seiyukai with himself. He was, like most of his countrymen, patriotic, but he could hardly be called scrupulous. Abuses he left alone; he was no great reformer; and he gave countenance to the institution of the political bully by having his own bodyguard of these ruffians.

His two chief Ministers were interesting characters: Mr. Tokonami, the Minister for Home Affairs, was the ideal bureaucrat. Upright and high-minded, his one object was to lead everybody along the path of patriotism and loyalty. Perhaps his ideas as regards independence of thought were open to criticism. Hara, like Terauchi, and Okuma before him, promised to give the Press his confidence, but he never restrained Tokonami in his suppressions of news and comment, in which he exceeded his predecessors. But Tokonami, whether promoting plans for amalgamating Shinto,

Buddhism and Christianity, turning gangs of rough characters into a patriotic society, officialising the young men's associations, promoting propaganda for pilgrimages to the Meiji shrine, or advising the professional story-tellers to tell such tales as promoted the noble sentiment of loyalty, always had one thing in view—the honour and solidarity of his country.

The Minister of Finance, Viscount (then Baron, but later plain Mr.) Takahashi, was the other most remarkable man in the Hara Ministry. Takahashi in his early days had been in America, where he had had hardships and adventures, being reduced at one time to menial labour, from which, apparently, arose the legend that he had been "sold as a slave." He had also been grossly swindled and left stranded by a man who had pretended to befriend him. However, he possessed a buoyant spirit. An unusual mastery of English was one of the results of his adventurous days, and he early displayed a taste for finance which at one time nearly got him into serious trouble over a Chilean silver-mine in which he had more faith than proved to be justified. After returning to Japan he won his way through office to the position of Minister of Finance, at a lucky time for him, because he had command of an overflowing treasury and a taste for bold measures. A more cautious man, less addicted to what he called a "positive policy," might have made more of the opportunity for putting Japan financially on her feet; but, after all, his greatest extravagances were in expenditure on the army and navy, which were not what he would have chosen to spend the war profits on if he had not been overborne by the Ministries of Defence, and he left the treasury still well filled, though declining, when he relinquished office.

The rice riots and labour troubles which brought about the downfall of the Terauchi Ministry have been described, and in introducing the subject mention was made of the resultant emergence of Trade Unionism and Socialism. After the riots the Government made some hurried and extravagant attempts to reduce prices. Not that it had been altogether neglectful before, but with the bureaucratic passion for regulating everything minutely it had hedged about the importation of foreign rice with so many restrictions that it would have been much better to make the business a Government monopoly. In the bureaucratic manner it also assumed that events would wait upon its deliberations, and on the very eve of the riots it sent Mr. Kawada Shiro, a professor of law, on a mission abroad to inquire into the reasons of the high price of rice. After the riots, the brokers, who had been mainly responsible, kept quiet and bought moderately, retailers were prepared to forgo profits rather than have their shops wrecked, and importation was facilitated. But the chief relief came from the general increase in wages. The war was still going on; contracts were in progress for supplying the Allies with 300,000 tons of shipping at the lofty price of 250 gold dollars a ton, and with the additional advantage that, in spite of the embargo on export, the United States, in consideration of this service, was to supply 300,000 tons of steel. With business going on at this rate, freights up to 1,300 shillings a ton, and a high price obtainable for everything that could be manufactured, employers all felt that it was better to satisfy the demands of their workers than to risk more strikes and riots. Some could ill afford such extravagances, but they had to fall in with the rest. The most fortunate were making such profits that there was no fear of wages ever overtaking them.

Naturally this was far from producing tranquillity, but we may interrupt at this point the narrative of how labour was affected by the war: for along with labour troubles the Hara Ministry succeeded to another legacy of its predecessor—a real participation in the war, but against a country that started out as an ally. The story of the intervention in Siberia is one that would need some very special research, and none of those concerned would feel any great pride to-day in an exploit which was much advertised at its inception.

THE HARA GOVERNMENT

European intrigue enters into the matter in no small degree, but little will be said on that point here except in so far as it is necessary to indicate its workings in a chronicle of the chief developments from the Japanese side. Almost immediately after the Bolshevik revolution, which was the death-blow of the hopes of Russia's allies that she would continue to play an active part in the war, a report was published in America, and said to be confirmed by the Japanese Embassy in Washington, that Japanese marines had been landed at Vladivostok. It was probably a *ballon d'essai*, and important only as pointing to the goal towards which the thoughts of those who were directing the war were tending. It is noteworthy, perhaps, that in December 1917 Mr. Inukai, the leader of the Kokuminto, in one of those moments of imperialism with which his liberalism was always chequered, declared that Japan ought to have a slice of Siberia as the reward of her services and the guarantee of her safety, insufficiently protected, he evidently considered, by the unprecedentedly large naval allotment of 260,000,000 *yen* just budgeted for. On December 30th a Japanese warship did arrive, unannounced, at Vladivostok, its commander informing the local authorities that it was for the protection of Japanese subjects but in no way hostile to Russians. During the next three weeks another Japanese warship and a British and an American cruiser arrived.

There was no immediate development. The new year was at hand, with its usual distractions in Japan. There was a plan afoot, of whose inspiration Japan was not guilty, for deporting all Germans from China for internment in Australia, but this, in the circumstances now developing, was postponed until after peace was restored! When the Diet opened at the beginning of 1918 (we have had to retrace our steps so far) the ministerial speeches included the usual tag from Viscount Motono, the Foreign Minister, to the effect that the Anglo-Japanese Alliance was the pivot of Japan's foreign policy. Perhaps this was the only reply that could be made to the publication by the Bolsheviks of the secret clauses of the Russo-Japanese Agreement of July 3, 1916. But Mr. Ozaki Yukio complained that Count Terauchi had so manœuvred as to prevent the Powers from seeking Japan's assistance in the war, and he demanded to know what Allied warships were doing at Vladivostok which could be doing much better service in the North Sea, and whether they were there because Europe distrusted Japan.

There was no great eagerness in Japan to enter the war by this back door now open at Vladivostok, and the prime responsibility for Japan's entering upon her squalid and disastrous adventure in Siberia could probably be traced to those European statesmen who, from the moment of the October revolution, were far more afraid of Bolshevik Russia than of Imperial Germany. In Japan, on the other hand, though men like General Baron Tanaka, Vice-Chief of the General Staff, were always declaiming about the menace of horrible ideas, and liberal politicians like Shimada Saburo, Ozaki Yukio, and Inukai were constantly attacking the Government for its harsh suppression of what it was pleased to call "dangerous thought," there was no such prompt reaction to an eruption of political ideas several thousand miles away, and no very general knowledge or tradition of the desperation of Russian nihilists. Nevertheless, the subject of intervening in Siberia soon became one of lively interest. So little was there any general enthusiasm, however, that the *Asahi*, perhaps the most influential paper in Japan, expressed some apprehensions lest, should Viscount Uchida, the Ambassador in Petrograd, be compelled to return as the result of the revolution, the Government might be hurried into some rash action. In more chauvinistic quarters, however, there was no reluctance to contemplate rash actions, one proposal being that, since the Bolshevik Government had repudiated war debts, Japan, in lieu of her money, should annex Siberia as far as Irkutsk, beyond Lake Baikal.

Soon the propagandists were at work, and Japan was fed with rumours of German influence spreading eastwards and with lurid accounts of the aims of the Bolsheviks. As a matter of fact, the revolution had spread to Siberia quite as fast as could be expected, the zemstvos and dumas, ready enough to be done with the autocracy, but apparently without any precise views beyond that, taking over the functions of government, and the more enthusiastic forming committees of public safety. As early as February 1918 there was formed an Amur Council of People's Commissaries.

Intervention in Siberia really began from the first signs of Bolshevik influence there. When Allied warships assembled at Vladivostok, the consuls in that port began to protest sharply to the zemstvo at the least sign of disturbance. China made an attempt to close the frontier, which would have been disastrous to Vladivostok, but passed trains through again when the Russians protested vigorously. General Horvath, the manager of the Chinese Eastern Railway, which traverses North Manchuria and extends from Harbin to Changchun, there joining the Japanese line, endeavoured to set up a Government at Harbin, which, though the centre of the railway administration, was, with the whole line, on Chinese territory. Colonel John Stevens and a corps of some two hundred engineers, who had been sent by President Wilson at the request of the Kerensky Government to reorganise the Siberian railway, but who had withdrawn to Nagasaki when the Kerensky Government fell, set out for Harbin on February 27th. Bolshevism rapidly developed. At Habarovsk, where the Amur railway turns south across the river for Vladivostok, a "coalition" Government was formed for the purpose of carrying on, but at Blagoveschensk, higher up the river, the local body was definitely declared to be Bolshevik. Some Japanese troops were immediately sent there "to protect Japanese nationals." The Kuhara firm had an office there, and there were rumours, never confirmed, that Bolsheviks had invaded it. A "White Guard" of some five thousand was formed, with a couple of thousand Cossacks and some odd Kerensky troops; but the peasants in all the country round turned out, troops came down from Habarovsk, and in three days after the Japanese incursion not only was Blagoveschensk "Red" again, but all along the Amur there was no longer any doubt as to the political complexion of the people at large. Even Vladivostok signified a wish to join up, but was too strongly held under foreign influence. Thus, nearly six months before formal intervention, a striking example was afforded of the inevitable result of foreign incursions, but the statesmen concerned were persistently blind to it.

There were some European statesmen who were so single-minded that they did not care for anything but the promotion of action which might damage the enemy, and these were anxious to drag Japan into the war by hook or by crook, especially when Russia made her separate peace with Germany at Brest-Litovsk. The rumours spread were without limit. In March German submarines, it was said, were reported at Vladivostok. Viscount Uchida, the Ambassador in Petrograd, who returned that month, was quoted as uttering a warning that intervention, whether by Japan or any other Power, would be disastrous to Russia—a true prophecy, if uttered, but one which Uchida himself did not, perhaps could not, act upon when he in turn became Foreign Minister.

The chauvinists in Japan who wanted intervention did not take the same point of view as the Western statesmen. It had been one of the dearest wishes of amateur and professional propagandists in England and France to know how they could interest Japan in the war, and they were fated never to discover, even though some of them journeyed to the Orient to find out. The Japanese themselves knew what line to take. Some irritation was caused by Allied representatives and armed forces arriving on the scene as soon as there was a real movement for intervention, but the Japanese were not very much hurt at these evidences of suspicion. The idea that the United States was stealing a march on Japan and promoting American interests in Siberia was a much more stimulating one. The advertisement of the "German menace" did not appear to make much impression, though, just after the Blagoveschensk affair, there was a report that two army corps of German prisoners were under arms at Irkutsk. Nobody, however, took this very seriously. Count Terauchi, the Premier, told the Diet that Japan was not so impotent that the prisoners in Siberia caused her any anxiety, and on March 23rd Viscount Motono, the Foreign Minister, told the same body that he knew nothing regarding the rumoured arming of the German prisoners in Siberia. Yet on March 27th Notes were exchanged between Japan and China settling the form of the secret Military Agreement, under which arrangements were definitely made for protecting—and crossing—the Sino-Russian frontier.

The Diet was prorogued at the end of March without any attempt to reach a serious decision regarding Japanese action in Siberia, but action was coming inevitably nearer; three Japanese were killed in a disturbance in Vladivostok on April 4th, and Japanese bluejackets were landed the next day, whereupon the Moscow Soviet asserted its pretensions to authority by protesting vigorously. The political oracle, Miura, pronounced against intervention, but in this matter he probably represented that fairly large school who, while ready to be boastful as to Japan's abilities, harboured a dread of foreign arms and preferred to find a good reason for not taking risks. But still the idea that Japan must be ahead of America in Siberia was taking root, and Viscount Kiyoura, who, when Minister for Agriculture and Commerce in 1904, had declared that the very purpose of the Russo-Japanese War was to open up new and great fields for trade and industry in China and Korea, now added fuel to the propaganda by warning his countrymen that, after the war, Britain would be Japan's economic enemy. The protection of Japanese and the forestalling of American and British economic activity in Siberia were far more effective slogans than any supplied by the European agents for intervention, one of whom, representing the *Daily Mail* in Harbin, exercised a lively imagination in informing the world exactly how near

Vladivostok the German armies had penetrated, and also declared that Japan's lack of interest in the war was due to the inadequate news service supplied her—efforts which elicited from Peking scornful indignation at the crudity and wickedness of the methods used for promoting intervention.

While this campaign of intrigue and rumour was being conducted, a new factor appeared which was to prove decisive as to intervention and at the same time to render that intervention a tragic farce. In Russia were some fifty thousand Czech prisoners. Unwilling to fight as Austria's conscripts, they had welcomed capture by the Russians and had maintained an effective organisation in Russia. After the revolution they were the mainstay of the Russian army for a while, but the Bolshevik revolution brought fighting to an end, and the Czechs expressed a desire to get out of Russia and take up arms on the Western Front. To this the Bolsheviks were not averse, as the Czechs were not of their persuasion, though most of them would have called themselves Socialists. Eighty trains were provided, and the Czechs set out on their journey across Siberia at the beginning of April, one rifle being allowed for every ten men. By this time railway organisation had almost come to a standstill in Russia, and the first of the Czechs to reach Vladivostok were fifty-seven days on their way, the rest being strung out all across the country. A small French military mission was accompanying the Czechs. Endeavours were made, it is stated, to convert them to Bolshevism, but it would hardly appear that there was ever very much mutual interest. Whether through instructions or misunderstanding, obstacles over and above the delays in railway mismanagement were put in their way, and the alarm was suddenly given that Moscow was playing them false. At Irkutsk, west of Lake Baikal, there was a conflict, in which the Czechs were easy winners, and armed and provisioned themselves at the expense of the Red Guards. Communication was opened with Moscow, where Lenin refused to parley with them, though

Krasnoschekoff, who was trying to organise the Russians in the Far East, without drawing any fine distinctions between their particular brands of Socialism, met the ten thousand Czechs who had reached Vladivostok and spoke to them on friendly terms.

The Czechs were now at open war with the Bolsheviks, and, after their success at Irkutsk, they crossed Lake Baikal and defeated the Bolsheviks on the eastern side badly, capturing Verkhneudinsk. They were now in possession of the whole line from Samara to the farther side of Baikal, in strong force in Vladivostok, and able to arm and provision themselves with supplies furnished by the Allies from Vladivostok.

And now there came about a development which has never been adequately explained, unless surmises that cover the probabilities and explain the facts may be considered adequate. American soldiers were pouring into France, and it was questionable whether the Czechs could be advantageously transported from Siberia to the Western Front, at a time when the shipping problem was so acute. The "oppressed peoples," especially those under Austrian and Russian rule, were being invited to enjoy the recognition of the Allies in their assertion of self-determination; the Republic of Czecho-Slovakia was duly recognised; the representatives of various nations at Vladivostok recognised the Czechs as a fighting force against armed Austrian and German prisoners; and the Czechs turned back and began a war on Bolshevik Russia.

When the Czechs were masters of the situation and had turned their faces westward again, a mighty cry arose that the Bolsheviks had dealt treacherously with them and that they must be rescued. In point of fact, Eastern Siberia was at this time showing signs of settling down on a workable basis. The peasantry had shown the invaders that only by fighting the Russian people could they interfere effectively with the Governments that had been extemporised at Vladivostok and along the Amur. But there was no reason for the Czechs to be squeamish, though they were far from being all of one mind, notwithstanding the good discipline that kept them, throughout, faithful to their leaders. One of these leaders, interviewed towards the end of June by a Japanese newspaper correspondent, gave voice to their suspicions that they were being kept in Siberia by the Allied Powers in order to extirpate Bolshevism. They appeared to undertake the task with no great reluctance, though, it is true, they had little option in the matter. On June 28th they made a sudden *coup* in Vladivostok, and disarmed the soldiers of the temporary Government, which, like all the East Siberian Governments, cared little for Leninite glosses on Marx, but waited anxiously for an opportunity to join the movement on which all hopes were set—the Bolshevik revolution. The remains of the old municipal council were set up as a government, the Czechs proclaiming that their action was rendered imperative by the oppressive measures taken against their brethren by Bolshevik organisations farther west. This was followed by a Japanese, British, French, American, and Chinese proclamation recognising the Czechs as being in military control of Vladivostok, and the occupation of a "neutral zone" by British and Japanese forces. The rapid growth of the American interest in the business led the Bolsheviks to declare that the Czechs were acting on American instigation. Citizens of the United States were certainly taking a lively interest in the developments, and members of the Young Men's Christian Association were as prominently among the Czechs as were the French officers, and more numerous. The Czechs followed up the Vladivostok *coup* by a prolonged raid along the Ussuri valley, to the north, and they were even heard of in the distant township of Yakutsk, on the Lena.

In these long midsummer days Ataman Semenoff appeared on the scene, fleeing from the Bolsheviks with some Tsarist cossacks in his train. Him the Japanese adopted as a chosen tool, and, through their influence, he troubled Siberia for many months, contributing more than any other single factor to the determination of the Russians to have nothing to do with foreigners or their myrmidons.

The agitation for a formal intervention was daily intensifying, especially in Britain and France, and the United States at last took the lead, in the hope that it would be possible, by this means, to make intervention useful to Russia and not pernicious. The demand for intervention had seized upon three leading reasons—the rescue of the Czechs, the saving of the vast war stores at Vladivostok from the hands of the Germans, and the giving of support to any tolerable form of government which might emerge from the welter. Unfortunately the Russian idea of what was tolerable was quite different from that of the invaders. The United States disclaimed any intention to carry intervention to the length of delivering an attack upon Germany from the east, and only regarded the preservation of the war stores at Vladivostok as being desirable in order to supply the subsequent needs of the Russian forces. But while the United States regarded as the chief object of the expedition the protection of the Czechs from the armed Austrian and German prisoners, it recognised that they were moving westward, and suggested to Japan that each should send not more than seven thousand men to act as a rearguard covering this westward movement. The train of thought may have been rather confused, but Japan did not cavil at that. What did cause dissatisfaction in Japan was the expressed "hope and purpose of the United States to take advantage of the earliest opportunity to send to Siberia a commission of merchants, agricultural experts, labour advisers, Red Cross representatives, and agents of the Young Men's Christian Association, accustomed to organising the best methods of spreading useful information and rendering educational help of a modest kind in order in some sympathetic way to relieve the immediate economic necessities of the people." This rankled a good deal, for Japan was herself short of every kind of necessity, and did not regard with any favour a benevolence calculated to make Russians regard the United States as their special friend; while as for the Y.M.C.A. men and other economic agents, they were from the beginning denounced as bagmen touting for orders and bargaining for concessions. Nor were the Japanese blind to the fact that here, as at Tsingtau, help which they did not require was rather too promptly supplied. In the Siberian adventure not only were American warships and seven thousand men sent, but British warships and a transport or two of troops, and even small contingents of French and Italians. Much was done to counteract the effect of this by arranging that wherever there were foreign troops there should also be some Japanese with an officer of higher rank than any others present. But much more effectual was the dispatch of seventy thousand Japanese troops over the Chinese Eastern Railway. A movement so overwhelming naturally evoked a request for explanation, and the explanation given was that this was in accordance with the Sino-Japanese Military Agreement, signed on May 16th, and still secret as to its terms, but under which Japan had to afford China assistance in case of her frontiers being threatened.

The Japanese preparations had been made before America thought of participating, and had even been preceded by a *ballon d'essai* in order to discover whether any American objections would be made. All the Japanese authorities were not at one in the matter, as might well be supposed. General Uehara, formerly Minister for War and now Chief of the General Staff, disapproved, and threatened to resign, but was overborne by his subordinates, Generals Oshima and Tanaka, who followed Count Terauchi, the Premier. The resignation of Viscount Motono in July was surmised to be due to his dissatisfaction with his colleagues' reluctance, but his death shortly after seemed to confirm the official reason of ill-health. Viscount Goto had succeeded him as Foreign Minister, and was quoted as declaring that Japan could never tolerate a Bolshevik Government in Russia. He was at any rate ready for intervention, but the attitude of some members of the Diplomatic Advisory Council was doubtful, notably that of Mr. Hara, so soon to become Premier, who yet, though holding office an almost unprecedented time, was not destined to live to see the end of the Siberian adventure. Some of the military men, and even the amateur fire-eaters, were very indignant at the Diplomatic Advisory Council's attempt to limit the scope of intervention.

All doubts had been settled before the American proclamation of August 5th, for on August 3rd the Japanese *Government Gazette* announced that Japan was preparing to follow the example already set by her Allies, out of her desire to see order speedily restored and the Czechs relieved from the obstructions to their eastward movement presented by the armed Austrian and German prisoners. That Washington and Tokyo conceived of the Czechs moving westwards and eastwards respectively is a striking commentary on the whole scheme. Increased activities began at once. Japanese troops went north from Vladivostok and cleared out the temporary Government from Habarovsk. The peasantry, who had before made such invasion impossible, seeing themselves confronted by an invincible force, submitted to fate and returned to their fields, much to the disappointment of the conquerors, who complained that, on the approach of the Japanese arms, the Bolsheviks disguised themselves as ordinary citizens. Both now and later, however, there were cases where, on a report that a village was Bolshevik, it was surrounded and obliterated, peasants and huts being put to sword and flame. Such were the evil fruits of propaganda. Nikolaevsk, at the mouth of the Amur, three hundred miles below Habarovsk, was occupied by a naval expedition. The Americans took over the management of the railway running north from Vladivostok. The Japanese had bigger things on hand, and within a fortnight of the *Government Gazette* announcing the imminence of preparations there were thirty thousand Japanese troops in North Manchuria. They also patrolled the Amur, capturing without resistance the "Bolshevik Navy" and seizing arms and ammunition wherever found.

In spite of their overwhelming force, however, the Japanese did not find it advisable to remain in Habarovsk more than a few days, but they left Kalmikoff in charge there. The forces in North Manchuria then went off to the rescue of Semenoff. This bandit, who had neither physical courage nor any military ability whatever, had but two talents—sycophancy and brutality. He showed the first in presenting to the Crown Prince of Japan a pair of Siberian eagles; of the second he was to give plentiful exhibitions under Japanese protection. Although the Czechs had won easy victories against the Bolshevik arms, they never attempted much in the way of administration, and they had got separated into two groups, the one in Vladivostok and the Maritime Province and the other an attenuated line from Irkutsk to Samara; from Chita to the Manchurian border, and also along the Amur line (a great "Y" of railway) extremer forms of temporary government, waiting for an opportunity to join up with Moscow, held sway. The Japanese forces put an end to that. The Czechs, under General Gaida, arrived in Chita from Irkutsk on September 3rd, and three days later the Japanese arrived from the east. Semenoff came marching victoriously up behind them, and was installed by the Japanese as dictator.

XIII

THE KOLCHAK ADVENTURE

Thus began the policy of assisting the Russian people to rally round a native Government of a kind agreeable both to themselves and to the Allies. The Japanese were absolved of any charge of setting up their own authority in Russia, at the cost of handing over the people to the brutalities of two rapacious and dissolute Cossacks. One thing at least was certain, that neither Semenoff nor Kalmikoff was tainted with the subversive doctrines of Marx or Lenin, though tortured and plundered bourgeois may have failed to appreciate the soundness of their political philosophy. Both made themselves notorious by wholesale murder and robbery. Semenoff in particular levied toll on every train that passed, and, being an amorous soul, earned notoriety by the dashing quality of his female companions. Kalmikoff was credited with a logical mind; in his view, if the whole population was Bolshevik, then the only remedy was to hang or shoot the whole population. The third Russian who had the countenance of the Allies was a far better man—General Horvath, the manager of the Chinese Eastern Railway. He kept to his job, so far as he was allowed, and, since some sort of administration was necessary, he assumed a vague kind of dictatorship over the railway, which, of course, was all on Chinese territory, though not under Chinese control.

So we find, in the early days of September, the Japanese with an army in Siberia and Manchuria, without Russian opposition and in a protective relationship to the Czech troops. From the Volga to the Behring Straits, Japan was in complete strategic control.

Success so extraordinary might well have been expected to fire the imagination of the nation; but the nation had truer instincts; it knew that nothing solid is ever so swiftly constructed, and it also knew that, notwithstanding the boastful war claims made in advance by patriotic demagogues, an extension of the empire in this direction was improbable and undesirable. Bitter complaints were made, especially by some of the high military officers, of the lack of popular patriotism. Troop trains started from the Japanese garrison towns without a single cheer, and there was no enthusiasm for intervention anywhere. Undisciplined minds even began to question the Government's right, under the constitution, to order conscript troops abroad on service unconnected with the actual defence of the country. Patriotism sank so low as to manifest itself in the form of a brutal attack by a gang of ruffians upon Mr. Murayama Ryohei, the aged proprietor of the *Asahi*, a leading newspaper long pre-eminent for the soundness of its information on foreign affairs. The attack was made on the afternoon of September 28th in the middle of Osaka, when Mr. Murayama was going home in a jinriksha. But for the courage of the puller of the vehicle the victim's injuries must have been far more serious than they were. Nobody ever doubted that the reason of the attack was that the *Asahi*, alone among important newspapers, had had the courage to oppose the Siberian adventure with vigour. But martyrdom combined with the stigma of being unpatriotic was a fate that few Japanese would care to court, and this political outrage was followed by the resignation of the most important members of the editorial staff. The incident was typical of the effect of the official cultivation of patriotism upon individual independence of thought.

Though all resistance was crushed and the Japanese and Czechs were in full control, there was no element either of peace or permanence in the situation. The Czechs were maintaining a front in the Volga region, and their base was at Vladivostok: between these points were thousands of miles of neglected and disorganised railway, the paralysis of which was accentuated by the presence of seventy thousand Japanese troops who used the trains for their own purposes and at their own caprice. Colonel Stevens with his corps of American engineers was waiting to fulfil the task for which he had been sent out a year before, and at the beginning of September an inter-allied transportation conference was held, over which General Takeuchi presided. It agreed that something must be done, but no nationality trusted any other to work the line for the general need, and throughout September and October Stevens was kept idle while the line deteriorated. At length the worst possible form of compromise was effected, each nationality taking charge of a section of railway, with the result that strikes, misunderstandings, bitter disputes, and chaos increased until the end of 1919, contributing not a little to the tragic failure of the whole preposterous enterprise.

At the height of the success of the incursion Vladivostok was put under martial law on September 18, 1918. Three days later the Vladivostok Government resigned. In every centre under their control the invaders again and again set up governments which they considered representative of the real Russia which only awaited a favourable opportunity to emerge from the nightmare of Bolshevism, and never, though these governments enjoyed but the briefest existence and maintained the most unsatisfactory of attitudes, was the obvious lesson of the futility of interference learnt. The invaders were certainly in no position to preach to the Russians on the virtues of amity and concord. The Americans were the most dissatisfied of all. This disagreeable and inglorious adventure was not the purpose for which they had entered the war, and, while keeping themselves within the limits of the proclamation of August 5th, they complained that the Japanese only wanted to go out shooting Bolsheviks, while the Europeans were intent on reinforcing a fighting front in Europe—two aims which the American Government had specifically disclaimed. To such a pass did relations come even in these early days of the intervention, that on October 12th an international censorship on messages dispatched abroad was organised, each nationality managing its own—a proceeding as futile as the sectional railway control, though less harmful.

All this time the Russians themselves were constantly endeavouring, in spite of the presence of foreigners in control of their scanty communications, to arrive, if not at a centralised form of government, at least at a general agreement and a working compromise. The finer points of Socialism were better appreciated in Western than in Eastern Siberia. The authority of the capital had been more felt there, and many regarded the release from the autocracy as being incomplete if it meant only subserviency to Moscow. But the revolution in Western Siberia also pursued its destined course from conservative democracy to Leninite Communism, its progress along that course being accelerated by every foreign attempt to promote reaction.

Soon after the Bolshevik revolution a Siberian Republic had been proclaimed in the arctic cold of Tomsk, and the duma assembled, but its authority never extended beyond the city. During the spring and summer that followed, while intervention was being prepared, a more radical and more vigorous government was set up in Omsk, under Vologodsky. So hopeful were its prospects that when, on July 23rd, less than a fortnight before the American and Japanese proclamations of intervention, it proclaimed the independence of Siberia, Irkutsk and Vladivostok declared their solidarity with Omsk, and even Semenoff and Horvath gave a nominal allegiance. Vologodsky, who visited Harbin in September, was rather embarrassed by this success, just as Horvath was by the helpful victories of the Czechs. Both of them saw in conditions favourable to their immediate security the greater possibility of interference with their independence.

Omsk, at last, was to provide the final object-lesson in the impossibility of making revolutions with rosewater. On October 7th the last effort of the moderates against the Bolshevik Government was seen in an All-Russian Constituent Assembly held at Ufa. Its method of representing Russia was to migrate to Omsk, where Vologodsky's Government complacently made room for it. It tried to make friends with the Czechs and Cossacks and to be liberal and comprehensive. But a new portent was arriving. Admiral Kolchak, spared by the mutinous fleet that he had commanded on the Black Sea, made his way to Siberia. He was an honest and patriotic officer, with a total incapacity for politics but anxious to restore what his class regarded as order in Russia. The Allies, dubious of such tools as Semenoff and Kalmikoff, hailed him as the saviour for whom all Russia was looking to save it from the usurping 5 per cent. of Bolsheviks. With their united benison he entered Omsk; but his method of gaining popular support was dubious. A Cossack regiment under Semenoff arranged a *coup* in Omsk, and on November 18th proclaimed Kolchak dictator.

Meanwhile in the east the hopes that intervention would bring pacification were proving more and more delusive. Sir Charles Eliot, the British High Commissioner, and Mr. Regnault, who fulfilled a similar office for France, arrived in Vladivostock and found the position an impossible one. Sir Charles, realising the mistake of the Czechs having been allowed to disarm the Russians, tried to effect a remedy, but only succeeded in restoring martial law, whereupon civil government disappeared. The official reports of the Japanese War Office describe a dangerous concentration of Bolshevik troops in Omsk early in September, and later on the consequent state of chaos supervening. There was an expedition along the Amur, the American troops co-operating in the capture of Habarovsk, and on September 18th the Japanese captured Blagoveschensk, bringing to a definite end the Council of People's Commissaries that had been organised in the previous February. As had been found earlier in the year, to attack the Russians in one place in order to make them less "Red" only resulted in a general reddening in the vicinity. After the capture of Habarovsk, the situation at Nikolaevsk became threatening, and Japanese marines were landed, but had to be withdrawn before the end of the month and replaced by soldiers sent down from Habarovsk, as winter descends early at the mouth of the Amur, making navigation impossible for the greater part of the year. The Japanese captures at Blagoveschensk included 300 prisoners, 55 river steamers, 326 railway passenger cars, 5,000 rifles, and 2½ million cartridges, according to the Japanese War Office statement, and this list is perhaps a more eloquent explanation of the expedition than the political chaos from which it was necessary to deliver the Russians. Between Blagoveschensk and Habarovsk Cossack and Japanese troops combined to obliterate Bolshevism, and it was reported that in the course of this operation they captured 1,500 Magyars.

This last item may be noted because, though there was a plentiful output of reports of all degrees of unreliability and imaginativeness, statements of this particular kind were extremely rare. There had been reports of the tens of thousands of Austrian and German armed prisoners, and their menace to Siberia was the very reason for the intervention. Sometimes they were more precisely spoken of, as towards the end of July, just before the intervention had officially begun, when it was reported that the Bolshevik force on the border facing Manchuli numbered 20,000, of whom 6,000 were Germans and 3,500 Magyars. Just after the report of the capture of Magyars in the clearing up of the Amur, the announcement was made in Japan that no prisoners were to be brought out of Siberia; it was also reported that when the friendly Russians caught Bolsheviks they let them go, but that they gave Germans and Austrians no quarter. The last statement is easy enough to believe, but the complaisance towards Bolsheviks is not compatible with the records of Semenoff and Kalmikoff, or even of the Japanese themselves. As time went on one heard less and less about the armed German prisoners,[1] until at last this bogey vanished from men's minds and was forgotten. Less and less was also heard of the great mass of the Russian people who hated the

---

[1] This is conspicuously noticeable in Colonel John Ward's *With the Diehards in Siberia*, where the armed Germans and Austrians are ever present to the mind's eye, but never appear in the flesh.

Bolsheviks and only wanted the opportunity of gathering round some steady rallying-point. They dwindled into the bands of Cossacks who took service under Ivanoff-Rinoff, the great exponent of pacification by the knout, Baron Ungern, brave but homicidal, Kappel, Semenoff, and Kalmikoff; and they included some old Tsarist officers and soldiers who were fired less by their ancient loyalties than by increasing fears of the vengeance of those against whom they had fought and by dwindling hopes of such foreign help as would set them up in safety and comfort under a régime which would leave the old classes in their old relations.

The last effort to rally the Russian people was made by Kolchak, the chosen favourite of the Allies. His beginning, it is true, was not auspicious. Instead of inviting the last anti-Bolshevik Government in Russia to rally to his standard, his Cossacks threw them out or flung them into prison. However, Kolchak went ahead, and presently had between two and three hundred thousand men under arms and in training for a great offensive against the Bolsheviks in the spring of 1919. Recruits were amazingly easy to get, but they proved astonishingly difficult to keep. Men joined up hungry and ill clad. They were well fed and well clothed, the Allies providing everything; and as soon as they were armed and in good fettle they vanished, marching off to their homes with their rifles.

But let us hasten to the end of this wretched tale. Kolchak began his dictatorship too late. The war in Europe had come to an end; there was now no question of the Czechs fighting Germans; they were fighting Russians; and for this there were subsidies forthcoming, but there were no ships to repatriate them.[1] Henceforth the Kolchak adventure was almost out of the range of Japanese history. The representatives of the Great Powers went to Omsk, and even past the Urals. They recommended the recognition of the Kolchak

---

[1] Some seventy British ships brought troops and stores to Vladivostok. The Japanese supplied as many for repatriation of the American armies from Europe. There were none obtainable for the Czechs till long after.

Government. But everything was now half-hearted. The spring offensive duly began, and there were some initial successes; but the Moscow Government was now mobilising its man-power, and, while Kolchak was being overwhelmed with every kind of worry, and his government was degenerating into a primitive tyranny, the Soviet forces were gathering strength for a decisive blow. They delivered it in the late summer, and from September onwards the history of Kolchak was a tale of rapidly accumulating disaster. The Czechs, wearied with Kolchak's methods and disgusted with being used as a cat's-paw, refused to sacrifice themselves in a cause that they saw was lost, and led the way in the retreat. The retreat led only into a chaos of conflicting authority and disorder. When the Czechs came pouring through and declared that they no longer recognised the authority of Kolchak, Semenoff hastened to denounce him also. The Cossack was always on the winning side. The flight only halted on the shores of Baikal, and the Bolsheviks came up in such force that General Janin, who was with the Czechs, set the crowning infamy on the whole transaction by surrendering Kolchak to his enemies. They incontinently shot him on February 7, 1920, and there was no longer any doubt about Russia being "Red" as far east as Lake Baikal.

XIV

SOCIAL DEVELOPMENTS AFTER THE WAR

The Siberian adventure had closed in shame and dishonour for all the participants, but it was to be long before Japan was to be free of it. Only very fitfully did it become a major interest in Japan, where there were many other matters to occupy public attention. Symptomatic of the times was the great Kyushu scandal, which dragged its slow length along throughout 1918. At Yawata, in Kyushu, near the coalfields, the Japanese Government set up a great smelting and steelworks. It was the foremost example of the policy of Government leading the way in industry. A plant so enormous could not, perhaps, have been started by private enterprise in a country coming late and inexperienced into modern industry, but there was always much dispute as to its management and much mystery regarding its finances. It helped Japanese industry and it hindered it, its position being an anomalous one and its policy a fluctuating compromise between trying to justify its existence by making a profit and benefiting industry at large without regard to commercial consideration. Early in February 1918 a sensation was caused by the suicide of the manager of the works, Oshikawa Norikichi. An official inquiry into the administration of the works showed that the suicide was, without doubt, the result of fear of imminent disclosures of corruption. Inquiries were pursued; everybody denounced everybody else in the hope of saving himself. Detectives even examined the books of drapers in order to find corroborative evidence that officials' wives had been the recipients of expensive presents.

The inquiry had to be stopped at last because so many people were involved that it would have become impossible to prosecute them all. Not that all were necessarily guilty; for, as we saw in the case of the Korean conspiracy, the growth of that gigantic mare's nest similarly had to be checked by closing the inquiry lest it became too vast to handle. The circumstances of the time have to be taken into consideration. The Yawata works was the greatest dispenser of both pig-iron and steel in the empire, and the price of these necessaries had risen to ridiculous heights. Dealers and users were prepared to give their souls for iron, and that bribes should be offered and taken was almost inevitable. During the trial there was such a shortage of iron that drain-covers, railings, and every visible and movable piece of iron was legitimate loot, and the accused officials must have reflected on the smallness of the sums for accepting which they were in trouble compared with the magnitude of those that they might have demanded in these latter days. But the war was over, the embargoes removed, and the price of iron approaching the normal before sentence was delivered. Officials were appropriately dealt with; and of the men who tempted them the leading names were Takata Shinjiro, Okura Hatsumi, and Kishimoto Ryutaro, all belonging to the great firms whose names they bore. All were sentenced to long terms of imprisonment, but were in reality not punished at all, being granted stay of execution of sentence—a device by which the most solemn vindication of justice can be turned into a farce. These sentences were pronounced on December 28th, when all the country was reading about another scandal—a still more corrupt story regarding land in Kyoto, publication of which had been forbidden in its earlier stages. In a time when all economic conditions were abnormal and when everybody was in a hurry to get rich, scandals were unusually rife. It was a part of the widespread demoralisation that must always accompany war. By the time the corrupt officials of the steelworks received their sentences for accepting bribes, the private dealers, who had been so ready to demoralise them, and who had secured shares in the 300,000 tons for which a bargain had been driven with the United States, were clamouring for a suspension of sales by the Yawata works until their large stocks were disposed of on a market which had suddenly lost its appetite. The officials appealed, and it was well on in 1921 before the case was finally disposed of, eleven of them, out of all this great army, at last receiving some punishment.

It cannot be denied that the armistice was regarded in Japan as a disaster. As at the opening of the war, the effects of a great and unprecedented event were very difficult to foresee. Consequently everybody waited anxiously to see what would happen. Happily there was no general panic. It took a month, indeed, before commercial men at large realised what the effect would be, and the first hard blows came from abroad, especially from India and Australia, in the form of cancelled orders. A number of merchants and manufacturers were ruined, dealing as they did in goods which the war had forced up to extraordinary prices. But there was no dramatic suddenness of ruin. Europe was at peace, but its manufacturers were in no position to take up their work immediately; soldiers were no longer being taken to France, but for a long time the trooping services were busier than ever taking them away. So the change came with a little breathing-space, and by the time the leading readjustments were made the post-war boom was in full swing. It could not revive a number of exotic industries: iron foundries of considerable size closed for ever; antimony and zinc mines were abandoned; Japan had risen to the position of second producer of copper in the world, but soon sank to importing, the seal of doom being put on export by the imposition of a high protective duty. But, on the other hand, Europe went on spending as lavishly as ever; goods which had been unobtainable for years were bought in enormous quantities; and Japan found a good market for many of her wares in countries which again began to supply her with the requirements which she had had to do without or to make for herself.

So the boom went on; not only did people soon begin to forget that it had suffered interruption, but since it was existing in a state of peace they forgot that it must come to an end. They even sought for reasons why it should continue, and the theory was popular that all commercial activities had been keyed up to a higher pitch than before, and that this intense activity was a normal condition. The boom in business, however, hindered rather than helped a restoration of normal conditions in the public services. Wharves again were congested with mountains of goods which it was impossible to get moved except by gangs of thieves who looted the piers by land and sea—a complaint which was heard not only in Japan, but in most of the great ports of the world. The postal service was worse than ever. All men of intelligence appeared to have found more remunerative employment, and letters were delivered weeks overdue, at wrong addresses, and even carried back to the senders. Telegrams became as bad; and the deep-sea cables, from the long neglect of wartime, were subject to constant interruption. Cables to and from Europe took two weeks and even longer; often they were not sent at all, and though proof was offered by injured senders money was never refunded. The telephone service was so congested that trunk calls often took twelve hours, and each day there was a large proportion of calls that never got through at all. Mr. Noda, the Minister of Communications in the Hara Ministry, freely confessed that the efficiency of his Department was about 2 per cent. of the requirements. The transport services were little better. Trains in Japan had been justly famous for their punctuality, though their speed was always very moderate; but now the time-table lapsed into chaos and the stations became as badly congested with goods as the piers. As for the tramway services, they were incredibly overcrowded, and at last it even came to a policy of removing the seats so that more people could be jammed into the stifling vehicles.

There were official rejoicings at the restoration of peace, and perhaps the perfunctoriness of these celebrations could be explained as being due to the influenza epidemic which spared Japan no more than it did the rest of the world. The most talked-of influenza tragedy was the death of Shimamura Hogetsu, a dramatist of the new school, which was

SOCIAL DEVELOPMENTS AFTER THE WAR 147

followed by the suicide of Matsui Sumako, a prominent actress—the more prominent since acting by women and in a naturalistic manner was an innovation in Japan. The two had been passionate lovers, to the advantage of their art, but to the sorrow of their families. Deaths did not interfere with the feverish commercial activities of the time, but provided a new variety of ostentation for wealth, black-bordered notices being very numerous in the Japanese newspapers inserted by the sorrowing relatives at astonishingly high advertisement rates. But while this tribute was paid to the dead, there was a scandalous neglect in the proper disposal of the remains: city crematoria were so overworked that the coffins stood in stacks for weeks at a time awaiting their turn.

This caused some horror, but its mere insanitariness might have passed unnoticed. In her conservancy problem Japan had never tried any alternative to the domestic cesspool, emptied from time to time by scavengers who removed the night-soil in carts. Those approaching or leaving the great cities by road are certain to encounter processions of these carts. To pass them is a nauseous experience, and, while their contents contribute greatly to the success of the intensive farming in which the Japanese are pre-eminent, the country, instead of being sweeter than the town, is rendered more noisome. But before the war the system was sufficiently well organised to enable all except those who either retired very late or went abroad preposterously early to escape encountering the carts in the city. Most organisations which, during the boom, got out of order were eventually restored, but not this one; and one of the most permanent effects of the war was that from that time onward the horrors of this primitive conservancy have been perpetrated at any time of the day or night and have shown as little respect for place as for time.

One of the most striking disorganisations of the time was in the currency. Gold had always been so carefully retained that it was never seen; but now silver, and even copper, approached vanishing point. The increase in wealth and wages found its expression in a flood of paper currency, which reached a denomination as low as twopence-halfpenny.

The war was no sooner ended than national self-consciousness was raised to a higher degree by the imminence of the discussion of the terms of peace. Prince Saionji was appointed chief delegate for Japan, but as some time must elapse before he and his suite could arrive in Paris, Viscount Chinda and Baron Makino, who were already on the spot, assumed temporary charge and took care of the propaganda, a department which, in general estimation in the belligerent countries, was all-important. It was recognised that whatever direct benefits Japan might gain from the war, her chief interest in the Versailles Conference was to keep upsides with China. So much sympathy had China won in America that there was a good deal of anxiety in Japan as to the result of the parleys in Paris. The Chinese delegation passed through Japan on its way, and was interviewed by officials of the Department of Foreign Affairs, much to the disgust of the progressive student body in China, who breathed out threatenings and slaughter at the idea that their delegation might betray them. Political indiscretion being a fine art in China, the delegation let it be known that it had been urged to say nothing about secret treaties between China and Japan, whereupon Viscount Chinda in Paris informed all the world that the report of there being secret treaties was "absolutely without foundation"—a disclaimer which proved rather unfortunate, since there was at least the Military Agreement—while Mr. Obata, the Japanese Minister in Peking in succession to Baron Hayashi, lectured the Chinese Foreign Office very severely on the intolerable imprudence of the disclosure of secrets by the peace delegates. Gradually making itself heard above the irresponsible clamour for territory as a condition of peace, the discussion of a demand for a racial equality resolution at the Peace Conference became a leading topic. In this connection Baron Makino tried to kill two birds with one stone by remarking for publication that the closing of all doors against Japan compelled her to look towards China for an outlet for her energies.

Japan's rapid rise and the reckless opportunism of her policy in China aroused a great deal of criticism and mistrust in America; unscrupulous armament advocates inflamed these feelings for the purpose of promoting military expansion, and Oriental exclusion became the slogan of the west coast. Hostility and mistrust in America were immediately reflected in Japan, and when, at the end of the war, the belligerent Powers were inevitably engaged in considering how best they could dispose of part of their swollen armaments, the continued and uninterrupted increase in Japan's navy was particularly marked. The hypothetical enemy, beyond any discussion, was the United States. Military men were keenly conscious that the army was almost obsolete: even coming in touch with details of second-rate European troops in Siberia had cured them of any remaining illusions on that point, but it was impracticable to expand the army. The strengthening of fortifications was possible, but manifestly meaningless; and the bringing of the army up to date was clearly a matter as much for training as for expenditure on the multitude of new weapons. The perfecting of the navy as a mobile force was more immediately practicable and, in the circumstances, more suitable. The idea of American hostility always conjured up visions rather of a naval struggle than of pitched battles, and even when military men indulged in fanciful essays (such as Lieutenant-General Sato Kojiro's *If Japan and America Fight*) they pictured a Salamis rather than a Marathon. Admiral Kato Tomosaburo, the Minister for the Navy, explained in the Diet that the "eight and eight" naval project was now found insufficient, and that it had been revised, the new plan providing for sixteen battleships and eight battle-cruisers; nor did anybody question whether, even with her increase of wealth as a result of the war, Japan could afford so powerful a navy as this.

By way of political diversion Mr. Ozaki Yukio at this time took up with great enthusiasm the advocacy of manhood suffrage. His party, the Kenseikai, joined in the cry, but the majority were professional politicians who cared little for such things except so far as they could use them for personal advantage, and Mr. Ozaki began to tire of party politics and to "plough a lonely furrow." As an exponent of constitutionalism and a student of English politics, Ozaki naturally turned to the ballot-box as a cure for the social discontent which was making itself manifest. Other leaders chose diverse remedies, according to their temperaments and habits of thought. Viscount Shibusawa at this time began to call conferences to discuss what should be done about the growing estrangement between Capital and Labour; for the economic upheaval of the war had swept away the last remains of the feudal spirit, leaving the country full of men who had made money and wanted to make more, and of landless casual workers attached to no master and to no place. Viscount Shibusawa's efforts bore fruit in the Kyochokai—the Capital and Labour Harmonisation Society. Generously capitalised, it was totally uninteresting to labour. It might have made militant trade unionism both unnecessary and impossible; but it never even began to exploit its magnificent opportunities. It frittered away time and money on the publication of a magazine, which nobody read, and the collection of futile statistics. Viscount Shibusawa had been a wonderfully successful banker and business man. Full of benevolence and gifted with urbanity, he was invaluable at arranging meetings for the promotion of international friendship; but though well equipped with maxims about the duties of capital towards labour, he seems to have had no conception of the requirements of the times.

Another political portent which the rice riots had thrown up to the surface was the existence of a pariah caste—the Eta. Learned discourses have been written on these people, who number between one and two millions. There seems to be little doubt that their degraded social position was mainly connected with the fact of their following trades (such as leather-dressing) which were inconsistent with Buddhism, though necessary to the social organisation. They were unlike an Indian low caste in that they absorbed into their community drunkards, wastrels, and disgraced men of better social standing; yet there seems to have been no way of emerging from the Eta ranks into something better, even though individuals among them acquired considerable wealth. Naturally they were a rough class, less cleanly and polite in their habits than the generality of Japanese. They had their own villages and their own trades, and in the great modern cities they tended to congregate in ghettoes and to be the scavengers of the commune. Accustomed to being treated with little consideration, they became indifferent to harshness and, in their villages and ghettoes, had little dread of the police, who for their part avoided interfering with them as far as possible, being rather at a loss in dealing with people who had no respect for their official position and even held the official sword in contempt. It was found, after the rice riots, that many of the men arrested in acts of violence were of the Eta class, and there was some spasmodic talk about society's duties towards them; Count Oki started a society called the Dojo-yuwa-kai for their amelioration; but nobody liked to tackle the question, which the Eta began to solve for themselves in a meeting held in Tokyo on February 23, 1919. The manner in which they strove to work out their own salvation will be described in its place; it is sufficient here to remark that the case of the Eta is only one more instance of facts contradicting the conventional moralising of political philosophers, who would like to believe, and who would have us believe, that violence and disorder only evoke repressive reactions against those who use such weapons in trying to remedy their grievances. The name "Eta" had long before been officially disused and *shinheimin*, or "new commoner," substituted; but not until the action of the Eta approached within measurable distance of leading a revolt was their position considered with the seriousness that it deserved.

Another social movement, entirely reactionary but important because of its strength, was the Roninkai, formed at the end of 1918 for the purpose of combating dangerous thought, under which term was included Trade Unionism, Socialism, and everything likely to cause perturbations to vested interests. Its leaders were Uchida Ryohei, Toyama Mitsuru, Sasaki Yasugoro, and Ogawa Umpei. Uchida and Toyama were the best known of these professional bravoes, who, of course, always extolled their own patriotism, and broke the laws only that law might be upheld. The "ronin" in Japanese tradition were masterless men, "careless of mortality and desperately mortal." Those in modern times who have adopted the description have wished to signify thereby that they stood for a strong policy and were ready to offer their own lives and interest in its pursuit. The attack on Mr. Murayama, of the *Osaka Asahi*, already described, was typical of the valour of this particular brand of patriot. Of the leaders Toyama was the most prominent. He had acquired wealth, lived in style, even entertained foreign notables, and laid down the law to statesmen with almost the oracular assurance of that other national hero, Viscount Miura, whose prestige, however, he could not emulate, since he stopped short of murder in his exploits. Moral and physical courage to criticise such patriots was rare, and Professor Yoshino ran no small risk when he attacked the Roninkai; some of the braves visited him, and he told them plainly what decent men thought of them and offered to debate the matter with them in public, a challenge which was taken up by Uchida Ryohei. Yoshino with a mordant wit made the subject of the debate "The Right to Assault." Naturally the audience did not go there to be convinced, and half of them did not even go because they were interested, for over two hundred policemen were present at the debate, which took place in a very moderately sized clubroom.

In Labour politics the Yuaikai, which began as a friendly society, was outrun and in danger of eclipse by the Rodo Domekai—more definitely a Labour Union; but Suzuki Bunji, the lawyer who founded the Yuaikai, was still the brains of the movement, and proved to be fully capable of taking a more and more advanced attitude with the progress of the movement. At one of the earliest meetings of the Rodo Domekai, in Tokyo, in May 1919, the typical form of Socialist meeting definitely developed. Osugi Sakae was there, a man of powerful mind, profoundly read in all revolutionary literature, and with a fanatical devotion to individual liberty. He had come somewhat unpleasantly into the limelight a couple of years before, owing to his being nearly murdered by a young woman with whom he had quarrelled and parted. She resorted to this desperate step after Osugi had formed a new connection with a young woman named Ito Noe, who was far better qualified to be the helpmeet of a social reformer, and who left her lawful husband in order to do so. At the Rodo Domekai meeting, where also a quarter of the audience were policemen, Osugi got into an altercation with the conservative element at the meeting and was flung out. The meeting went on, but in spite of this ejectment the speeches continued to offend the police, who stopped them one after the other, until the assembly broke up in a storm of indignation. This became the type of Labour meeting henceforth, and though the most passionate outbursts greeted these prohibitions, disobedience and force were very rarely attempted.

XV

THE INDEPENDENCE MOVEMENT IN KOREA

THE year following the armistice was one of intense restlessness all over the world. There was a belief that, even if the war had not brought in a new heaven and a new earth, at least the former things had passed away, and this feeling spread even to that social and political backwater, the "hermit kingdom" of Korea. General Hasegawa was now ruling in the peninsula, and, like most military martinets who find themselves in high administrative office, his mind could not soar above the barrack-room idea that inflexible discipline is all that is needed in the government of a people. The Koreans, however, were acquiring a more varied outlook. Many Korean students had come to Tokyo to seek their education, and there acquired many ideas besides those imparted in the Imperial University. At a meeting which they held on January 7, 1919, at the Young Men's Christian Association, they discussed the new principle of self-determination which President Wilson had been recommending for the European peoples and acclaimed it as eminently suitable for Korea. On the 21st of the same month the former Emperor of Korea died. As a sort of State prisoner he had survived for over twenty years the murder of the Queen—that night of horror when, held back by the points of the swords of Japanese bravoes, he had heard the murderers at their work in an adjoining room. Thenceforward, whether exhibiting to the world an imperial independence or living on a State pension, he had known no personal liberty, but two days after his death eulogies from the Government and the Opposition were pronounced upon him. His friendship for Japan was extolled, and the political wisdom inspiring him to conclude with Japan treaties which had assured peace and tranquillity to his people.

How little confidence the bureaucracy felt in that tranquillity there was no lack of signs. On January 28th the Press throughout Japan was warned by the police that it must say nothing about a self-determination movement in Korea. Korean students who had imbibed disturbing ideas were always being rounded up and newspapers referring to subversive thought in the peninsula were suppressed. In the Diet on February 20th the Director of the Colonisation Bureau, in reply to a question, said that dangerous Koreans known to the police existed in Siberia to the number of 250, in Manchuria 800, and in Hawaii and San Francisco 500.

Official ethnologists and historians began to seek for a satisfactory common origin for the Koreans, one authority, Takagi Masutaro, coming to the conclusion that there were excellent grounds for believing that just as Amaterasu, the Sun Goddess, was the divine foundress of Japan and ancestress of the Japanese, so her younger brother, Susa-no-o, stood in the same creative office for Korea. These ideas, it was thought, would greatly promote the effectiveness of the erection of a National Shrine in Korea[1] and enable the Koreans to appreciate their good fortune, besides adding to the glory of Japan.

The obsequies of the Emperor Yi were the signal for a rude disturbance of that tranquillity which his wisdom had conferred on his people. Signs of popular mourning had made the police anxious, for they interpreted the vehement grief expressed as a sign of dissatisfaction with the Japanese régime rather than of abandonment to the pain of a personal loss. Nor was this view altogether wrong. The Emperor Yi had never been a popular or enlightened monarch, but in his death his people, especially of the younger generation, saw a symbol of the passing away of Korea itself, just as the national spirit had reawakened. As though to arrest that passing, some thousands assembled before the palace where the dead monarch lay in state, on March 1st, two days before the date officially set for the funeral. They swept tumultuously

[1] The Chosen Jinja was formally dedicated on October 18, 1925.

into the palace grounds, and were driven out again by the Japanese guards, with no lack of roughness. On March 3rd the programme for the funeral was carried out in all points according to arrangement. Seven thousand Japanese troops lined the streets, Japanese and Korean notables participated in the procession, and the people came after, till there was a continuous line along the two miles from the palace to the place of burial.

From that day there began a month of strange and terrible scenes. Chiefly in the capital, but in every considerable town, and even in villages, Koreans met together, sometimes with banners or the flag of the old régime, and formed processions, shouting "Mansei." This was the Korean equivalent of the well-known Japanese cry "Banzai," meaning, literally, "ten thousand years," and comparable with "May the King live for ever." Many women and children joined in these processions, which were never armed. Perhaps it is too much to say that if these processions had been left alone there would have been no violence. There were many petty tyrants who were bitterly hated for their harshness and cruelty. Men placed in unchecked power over others always develop the worst qualities of human nature. Even the gentler ones had the Japanese passion for orders and regulations, and irritated the Koreans, who preferred above all things to be left alone. Police and gendarmes realised this well enough, and from end to end of the country they were panic-stricken. Processions were fired into as soon as they uttered their slogan, the fire brigades were called out and chased the fugitives with their bill-hooks. Swords and bayonets were as freely used, and in Seoul public safety was secured with machine-guns. The advent of troops only made it worse, and in some cases there were massacres. One of the worst cases was at a village in the Suwon district, where the local Christians were surrounded in their church, shot down, and the church burnt over them. It was said in extenuation, first, that a policeman had been killed in the neighbourhood, and secondly, that the troops were newly arrived and did not understand that the Koreans were fellow-subjects, conceiving rather that they were in an enemy country. Similar scenes, however, were witnessed in localities where these predisposing causes could not be pleaded. The severities were not confined to the dispersing of the processions. Thousands were arrested and imprisoned, not only for demonstrating, but taken from their homes on suspicion. The methods of interrogation were mediæval, and so were the punishments. Many died under the blows of the "paddle," a kind of thick rod, the excuse for using which, when corporal punishment had long been abolished in Japan, was that it was a Korean and not a Japanese institution, and that there was no prison-room for the housing of so many delinquents.

Severe restrictions were imposed on the Press in Japan regarding the reporting of these things, "lest it cause a disturbance of popular feeling in Korea." But the Press as a whole was only too ready to believe that the Koreans were monsters of ferocity, though a few enlightened journalists and politicians demanded investigation and reform. General Hasegawa, interviewed on the subject by a group of Japanese journalists, declared that the disturbances were solely due to the instigations of Bolsheviks. He was remarkably like the typical military reactionary all over the world: distant and invisible dangers were plain to his mind's eye, but to salient facts right under his nose he was entirely blind. There were many like him in Korea; the most preposterous of petty tyrants could never understand that his own actions provoked public sentiment against him: always the instigation had to come from some malign source. At this time there was much hostile feeling towards the United States, and while the Bolsheviks were the only people that a man in General Hasegawa's position could safely blame, less responsible people freely aired the opinion that American money was causing the mischief. Indeed, an American missionary named Mowry was arrested on a charge of harbouring rebels, these rebels being his own students, who had stayed in his house before they were wrongfully arrested. He was tried with unusual expedition and sentenced to six months' imprisonment. He appealed, of course, and it was not till March 1920, a year after the "rising," that he was finally sentenced to a fine of 100 *yen* and forbidden to continue teaching. Failure to assist the police or to act on their advice was mentioned as being his real fault. An English missionary named Thomas was, at the time of the disturbances, assaulted at a venture by some Japanese policemen and soldiers. He received 5,000 *yen* (£500) compensation from the Government. From these incidents the position of the Koreans may be inferred. But by the autumn of 1920 an official was quoted as remarking that Mowry and Thomas had been dealt with as they were in order to show who ruled in Korea—a fact of which the Koreans hardly needed such reminders. An interesting sequel was a series of strikes in mission schools, officially explained as being due to the students' discontent with the quality of education given as compared with the Government schools. The reason would have been more convincing had the supply of Government schools been sufficient to make the mission schools unnecessary. The influence of the schools was further weakened and their *raison d'être* sidetracked by a new series of regulations which made religious teaching practically impossible.

The "rising" was suppressed with ruthless severity, but the martyrs did not suffer in vain. General Hasegawa was removed. For some time the advisability of putting General Akashi, formerly head of the gendarmery in Korea, in his place was discussed. He knew the country, and would have been a very capable man for suppressing rebellions; but wiser counsels prevailed.[1] It was recognised that General Akashi's gendarmes had been one of the principal sources of the trouble, and that, on the other hand, there was no rebellion to suppress. The happy choice was made of Admiral

[1] General Akashi died in Formosa in the following October, and General Count Terauchi in November.

Viscount Saito. He was also a service man, it was true, and a new rule had been made permitting others than admirals and generals to occupy gubernatorial posts in Korea and Formosa; but it was one thing to make such a rule and quite another to find a suitable civilian, so many of Japan's choicest men having adopted the profession of arms. Viscount Saito proved a suitable Governor-General. Embittered irreconcilables tried to murder him, but he kept on steadily with his work of reform, hindered chiefly by his conservative officials who were firmly convinced that they knew better than any Governor-General could tell them the best way to treat Koreans.

Admiral Saito tried to introduce a new spirit into the administration rather than to make any great reforms in its machinery. From Tokyo communications went to the authorities in Vladivostok and Peking requesting them to suppress the recalcitrant Koreans who had crossed their respective borders and who became anything from bandits to "provisional governments." A fresh emigration took place into Chientao, not on the same scale as at the time of the annexation, but sufficient to sow the seed of future trouble.

XVI

JAPAN AND THE PEACE OF VERSAILLES

THESE events, while they were like a flame passing over Korea, were never more than of secondary interest in Japan, where other excitements following the war held the public attention. Too fervid patriots raised hopes doomed to disappointment by loudly proclaiming that Japan had won Shantung and the German Pacific colonies by conquest, and there were others, like Dr. Tomidzu, nicknamed Dr. Baikal, who insisted on the annexation of Eastern Siberia. A more definite and hopeful interest was aroused by the announcement that the Japanese delegates at Versailles were instructed to introduce a racial equality clause into the Covenant of the League of Nations; and there was a still keener interest in the anticipated struggle between the Japanese and Chinese delegations over the question of Shantung. Japan was not much interested in the terms of peace in Europe, and would have agreed easily enough to a generous treatment of the enemy countries or equally readily to their partition among the victors. Whether the diplomatists really desired to see their racial equality issue incorporated in the League Covenant is doubtful. A keen observer expressed the opinion at the outset that this was merely a demand to be withdrawn in favour of something more vital.[1] Racial equality was itself a rather vague term. Everybody would be ready to concede that we are all "equally God's creatures," but those countries which saw in the motion an endeavour to secure the free entry of Oriental labour were not inclined to incorporate this

[1] Mr. J. M. Keynes (*The Economic Consequences of the Peace*) has explained this principle. A motion is put forward and rejected. Another is proposed and is about to share the same fate, but a reproachful look, as if to say, "What, are you entirely hostile?" ensures its passage.

affirmation of equality in any international treaty. Prince Saionji arrived in Paris on March 2nd, and within a week public interest in the question was stirred up by messages that the racial equality issue was to be dropped. Viscount Ishii, Ambassador in Washington, however, was quoted as hinting that the equality clause was an essential condition to Japan's joining the League, but towards the end of the month there were fresh reports of the question being withdrawn for the present, to be raised later. So much canvassing and lobbying went on that the fate of the resolution was really known before it came to the vote at the meeting of the Commission on the League of Nations. Viscount Uchida, the Foreign Minister, breaking the news to the Diplomatic Advisory Council, said that at first the Imperial Government had had in view the impartial and equal treatment of all participating peoples in the League of Nations in matters of immigration, residence, mining, and coastal trade, but that this was modified owing to America's objections to the immigration clause. It was rather a curious assortment of equalities, and it was pointed out that Japan herself was an outstanding opponent of them all, since she did not allow Chinese immigration, foreign ownership of land, or participation in the coastal trade, and permitted mining only on unacceptable conditions.

When the news came that the resolution had been presented, and had secured a substantial majority of votes, but not those of Britain and America, and that President Wilson had ruled that unanimity was necessary, there was a real feeling of injury. Japanese critics had always been inclined to unnecessarily depreciative comparisons of their own country with others, especially in such matters as wealth, the standard of living, the amenities of life, and strength of armaments. Behind the bluster of the very noisy patriots, too, there could always be discerned a dread that perhaps Japan was not quite so great as they asserted. But the question of racial equality had never been raised—indeed, the protagonists of exclusion of Orientals had always been careful to explain that the question was a purely economic one, concerned mainly with the standard of living of the working classes. Even the rejection of the resolution by the League Commission did not amount to an expression of opinion on the subject, being purely negative. Nevertheless, the fact of Japan having brought the matter forward and of its being rejected was not unnaturally interpreted by Japanese as an affirmation that the Japanese race was inherently inferior to the European. It was a blow to national pride, but the vast majority were sufficiently occupied with more pressing personal affairs to prevent them from taking it greatly to heart, and they probably recognised that it had been unwise on the part of the Japanese Government to court such an issue. The militarist *Kokumin* declared that the nation was, as a result of this insult, like a bloodthirsty animal seeking its prey, and milder papers, which had made ribald jests about Prince Saionji being accompanied to Paris by his pretty maidservant, now said that it would be well if he had insured his life, as he could expect nothing but assassination when he returned to his indignant country: and this was no idle tattle, for the most eminent statesmen in Japan go in danger of their lives when the idea gets abroad that they have failed to exalt their country sufficiently.

It is doubtful whether the diplomatic creation of a grievance in order to gain a compensating support on some other issue was really necessary, and it is also doubtful whether even this spectacle of a proud nation undeservedly humiliated would have evoked enough sympathy to ensure the concession of Japan's more vital demands. Yet the struggle between China and Japan seemed somewhat academic. Japan repeated her promise to return Kiaochau to China, but demanded that the German rights and interests should be surrendered to her and the matter be left as one for settlement between her great but impotent neighbour and herself. To this the Chinese delegates were unalterably opposed. Both sides issued large quantities of propaganda literature dealing especially with the history of Japan's actions in Shantung during the war and with the Twenty-one Demands, for the benefit of the world at large as well as of the multitude of delegations present.

The Japanese were not good propagandists: they could never place themselves in the attitude of the man who looked at any question from another point of view. Linguistically they were generally inferior to the Chinese also, and when they hired foreign scribes to plead for them, they almost invariably made the most unfortunate choice. Besides, the attitude towards China during the war was almost beyond explanation, especially with old Okuma at home still blatantly declaring that Kiaochau properly belonged to Japan. So it appeared that they had courted humiliation in vain. At this moment Italy indignantly withdrew from the peace discussions owing to the other delegates not being prepared to agree to her territorial demands. Here, it seemed, Japan's case was saved, for the five Powers—America, Britain, France, Italy, and Japan—could hardly continue their discussions if there were two withdrawals. President Wilson, however, was unable to bring himself to the point of agreeing to the Japanese demands, even though it was hinted that Japan might follow the example of Italy: and, after all, Japan's interests in Europe were not so intimate that her withdrawal really made much difference.

So Japan was forced to play her last card. On April 22nd the delegation pointed out that on February 16, 1917, Britain had signed a Note guaranteeing support to Japan's claims in respect of German rights in Shantung and in the Pacific islands north of the equator. Mr. Lloyd George admitted that it was so, and this ended the discussion.

In the eyes of the world all this greatly injured Japan, and even the sympathy that had been widely felt over the racial equality issue turned to distrust. As for feeling in China, it became intensely hostile. There was propaganda, boycott, and even rioting. Nor was Japan in the least inclined to diminish the demonstrations. They were popularly exaggerated to a ridiculous degree, and a *casus belli* would have been very popular. Had the Japanese authorities wanted to find one, there would have been no difficulty. At Kuanchengtze, near Changchun, on July 18th, there was a serious fracas between Chinese and Japanese soldiers. Indeed, considering the manner in which Japanese garrisons were maintained in all sorts of places in China, it is surprising that there were not many more such incidents. In this instance the Chinese appear to have been to blame. They were commandeering carts in the railway zone—for at this time so utterly had all railway service except that for the carriage of Japanese troops broken down that it had become usual to make the long journey from Changchun to Harbin by cart instead of by train (whereupon the South Manchuria Railway put a tax on carts). A Japanese sentry asked the Chinese what they were doing, and was set upon and beaten. Some Japanese soldiers hurried to the spot, and soon there was a miniature battle in which eighteen Japanese were killed. After a great deal of discussion the affair was settled in the usual manner, by indemnities and apologies. In Shanghai, besides boycotts and burnings of Japanese goods, there was an incident which was very emotionally treated in Japan. A photograph of the Emperor from some illustrated paper was disfigured and stuck on a telegraph-post with insults scrawled below it. In the Japanese Press this was not even described, but was referred to as the unmentionable crime, at the thought of which every loyal Japanese swallowed hot tears.[1] But this passed off with an official apology. There had been a very fierce debate in the American Senate on the Versailles Treaty, in which the Shantung settlement had suffered special

---

[1] Japanese respect for royalty is markedly insular. During the war, when news came that King George, visiting the front line, had been thrown from his horse, the *Osaka Puck* published a picture of the King on a large barrel-shaped nursery horse with three soldiers pushing behind—a vulgar, schoolboy sort of drawing, with appropriately scurrilous remarks. Not the least notice was officially taken of this impropriety.

condemnation. The severity and vehemence of the criticism was as much the measure of the senators' political hostility towards President Wilson as of their humane feelings; but there was in truth so little that could be urged on the other side that Japan writhed under such a lash of invective as has seldom been applied in any legislature to the back of a friendly country. The Chinese, therefore, were enabled to give unrestrained expression to their feelings; and Dr. Sun Yat-sen, who had on occasion used Japan as a place of refuge and whose friendship for Japan even aroused the suspicions of some of his patriotic countrymen, declared that the Shantung settlement would rankle in the Chinese mind for a hundred years. The Japanese were not slow to respond. Wherever there was a large number of Japanese in China, they would meet and demand protection, telegraphing their resolutions to Tokyo. China was full of Japanese propaganda newspapers, in Japanese, Chinese, even in English, all so unskilfully conducted that they exacerbated feeling against Japan. Naturally Japan felt little inclined to forgo even the slightest advantage won; and as the Treaty of Versailles gave her the right to confiscate enemy property she did so, in spite of her solemn promises at the beginning of the war that enemy subjects should be undisturbed in their possessions. A part of the proceeds of these forced sales was afterwards refunded, but the incident did Japan's credit much harm even in the eyes of her allies, as she had suffered no such war losses as gave her even the shadow of an excuse for the breach of a spontaneous pledge. In one direction confiscation was encouraged by Japan's allies: the perpetual leases, of which Germans held a few in Yokohama and Kobe, under the old treaties, were extinguished, as well as the leases that Germans held in Chinese treaty ports. Much official corruption accompanied this breach of faith. Sales of German property were scandalously manipulated, and several officials ultimately went to prison for accepting bribes. But Japan did not actively participate in the last shameful act of deporting the Germans from China. So anxious were the statesmen of Europe to insult a fallen enemy, and so eager were the merchants in China to be rid of possible competitors, that they did not stop to consider the fatal blow they were dealing European prestige by these actions.

XVII

STRIKES, TRADE UNIONS AND PATRIOTIC SOCIETIES

IMMEDIATELY after the signing of the Versailles Treaty the restlessness which pervaded the whole world manifested itself in industrial strikes, and Japan had rather more than her share. In Japan, however, they were largely prosperity strikes, though the workers were constantly irritated by prices rising even faster than wages. In June the price of rice was higher than ever. Viscount Takahashi, the Minister of Finance, considered grandiose plans for a Government Rice Monopoly, but Mr. Yamamoto, the Minister for Agriculture and Commerce, favoured a *laissez-faire* policy. After the signing at Versailles public processions and entertainments were organised, picturesque affairs in which the *hetairai* figured largely, but these were hardly over when the streets were full of other processions of a less jocund character. There was such an epidemic of demonstrations as Japan had never known.

Capital as well as Labour had become self-conscious. Distinguished men would write articles and make speeches on the proper use of wealth; but, as always happens, that proper use was always something in the future and waited for Labour to say that it wanted amelioration here and now. There was much nervousness concerning dangerous thought. At the beginning of the year the girls in a filature at Nagano were reported to be singing a seditious song about the tyranny of capitalism, and steps were promptly taken to stop it. To the Western ear the Japanese "Labour Song" is even more dreary than the "Red Flag," but such mournful chants were believed by the police to be highly stimulating. Some students made a suffrage demonstration with red flags on February 11th ("Constitution Day"), and this had a rather chilling effect, as the authorities were particularly averse to students being interested in politics, and constantly tried to extirpate advanced propaganda from the universities. Besides Mr. Ozaki Yukio's enthusiastic advocacy of manhood suffrage, each political party evolved its own particular scheme for an extension of the franchise, by which it was hoped that the proletariat, satisfied that there was a good time coming in the indefinite future, would cease from troubling. But when the Diet dissolved, all interest seemed to be lost. The working class had never had any, and were somewhat sceptical about the plan. Just before the Diet closed, the question of the Police Regulations and the legality of trade unions and strikes was brought up. Mr. Kawakami, the Director of the Police Bureau, said that in view of the spread of dangerous thought it would be unwise to curtail the powers of the police. No. 17 of the Police Regulations was the chief point at issue. Strictly interpreted, this could be, and was for a long time, so used as to suppress strikes and Labour Unions, and it was the subject of a prolonged struggle, only being revised when it was no longer practicable to enforce it.

In July, Regulation 17 was openly defied. Railway workers, teachers, printers, people in the most diverse occupations, went on strike, and not infrequently there was some window-breaking. Workers in the great Mitsubishi and Kawasaki Dockyards held meetings in temples—rather a favourite resort in the lack of public halls—but did not get under way so soon as the employees of smaller concerns. The Okamura Denki, an electrical works, was one of the first big strikes, but perhaps more significant was the coming out of Government employees. That postmen should strike was perhaps not extraordinary, but there was some alarm when the workers in the military arsenals came out. There was even a soldiers' strike in the Matsuyama barracks, and it was dealt with in an exceptionally lenient manner; searchings of heart were going on, and it was thought advisable in this instance to remove an exceptionally tyrannical officer rather than to punish his rebellious victims. But what aroused most public attention was the good organisation shown by the Tokyo printers, for when they went on strike there was not a single newspaper produced in the capital for over a week.

Labour simultaneously took an active part in the disputes over Japanese representation at the International Labour Conference at Washington, a meeting which was practically boycotted in America and not taken any too seriously in Europe, but which was a very important event for Japanese labour. The Yuaikai demanded in vain that it should be allowed to send a representative, and a typical incident of the agitation was a brutal assault on a meeting of some Labour men in a Tokyo theatre by a gang of professional bullies. Another incident reported at the time was the murder of the captain of a sailing ship and his wife by the crew, who, attacked by the prevailing epidemic, had gone on strike; but probably this was only an ordinary mutiny. Violence on the part of the strikers was very rare when the magnitude of the disturbances is taken into consideration. It was not till September 19th that the 15,000 employees of the Kawasaki Dockyard walked out. They conducted a model strike. Their demands were submitted, the chief of which were concerned with rates of pay, and especially with hours of work, the eight-hour day being their essential demand. Committees were formed not so much for the purposes of picketing as for the keeping of order. Everything was excellently managed, but the strikers had no funds, and a week without pay was enough for most of them. The heads of the Dockyard were probably well informed regarding the condition of affairs, but they agreed to the eight-hour day and to a number of other demands at the same time as the strikers, unable to keep up the strike longer, returned to work, on September 29th. In November the yard distributed $4\frac{1}{2}$ million *yen* among its employees, and there was an edifying exhibition of mutual politeness. The previous year the yard had paid a dividend of 40 per cent. besides laying by large reserves.

Now, however, though the Kawasaki Dockyard could still afford largess on such a scale, it was preparing for the slump. Freights, though but a tenth of the war-peak price, were still high, and there was no difficulty in chartering ships. But as soon as the war ended it was plain that, however long the boom might last, there would presently be a slump in shipping. The excesses of shipbuilding in the United States alone made this certain. At first some of the big shipbuilders and shipowners discussed the formation of a concern to be called the Sentetsu Kokan-kai, or Steel and Ships Exchange Association. That did not appear very promising, but in due course the Kawasaki Dockyard and Messrs. Suzuki & Co., both large shipbuilders and owners—for the yard had built a number of steamers in readiness to supply the insatiable demand of the latter days of the war—succeeded in creating the Kokusai Kisen Kaisha (International Steamship Co.), into which they put their merchant fleets as capital at 350 *yen* per ton, and on this basis sold shares or borrowed from the banks so as to have their hands freer for other operations.

There was still an immense amount of money in Japan. In some directions there were most pressing embarrassments. Prices soared and slumped in an incalculable way, and one of the crises of the time was in connection with a heavy slump in cotton yarn. There were intricate complications, what with forward buying and forward selling, and there were long and sometimes acrimonious negotiations between brokers and millowners before a workable compromise was found. But the boom was still in being, and was in some ways intenser than ever. Every day saw new companies formed; there were such shortages that prices of commodities shot up like rockets; many concerns increased their capital for no discernible reason except that they could sell the new shares at a premium. The most cautious, who considered the possibility of trade slumps and currency depreciation, were the most reckless investors of all, owing to the means they took of providing for the future. It became the fashion to invest in land, as something that was always valuable and which could never dissolve into thin air. Among the squanderings of these investments there were some which had a permanent value. River banks and beds form the most promising areas for the development of residential sites, for which there was a tremendous demand. Japan's rivers are mostly torrents, higher than the plain through which the last few miles of their course runs, and consist, normally, of a small trickle of water through an immense stretch of stony river-bed. River-training reclaims large areas of land which, being a little above the fields, is very suitable for building. Areas of this sort were reclaimed by some building companies, and others developed various uncultivated slopes. In some cases the work was completed and a new suburb established, but usually at such a cost that the company could pay its way only by charging rents as extortionate as in the overcrowded cities. In most cases there was little left after the boom had passed but scars of unfinished clearing and half-made roads and the weather-stained boundary posts bearing the name of the company. These land companies were more prolific than most lines of investment in frauds and misappropriations, and what began with champagne and congratulatory speeches finished in the discomforts of a Japanese prison.

Amidst all this turmoil of Capital and Labour, the formation of the Kyochokai, or Harmonisation Society, was completed by meetings of great capitalists at the Bankers' Club and the Imperial Hotel, and a capital of 10,000,000 *yen*. Never did so much money make so little impression. And as the strikes died down for a while the appointment was completed of the delegates to the International Labour Conference at Washington. The Labour Unions managed to send one Domae, a workman of sound views but without linguistic attainments, who, through a volunteer interpreter, told the Conference something of the hardships of the Japanese working class. The official representative of Labour was Mr. Masumoto, a director of a shipbuilding yard, and consequently bitterly opposed by Japan's Labour men, who celebrated his departure by holding a mock funeral service for him. Mr. Masumoto was almost as good a selection as the Government could have made, for he knew what work was, and had also worked both as labourer and journeyman in England. He was, moreover, an enthusiast for the amelioration of the working class. The opposition was none the less bitter on that account, and, though it failed of its immediate purpose, it went a long way towards the subsequent establishment of the principle that Labour delegates could be better chosen by Labour organisations than by the bureaucracy. Mr. Muto Sanji, the managing director of the Kanegafuchi Spinning Co., Japan's model cotton-mill, and at the same time her most remunerative one, was delegate representing Capital. Mrs. Tanaka Takao, a niece of Viscount Shibusawa, was selected to represent Japan's working women. Her chief equipment for the task was a visit to various factories, and at the Conference there were uncomplimentary recriminations between this sympathetic but imperfectly informed lady and the benevolent capitalist who stood for paternal relationship and efficient organisation. As at all international conferences which almost necessarily lack plenipotentiary authority, the resolutions passed were rather pious hopes for the future than calls to immediate action, but this meeting at Washington had the effect of informing the world at large that Labour in Japan was now a body at least partly organised, and with aspirations similar to those of Labour in the Occident, not a mere inarticulate horde of coolies.

October 1919 saw the beginning of a movement that threatened to have serious consequences, but which proved to be of no particular importance, though its historic origin is of respectable antiquity. Lord Redesdale, in the *Tales of Old Japan*, tells of the *otokodate*, or "manly fellows," of old Yedo. They have been called a sort of low-class *samurai*. They were bullies and swashbucklers, but had a sort of rough chivalry, and their leaders were men of no little influence.

Their most prominent function in the old days was that of settling quarrels between the *daimyos* and their train of coolies. The feudal lords had to make an annual visit to Tokyo (then known as Yedo), and performed the journey with their principal retainers all in palanquins, with much baggage. The *daimyo* procession was one of the great sights of the country roads, and is still a favourite subject in decorative art. The hundreds of coolies who supplied the draught power for these journeys were often mutinous in the capital, and a Japanese gentleman has always a particular abhorrence for an altercation with the lower classes. So the *otokodate* were often called in to mediate in these disputes, and appear to have enjoyed a certain amount of confidence from both sides, having no fear of or bias towards either. In modern days the descendants of these *otokodate* had generally called themselves *kyokaku*, or "dare-to-dies," and had developed a hereditary inclination to become contractors' men and gangers. It was estimated that there were some half-million of them throughout Japan, about one in ten counting himself a leader.

Somebody conceived the idea that these men might, if formed into a patriotic society, be of considerable use to the Government in these disturbed times, as they were likely to stand for "law and order and no damned nonsense." So, in October 1919, an invitation was made to a number of the most prominent leaders to dine with Mr. Tokonami, the Home Minister. Now, no scheme could be more characteristic of Mr. Tokonami than this, but either some too zealous lieutenant issued the invitations prematurely or Mr. Tokonami was advised meanwhile that the *kyokaku* were not the men their forefathers had been. When the guests presented themselves they were politely told that there had been some mistake and that the Home Minister had not invited them. The braves manifested no little indignation, but did not lose their dignity, and, on the understanding being thoroughly established that there was nothing official about the matter, Mr. Tokonami met and talked to them, and they were duly fed. They were then formed into the Kokusuikai, or National Essence Society. Perhaps through this initial damping of enthusiasm, or more probably through inherent incapacity, the society never fulfilled the hopes that attended its birth. An air of respectability was conferred on it by retired generals and such-like accepting the office of president, but it failed from the beginning to command any confidence. Labour leaders protested vigorously against its creation, for they regarded it as an organisation of bullies designed to break up Labour meetings and overawe strikers. There were many cases where the Kokusuikai rushed in to settle Labour disputes, but they were very coldly received. Employers had as little faith in them as Labour had, and preferred the mediations of the police. The police looked on them with equal coldness, clearly regarding them as interlopers. They lost all prestige in an effort to teach the *eta* (Japan's despised caste) a lesson, and the most creditable show that they made was when they marched in rank, marked with a distinguishing sash, at loyal celebrations.

It has been mentioned how, as the great Yawata scandal came to a close, another serious case of official corruption came to light, Mr. Kiuchi, an ex-Governor of Kyoto prefecture, and several others being charged with making illicit gains. This case did not come to an end till the close of 1919, and was remarkable not so much for the corruption exposed —that, unhappily, was only too common—as for the charges of torture made by the accused against the police and procurators. Accusations against the police made by men of no particular account and bad character were common enough, and were invariably brushed aside as unworthy of investigation. But the charges made by Mr. Kiuchi and his associates could not be so contemptuously regarded, in disgrace though the accusers were. The Tokyo Barristers' Association took the matter up, and it looked as though a reform was about to be effected, but in the end the Government refused to prosecute and the barristers proved amenable to the argument that it would not be well for the prestige of the Department of Justice to suffer from such exposures, and to promises that an inquiry would be made and punishment meted out if necessary. They do not appear to have entertained the idea that an exposure of guilty officials and their condign punishment would maintain the prestige of the Department much better than allowing the public to continue in its belief that torture was the usual procedure and that police and procurators were the chief lawbreakers. It is always difficult for an Occidental to understand just what line of conduct the necessity of "saving face" will dictate, and it is possible that the Department of Justice was not averse to being feared, and considered that the difference between fear and respect was not so great as to warrant a casting out of fear in the hope of increasing respect.

XVIII

THE EMPEROR

TOWARDS the close of this year of intense and varied activity the Head of the State suffered a breakdown in health from which he never recovered. The Emperor had always been of delicate health, and, though he was the only son of the Meiji Tenno, it was only after a consultation with physicians as to his prospects of growing up to manhood that he was declared heir to the Throne. He grew up, married, and became the father of four sons, the last of whom was born not long after the Coronation in 1915. But though for a long time he fulfilled the arduous duties of a modern monarch, his health was gradually giving way. At the autumn manœuvres in 1919, which were held in the Hyogo district, His Majesty was in supreme command, as usual on such occasions, and he displayed a great interest in the equipment, the rationing, and the burdens of the common soldier; but this, while gracious and kindly, was a departure from the routine of a Commander-in-Chief which may have foreshadowed the coming disaster. It was very shortly after this that it was found necessary to treat the Emperor as an invalid. Hopes were held out for some time of his recovery, but they were disappointed. The Emperor failed in both mind and body. His speech was affected, and his memory left him, and though his physical functions were normal, his nervous system failed, so that he walked with a dragging step. From this time onwards His Majesty lived chiefly at the imperial villas, the Empress constantly attending him.

XIX

THE MASSACRE AT NIKOLAEVSK

It is time to direct our attention once again to the Siberian expedition. As a contribution to the war it had no longer any justification. From time to time it was the subject of bitter complaint. Viscount Kato, who had presented the Twenty-one Demands to China, who was quite unrepentant on that subject, and whose hectoring style was now being out-hectored by Mr. Obata, the Minister in Peking, denounced the Siberian expedition as wholeheartedly as the most thoroughpaced pacifist. He dwelt on the purposelessness of the quest, on the sufferings of the Japanese soldiers, and on the deep discontent that had been growing for a long time. As he was leader of the Opposition, such denunciations might have been merely political, but others less interested in party politics spoke of the expedition in the same strain. Among the soldiers Siberia was as unpopular as if it were a penal settlement. They were totally unaccustomed to such a climate, and, though it was glorious to die in battle, there was no glory in the rather too frequent accident of freezing to death on sentry-go. The official pronouncements on the subject were to the effect that it was true that the menace of the German prisoners of war had been extirpated, but that the Czechs were still in Siberia, and that for various reasons the safety of the Czechs, the security of the railway, the protection of Japanese residents, the dangers threatening from Bolsheviks and Bolshevised Koreans on the Korean border, it was still impossible for Japan to withdraw her troops as yet. As for Admiral Kolchak and the Omsk Government, that promising project had unfortunately come to nothing, but the supply of stores, for which payment was guaranteed, still went on, playing its part in the paralysis of transport which brought Kolchak to his death. Another contributory factor to this disaster was Semenoff's insubordination, but when Kolchak endeavoured to remove him the Japanese prevented him, and when he arrived in full retreat they compelled him to appoint Semenoff Commander-in-Chief—after which he was left to the vengeance of his enemies. Semenoff appealed to the Czechs, now streaming eastwards, not to desert him—for seeing the fate of Kolchak he began to fear for his own—but the Czech commander advised him to appeal to the patriots of his own nation who had hitherto crouched behind the protecting line of Czech bayonets, or to the heroes like himself who had kept as far from the firing-line as possible.

While the curtain was being rung down over the last act of the Kolchak drama—his inglorious retreat, disgraceful betrayal, and pitiful death—the truth about the dreaded prisoners of war began to leak out. The "menace was extirpated," according to the official formula, but the prisoners were found to be still there. Of Germans there were 5,000, Austrians 100,000, Magyars 90,000, Turks 15,000, and Bulgars 2,000. These were in prison camps, scattered along the Siberian railway zone from Petropavlovsk, in the west, to the neighbourhood of Vladivostok, in the east. There they had been for four years, guarded by Russian soldiers of the worst type, fed like pigs, housed worse than pigs, and becoming year by year more and more ragged and filthy. Though still numbering 220,000, a third of the original company had died of smallpox, typhus, and hunger, and thousands of others were sick and out of their minds with horror and despair. The Bolshevik revolution might have liberated them but for the intervention. In such conditions misery intensifies with the passing of time till death brings release or madness forgetfulness. The horrors of the last two winters these unhappy men owed to the 100,000 Allied troops who were sent to fight them but never even looked for them. The anti-Bolshevik administrations that the invaders set up simply kept things as they were, and neglected even the inefficient provision previously made.

The Japanese military men came to know of the prisoners' existence and even saw some of them, but they were quite indifferent to their sufferings. American officers saw one or two of the camps and reported on them, but had no means of relieving them. At length the Danish and Swedish consulates in Vladivostok appealed for aid in the autumn of 1919, and began to give some relief, while the Japanese were moved to clear out one or two of the camps and bring the prisoners to better places. The American Red Cross also began relief in December 1919, on the eve of the final departure of the American troops. It was left for the Germans, more than a year after the war had ended, to send a really effective Red Cross unit into Siberia and to begin to get the prisoners out.

Such was the menace that formed the excuse for the intervention. As for the other excuse—the rescue of the Czechs—these very capable warriors were all rescued before the end of 1918, but by the end of 1919 not one-third of them had been repatriated. They were no longer wanted for the Western Front, nobody was interested in them any more, and nobody had ships to spare for the task. Though well able to look after themselves, they could not get away, and the longer they stayed the more hostile grew their feelings towards their rescuers.

The British units were withdrawn, the Canadians in a state bordering on mutiny. The Americans followed, in much the same frame of mind, after General Graves had made strong protests against the continuance of an occupation which did great harm and contained no possibilities of doing good. The Washington Government negotiated with Japan regarding withdrawal, but was informed that Japan's position was not the same as America's. America thereupon abandoned the whole affair, with the expression of a pious hope that Japan would also evacuate when it became convenient. On January 12, 1920, Washington formally notified Japan of her intention to withdraw immediately. Japan maintained the necessity of holding the existing line against the eastward flood of Bolshevism, and pointed to the indubitable fact that there were still immense piles of war and other stores in Vladivostok, though some inroads had been made in these by enterprising merchants who bribed whatever officials happened to be in control to let them make shipments.

The Siberian intervention had taken on a new phase. The Americans were interested only in getting out, and the Japanese only in such opportunities as this evacuation might afford for taking a more definite line of action. General Takayanagi, of the General Staff, informed the public that neither the rescue of the Czechs nor the protection of the railways was Japan's real objective, but something far greater, which time would reveal. The General doubtless represented the forward school, but repeated failures were soon to discredit the powerful clique for whom he spoke.

During the period of the American withdrawal, which lasted from the 17th of January till the 3rd of April, there were important developments in Siberia. Soon after the first transport left there was yet another revolution in Vladivostok. General Rozanoff, one of the Russian military officers put into power by the interventionists with the fatuous idea that the people would loyally rally round them, proved to be an intolerable tyrant. At the beginning of February there was a revolt against him, in which the Czechs took part. He fled to the Japanese headquarters and was thence helped to proceed to Japan. Here he was an object of popular curiosity for a few days, and afterwards faded out into his natural obscurity.

A series of naval movements began at this time, which attracted attention at Moscow, but of which the significance was to appear only at a later date. The dispatch of warships, accompanied by an icebreaker, for Alexandrovsk, in Saghalien, was reported in the middle of January, and again on February 9th, the arrival of this second squadron being announced on February 15th. A protest came from Moscow, and the reply was made that the ships had been to Alexandrovsk only to obtain assurances of the safety of Japanese there, and had been withdrawn. That they could operate to any effect in this icebound region is very doubtful, and apparently the withdrawal was really necessitated by the impossibility of movement near the shores. Of their later attempts we shall hear presently.

In the very depth of winter there began in the Far North a general revolt against the intervention, and especially against the brutal Cossacks set up by the Japanese as administrators satisfactory to the mass of Russians, who still, according to the official formula, hated the Bolsheviks and Bolshevism.

In Eastern Siberia for some little time there had been reports of the doings of the "Partisans," and there was much uncertainty as to the exact political complexion of these bodies. Actually they were bands of peasants, co-operating for self-protection. So far as they were political they hoped for the establishment of the Soviet rule, for they had suffered outrageously under the tyranny of the subsidised Cossacks who were supposed to be saving them from the horrors of Bolshevism, and they had no reason whatever to love any of the foreign troops who were in occupation of the country. It was in the course of Japan's dealings with the Partisans that her chief misadventure occurred.

Nikolaevsk, at the mouth of the Amur, was a somewhat squalid port. Only approachable for six months of the year, it was nevertheless an important fishing station in the summer months, and there were many Japanese inhabitants as well as Chinese and Russians. One of the first acts of the intervention had been the occupation of Nikolaevsk with a couple of companies of troops. Almost immediately the naval supports had to be withdrawn because of the ice blockade. By land it was equally isolated, transport from Habarovsk, where the Amur railway turned south to Vladivostok, being almost impossible. So the Japanese occupation ran into its second winter, and the place was left once more to its isolation. There was wireless communication with Harbin, whence some news trickled through.

In January, in spite of the arctic cold, the Partisans in the neighbourhood began to take action against the Japanese, of whose high-handed methods they had had enough. A young man named Tripitzin, as much bandit as patriot and altogether too much of a firebrand, gathered about three thousand followers and marched on Nikolaevsk. If they, who were accustomed to the rigours of the winter, could move, they would be able to have their own way at least so far as Nikolaevsk was concerned. A wireless message on February 21st said that the Japanese troops were cut off —apparently from the rest of the town. The Japanese commander at Harbin telegraphed on the 23rd that the garrison was not to interfere with Russian affairs and not to fight unless attacked. It appears, however, that they endeavoured to make a *coup*, perhaps only in order to get all Japanese together under military protection. On the 25th there was a message saying that all was well, but this was the last word from the beleaguered garrison. It was learnt later that on the 29th the Russians were attacking in force and in such superior numbers that the Japanese had to surrender. A request was made that they be allowed to keep their arms, and this was agreed to. On March 3rd Harbin received a wireless message stating that the garrison and the Partisans had made an agreement not to fight any more.

What happened thereafter it is very difficult to say. There were alarums and excursions in the Russian town, and it appears that on March 14th the Japanese fired on the Russians. Whether they had reason to fear an attack, or whether some shots coming over made them believe that an attack was actually being launched, is not certainly known. The Russians were infuriated at the firing, and attacked in overwhelming numbers. The Japanese defended themselves with their customary courage, but they fell fast, and it was soon seen that the position was a hopeless one. The Japanese Consul's wife shot her little daughter and herself rather than fall into the hands of the enemy. The Consul himself fell. And about 140 survivors out of a company numbering, military and civilians together, about 600 a couple of months before, surrendered and were flung into prison.

Though there was no more communication by means of the wireless telegraph, some news of this disaster was carried to the outer world by refugees and perhaps by Partisan participants. But while rumours reached Japan of the death of the Consul and of a general massacre, nothing was certainly known, and succour was impossible. Habarovsk was too far distant as a base for relief when the river was icebound, even had it been free from the troubles that beset Nikolaevsk. In February the town was taken by Partisans. The Japanese and Kalmikoff's Cossacks turned them out, but they returned in such force that the Japanese found it necessary to withdraw to save themselves from being overwhelmed. In the first days of March they entrained for the south. Kalmikoff now found himself in similar plight to Kolchak, by whose murder he had hoped for advancement. With no Japanese bayonets between him and his enemies, and the railway occupied by Japan's transport, he destroyed as much of the line to the westward as he could—for Blagoveschensk had also fallen into the hands of the Partisans, and they were advancing to join hands with Habarovsk —and he fled across country. On entering Manchuria the Chinese captured and interned him. The Japanese, who no longer had any illusions as to his military capacity or political influence, and who had had frequent occasion to reprove him for his tortures and butcheries, were as glad to be rid of him as they were to be rid of Kolchak. In an attempt to escape from his Chinese prison he was shot like a dog by the sentry, and no word of regret was heard from any quarter.

The revolt against the occupation had been successful all along the Amur, and was disquieting in Ussurisk and Vladivostok. It was inspired by the American evacuation, and was successful because of the Japanese inability to compete with the Russians in winter campaigning. As the last American transport left Vladivostok at the beginning of April the Japanese Government published a proclamation announcing its intention to withdraw from Siberia as early as possible, its desire to do it immediately being hindered by the necessity of preserving the safety of the Czechs, the Japanese residents, and the Korean border. Simultaneously, on April 2nd, a series of demands were laid before the Vladivostok zemstvo, which had been summoned to take over charge when Rozanoff fled, this impotent body being required to assist Japan and suppress anti-Japonism. Two days later the Japanese seized control and disarmed the Russians. During the next two days a series of similar *coups* were made along the Amur railway. Nor was all this accomplished bloodlessly. At Nikolsk machine-guns were in action, and the recapture of Habarovsk was described as a massacre. But though the last remnants of Russian independence were being crushed in the east, on April 6th there was proclaimed at Verkhneudinsk, at the southern end of Lake Baikal, the Far Eastern Republic, a piece of constructive statesmanship accomplished under great difficulties, which for a season was permitted to exist as a buffer State, but which was really only holding its tolerated position until it could reunite with Soviet Russia.

Japan was in complete control of the great circle formed by the two railways between Chita and Vladivostok—the Chinese Eastern Railway crossing Manchuria and the Amur Railway, following the course of the great river to Habarovsk, where it turned south to Vladivostok—an all-Russian line built largely for strategic reasons. But there was still no news of Nikolaevsk. The Mikasa and Mishima left again for Alexandrovsk early in March, but were still unable to "suppress Bolshevism in Saghalien," as had been given out in Japan, or to "see that Japanese residents were safe," as had been reported to Moscow. Yet another departure was announced on April 10th; arriving at Alexandrovsk on the 22nd, they sent aviators over the town dropping "reassuring leaflets," and on the 23rd the troops were landed and took possession. This completed the Japanese reply to the revolt of the Russians against the intervention, though an incident farther west has still to be related. In the course of their crushing of the general revolt during the first days of April they came into conflict with the Czechs at Hailar. The Czechs were managing their own transport to Vladivostok, and the disagreement about rolling-stock and the right of way was so strong that there was a battle at this point between the Japanese and the men whom they were rescuing. The party of Czechs concerned were compelled to surrender their arms and apologise, but their concentration in Vladivostok continued, and their transport to Europe was by this time fairly well organised.

Nikolaevsk was outside the circle formed by the railways, and silence still reigned over this isolated port. Spring comes late in that region, and it was not until May 14th that Japanese troops succeeded, with the help of the ice-breakers, in landing at Decastri, south of the estuary of the Amur, whence it took them nearly three weeks to reach Nikolaevsk. A troop, however, always moves more slowly than a solitary scout, and there were stray Partisans on the look-out, who carried word to Nikolaevsk that vengeance was approaching. Tripitzin knew that he could not hold his own against the Japanese reinforcements, and prepared to make himself scarce. The inhabitants must be left to shift for themselves, but there was some discussion as to what should be done with the prisoners. The deciding voice was that of Nina Lebedeva, the companion and paramour of Tripitzin. This bloodthirsty young woman insisted upon a massacre. She contended that the Japanese had broken their parole and deserved death, and that nothing worse could happen on that account. The rest agreed. The sufferings of the captives during the preceding two months must have been intense, and now, just as a whisper of hope had gone round, their jailers became their murderers. Not one was spared, and before scattering over the countryside the Partisans fired the town. When the Japanese arrived on June 3rd, ten days after, they found the remains of their comrades, often charred, in the burnt-out ruins of the port. Some had written last messages on the walls of their prison. A few wretched inhabitants camped among the ruins, and the rest had found shelter at the little township of Mago, thirty versts above Nikolaevsk.

The news of the massacre was received with grief and indignation in Japan, but the Siberian expedition had been so long unpopular that the public at large felt more indignation against their own Government, which allowed itself to be dragged into such adventures by the military men, than against the Russians. Vengeance meetings were organised everywhere and impassioned speeches were made in which seven hundred was generally accepted as the number massacred; but they fell flat: the public was weary of Siberia, and was little moved by the organised propaganda in the newspapers.

Though only uncertain rumours had reached Japan as to what was happening in Nikolaevsk, the news of the relief expedition found its way to Moscow. Mr. Chicherin, the People's Commissary for Foreign Affairs, seems to have regarded Japan's naval activities on the coast with more anxiety than her military movements in Trans-Baikalia, and his protest against the naval visit to Alexandrovsk was followed up on March 23rd by one against the Mikasa expedition, proposing that the garrison in Nikolaevsk, whom he charged with attacking the Russians, should negotiate for peace.

It was too late for negotiation, the remnant being in prison, but no news leaked out until the final massacre became known. Moscow did not know of Tripitzin's actions, and only his immediate followers approved of them. A local administrative body which was formed in the spring hunted down the desperadoes and shot Tripitzin, Nina, and twenty-two of their followers. This, however, did not satisfy the Japanese authorities, who announced the occupation of part of the Saghalien Province as security until satisfaction was given. "Saghalien Province" was supposed to include Nikolaevsk, but in practice it was only the island, its capital Alexandrovsk, and Decastri, on the coast of the mainland, which were occupied. A sharp protest from Washington was the result of this action, the United States' expectation that Japan would evacuate at no distant date being expressed in terms so brusque and uncompromising that they caused more indignation than the massacre, and materially helped the strategists, who were bent upon making Japan spend more than half her revenue on the navy.

Three items may be added before we leave the Japanese in undisputed control of Eastern Siberia for a season. The American Red Cross left behind them four million dollars' worth of stores which they had been unable to distribute and which appeared in the Vladivostok shops in due course, sometimes with the donors' names still attached. A shipload of Russian children, "rescued from the Bolsheviks," were sent more than half round the world by sea and delivered to the Soviet Government at Petrograd. In May 1920 it was reported to the Council of the League of Nations at Rome that unless the prisoners were removed from Siberia before the winter none could survive.

XX

SHANTUNG AND THE CONSORTIUM

THE years 1919 and 1920 were so crowded with activities that it is difficult to disentangle the significant ones even for the purpose of making such a mosaic of fragments as this without a chronological chaos resulting. One of the great causes of this ebullition was the wealth that had been brought to Japan by the war. In 1919 exports and imports each totalled over two thousand million *yen*, and as 1920 dawned, more than a year after the armistice, there was a greater craze for investment than ever. Banks increased their capital most recklessly, and their agents competed for the business of financing merchants and manufacturers. There was an orgy of company flotation and of capital inflation of already existing concerns. Even concerning things that had hopelessly slumped, like iron-smelting, there were plans for gigantic combinations to save everybody, generally at the expense of the Government.

Japan's condition was not peculiar to her. There was a post-war boom nearly all over the world. The cessation of the war, followed by the return of the troops, set free an immense number of ships which were kept busy in clearing off four years' arrears of commerce; but while shipping thus suddenly increased, it was not so easy to increase harbour accommodation. In the Japanese ports, as elsewhere, goods piled up in mountains on the piers, and in Kobe, Japan's great import entrepôt, consignees were complaining that six months after landing they were still unable to get delivery of their goods. Theft was almost unchecked, the plunderers taking away their booty in carts and lighters.

An incident of this time is worth relating as indicating an attitude of mind which perhaps is necessarily characteristic of a country which has passed from a condition of isolation to one in which the cultivation of an intense nationalism is considered necessary as a substitute for the older form of protection. The Koheikai, describing itself as an association of the principal importers, but actually including several shipowners and at least one stevedoring company, circularised shipowners in England and America informing them, quite libellously, that the delays were due to their employment of a foreign stevedoring firm. As a matter of fact, the stevedores in question had been operating since days when Japanese commerce could ill have done without them, and at the date of this circular the firm had few foreign employees and a small proportion of foreign capital. Other manifestations of commercial jealousy even of those foreigners who were promoting Japanese trade were seen in connection with the official inspection of exports. This system of trying to maintain a reasonable standard of quality was being extended to a large variety of goods, and achieved very little. Foreign export merchants established in Japan had always maintained their own standards, and at this time of a boom in trade manufacturers would deliver goods to these foreign exporters all ready packed and marked "Passed for Export." When the exporter insisted, nevertheless, on opening the goods and examining them for himself, his right to do so was denied, and he was accused of insulting Japan and her officials. Examination always disclosed the fact that they were unfit for acceptance. The indifference and unscrupulousness with which, during the boom, grossly defective goods were exported were constantly denounced by prominent men, but their warnings had no effect, and Japan's reputation for commercial honesty suffered greatly.

The boom came to a sudden end in the middle of March 1920. Again the situation was world-wide and not merely local. It began with a panic on the share-market, which almost instantaneously wiped out enormous amounts of fictitious capital. Yet there were very few bankruptcies. For a time there was a commercial and financial paralysis, but Japan had her own methods of dealing with such a situation.

All money was banked, and all the banks had lent money to industrial and commercial concerns. Nominally, when the crisis came, all stored merchandise, most of the ships and most of the shares, were the property of the banks with whom they were pledged for advances. Actually the banks dared not foreclose or force sales. Bankruptcy is greatly dreaded in Japan, and the judicial authorities do not facilitate its declaration. Even when there is a run on a bank which cannot be met all that is done is to close for three weeks —and the weeks sometimes run into months—while feats of legerdemain and compromise are effected, when the bank reopens without, apparently, having suffered greatly in credit. At the time of the collapse in 1920 banks and their creditors acted on the excellent principle of all hanging together lest they should hang separately. For years bad debts remained on the books even of first-class banks as assets, and the necessary depreciations were adjusted slowly. The procedure has obvious advantages, but its benefits are more than counteracted by the temptations with which it is beset. So far as foreign commitments were concerned, the situation was saved by the large holdings of gold abroad in readiness for the settlement of bills. The *yen* also stood very high in relation to other currencies, so there was an ample margin for depreciation without its having the appearance of being anything but a resumption of normal conditions.

At this period also relations with China were worse than ever. Mr. Obata had succeeded Baron Hayashi, and his manner with the Chinese Foreign Office was minatory in the extreme. His lieutenants followed his example, and Mr. Funatsu, the Consul-General at Shanghai, went so far as to demand that the Chairman of the Chinese Chamber of Commerce at Tientsin be superseded because of his hostile criticism. Demands were frequently made of the Chinese authorities, both by Japanese officials and by meetings of Japanese residents in China, that they suppress all manifestations of hostility to Japan, while everything was done that could exacerbate such unfriendly feeling. The "Fuchow incident" was the subject of a good deal of acrimony. In this affair Japanese and Formosans were the aggressors, and when China demanded damages for bodily hurt and destruction of property of her subjects the Japanese Minister brusquely replied that it was China who was to blame, as the affray came about through her neglect to suppress anti-Japonism. It was finally settled, after months of negotiation, by apologies on both sides.

The Shantung settlement was naturally the sore point. China had declined to sign the Versailles Treaty, and on this ground refused to recognise any settlements contained therein in which she was concerned. Japan had repeated her promise of retrocession, but did not withdraw. In April 1920 she sent something like an ultimatum to China on the subject, but in June said in a much milder manner that she was prepared to negotiate on the subject at any time. The Chinese contention was that there was no need for negotiation—that all that Japan had to do was to withdraw. Japan, however, had become too deeply involved to make withdrawal easy. Her nationals had invested heavily, acquiring many large and valuable city and waterside leases at Kiaochau; Japan was operating the railway, and had a garrison at the important junction of Tsinan, where it joined the Peking–Hankow line. Japanese cotton-mills and other industrial enterprises had come into being where the Germans had once ruled, and the idea of retrocession on any terms was unpopular, while the Japanese Government would have had much difficulty in keeping faith with its own subjects if a withdrawal were effected without negotiation. Persistent reports to the effect that yet another Japanese loan to China was being negotiated showed that there were ways and means of smoothing things over, but the fact that the latest ten million borrowed dollars were to be for the improvement of Marshal Tuan Chi-jui's "model army" did nothing to improve feeling, nor did the fact that the subservient clique known as the Anfu Club had fled from popular indignation and sought sanctuary in the Japanese Legation contribute in any way towards a friendly settlement.

Loans to China were no longer popular in Japan, as there seemed to be some doubt as to the feasibility of taking appropriate steps when the inevitable failure to pay the interest should happen. Among all Chinese politicians loans in general and the Nishihara loans in particular were anathema. They as well as the Japanese militarists knew the history of the Egyptian loans.

That China could make progress without loans, however, was an idea that Western statesmen and economists could not envisage. The international syndicate that was in operation when the Great War broke out had to be revised. America had become the world's chief moneylender, and whereas President Wilson's attitude had previously been one of disapproval of such loans as could be turned into diplomatic levers, he was inclined, after the revelations of Versailles, to regard American participation in international loans to China as necessary for the debtor's safety. Very soon after the conclusion of the peace treaty, therefore, steps were taken to form a China Consortium, which should monopolise all future Chinese loans, and should see that the money was not spent on enriching military satraps and financing civil war. In the formation of the Consortium, Mr. Thomas W. Lamont, of Messrs. J. P. Morgan & Co., was the leading figure. Mr. Lamont visited China and discovered that the militarists were ready to borrow anything and to promise everything. The final arrangements were completed in Tokyo. There had been much debate over the question whether Manchuria and Mongolia, as areas in which Japan had special interests, should be excluded from the area over which the Consortium should operate. For this purpose certain negotiations into which Britain had attempted to enter with China regarding the status of Tibet were represented as intending to establish a British suzerainty over Tibet, and, as some Japanese critics expressed it, Britain's pretensions regarding Tibet were "even worse" than Japan's respecting Manchuria and Mongolia. It appeared somewhat uncertain whether the exclusion of Manchuria and Mongolia meant South Manchuria and Eastern Inner Mongolia, according to the terms of the "Twenty-one Demands" treaty, or whether it referred to the whole region covered by these two names. From the constant references to the magnitude of the supposed British operations it appeared as though the Consortium might be used as a means of establishing the claim to special interests in the whole region, in which case China would be almost encircled by British and Japanese influences. However, these interesting speculations came to nothing. On March 11, 1921, the agreement was concluded, and Mr. Lamont announced that, with the exception of business in connection with four feeder lines to the South Manchuria Railway, the Consortium covered all the ground. He expressed a sympathetic understanding of the contentions raised in some Japanese quarters, especially among the military men, regarding Manchuria's importance to Japan, but said that Japan had, in the end, waived special claims. Curiously enough, on the same day, Mr. Kajiwara, of the Yokohama Specie Bank, informed a meeting of bankers that Japan's claims had been successful. The only feasible explanation seemed to be that while the Consortium Agreement made no mention of any special claims or exceptions, there was a "gentlemen's agreement" on the subject. However, little in the way of corroborative evidence ever emerged, for the Chinese very effectually boycotted the Consortium, and it never even began to fulfil its intended function of financing the economic resuscitation of China. Its chief function was to demonstrate that, though China might be in chaos and disunion, it was no longer possible for the Powers to do as they pleased, even though they were united in benevolent intent.

The manner in which Labour became class-conscious has already been described. The connection between social theory and Labour was naturally much the same in Japan as in other countries. As regards the working class, they were naturally docile enough, and seldom thought of questioning the wisdom of the police. Educated theorists were much more dreaded. The year before the Taisho Tenno came to the Throne a dozen anarchists had been executed. Their trial was secret, but it was rumoured that they had conspired against the life of the Meiji Tenno. The drastic measures taken, however, seem to have frightened the police quite as much as the political extremists, and after the Bolshevik revolution in Russia there was great nervousness regarding "dangerous thought." This dread was manifested often in grotesque ways. An army officer was compelled to divorce his wife because she was the sister of a well-known Socialist. A portrait of Osugi Sakae, a popular leader, was not allowed to be exhibited at the Teiten—the annual art exhibition held under the auspices of the Education Department. Much more serious was the condemnation to four years' imprisonment of a Christian pastor named Utsunomiya, in Wakayama prefecture, who with his small flock had all things in common. His following of this venerable precedent is believed to have been less contributory to this severe punishment than his heterodox views on the theory of monarchy.

In spite of every device for the suppression of dangerous thought, such thought became more and more popular; 1920 came in with a flood of suppressions and prosecutions, but these only increased the vogue. Mr. Morito, an assistant professor at the Imperial University, Tokyo, was prosecuted for translating some of Kropotkin's works, and, after a trial that lasted for five months, was given two months' imprisonment. Miss Kamichika, whose misadventure with Osugi Sakae has been related, also got into trouble for translating an interview with Kropotkin, who was now regarded as an extraordinarily disturbing person. Translations from the writings of famous Socialists became, indeed, objects of so much fear that it was even reported that a rendering into Japanese by Mr. Sakai, a Socialist as prominent as Osugi himself, of Morris's *Earthly Paradise*, was banned.

Perhaps it was not really quite so ridiculous as this, however, as Mr. Sakai would be unlikely to take the trouble to translate what must have been to him one of the least interesting of Morris's works.

The Diet, which met for the annual session at the beginning of 1920, showed distinct progress in the art of being unruly and clamorous, and towards the end of February it was summarily dissolved. This was a very high-handed action to take, though from the legislative point of view it did not greatly matter. Dissolution before the budget was passed, and when it was too late to hold a general election and present the budget to the new assembly, involved the repetition of the previous year's budget. Herein the Japanese constitution—an eclectic composition—followed the Prussian model; but in times of such violent change nothing like a real repetition was possible, and the Government actually had to take enormous liberties that had only the subsequent sanction of a new and subservient Diet.

The most interesting point about the dissolution of the Diet, however, was the reason which Mr. Hara, the Premier, declared had prompted the Government to seek the imperial consent for such a measure. It was owing, he said, to the increase in dangerous thought, and he illustrated the manner in which subversive ideas had penetrated even into the legislative chamber by pointing to the fact that each of the political parties, all striving for popularity, had introduced its own Suffrage Bill into the House, and that these Bills were dangerous because they aimed at the destruction of class distinctions. So spoke Japan's "Great Commoner" after holding office for two years.

A year before this the Government had reformed the constituencies, making most of them smaller, and so increasing the number of members of the Diet, which now reached 464. The three principal parties in the first Diet elected under this new arrangement numbered: Seiyukai 281, Kenseikai 109, and Kokuminto 30. The Government party thus had an absolute majority, and the Diet gave little more trouble.

The new Diet met at the end of June, but though its session was brief and the members were obedient, the session was not altogether happy. Viscount Takahashi, the Finance Minister, was profoundly dissatisfied with the manner in which the costs of the Siberian expedition were piling up, and General Tanaka, now Minister for War, could find no better excuse for holding the whole triangle of Chita, Habarovsk, and Vladivostok than that it would not be in accordance with the principles of Bushido to abandon Semenoff. Nobody reminded him that he had had no such scruples about abandoning Kolchak and Kalmikoff. Only a month later, when it became obvious that Semenoff had neither courage nor following enough to remain in Chita without a Japanese garrison, General Takayanagi assured the anxious inhabitants of Vladivostok that he would not allow Semenoff or the troops of General Kappel (the best of a bad lot, who had fought Kolchak's rearguard actions) to enter the town. Bushido proved to be subject to variations according to the military situation.

The Government had its majority in the Diet, but there was a struggle going on within its own circle. From the beginning the Premier had been desirous of keeping the Siberian expedition small; the Minister for War had insisted on it being large. It is fairly certain that the civil power would have been very glad to get out of this bad Siberian business, but they could not do so without the consent of the military. There were rumours of Takahashi resigning, of the whole Cabinet resigning. They did not want to do so, and after General Tanaka also threatened to resign they all came to heel, for that would have meant resignation in real earnest for the entire Ministry. General Tanaka's reason for suggesting resignation was to show his "sense of responsibility" for Nikolaevsk; and the strategy which led to the disaster was indeed so egregious that the heads of the army deserved to be broken for it. But the talk of responsibility had become a farce. Traditionally there was a high sense of responsibility in Japan. If a drunkard staggered into the path of an imperial procession, it would be the correct thing for the Chief of Metropolitan Police to offer his resignation, with protestations that it was because of his own lack of virtue that one of his subordinates had been so negligent as to allow such a thing to happen. Naturally such resignations were often declined, and by this time it had become customary to offer what they called *shintai ugakai*, or offer of resignation, which signified clearly enough that the party concerned did not wish to resign and would, indeed, have been horribly chagrined if the offer were accepted. Certainly General Tanaka had no intention of resigning on account of an incident which seemed capable of being turned to such excellent account. The military men dug in their heels in Siberia, and accumulated increasing discredit for another two years before Nemesis drove them out. Russia proved once more to be the grave of military reputations.

The question of what is "public opinion" and of what nations think collectively is always a very difficult one. It appears plain enough in the light of subsequent events, but when we actually review what is on record of contemporary thought and action we find little justification for the historian's assumptions that at any particular moment the whole nation was moving in any particular direction. At this period in Japan we find an enthusiastic promotion of Socialistic ideas and the cult of Emperor-worship in full blast simultaneously; religion flourishing in an amazing and varying fashion, and an attitude of mind in which it had no part whatever; Kagawa trying to put Christianity into practice in the slums, and an ostentatious extravagance hitherto unknown; pacifism and pessimistic introspection side by side with national egotism and a desire for war; a growing sense of constitutionalism and a hardly disguised usurpation of power by the military satraps. This last contrast is one of the most perplexing of all. In October 1919 Baron Shidehara was sent to Washington as ambassador. So sincere a promoter of international friendship could hardly have been chosen by a Government whose intent was other than peaceful; yet such was the power of the military party and so extravagant were its ambitions that the student of this period might almost be excused if he regarded the appointment as being dictated by a super-Machiavellian policy. Certainly the most important question of the day seemed to be that of piling up armaments. The army estimates for the fiscal year April 1, 1919, to March 31, 1920, were 144,000,000 *yen* and the naval estimates 249,000,000. The peace treaties were signed, the League of Nations formed, and the Czechs were "rescued," but the estimates for the next year increased to 210,000,000 *yen* for the army and 352,000,000 for the navy, besides a provisional allotment of 200,000,000 for the Siberian expedition which was always about to be withdrawn. Military activity was as keen as though a real war had been in progress instead of the travesty of war in Siberia. The expedition to Siberia, the free hand won in Shantung, Mr. Obata's continual and undisguised browbeating of the Chinese Government, the acquirement of the German island groups, the increased feeling over immigration in America, and the sharp dispute over the possession of the island of Yap—all these things brought about an attack of national egotism and pugnacity. The not very sapient remark of some picturesque journalist that the world's centre of gravity had shifted from the Atlantic Ocean to the Pacific assisted in the process of attracting attention to the possibility of war between America and Japan. The question attracted a great deal of attention in America, and on the Californian coast everything in the way of increasing armaments was very popular because of the business that such activities would bring. It was noted that during 1920 nearly six thousand Americans visited Japan. The great bulk of these were tourists or business men, but the groups that came with Mr. Lamont and with Mr. Vanderlip, and later on a group of Congressmen, besides numerous independent travellers, were all keenly interested in the prospects of war. In public it was the fashion to declare that such things could never be, the declaration being varied in every possible way according to the speaker's temperament or idea of tactfulness; but in private anxiety was often expressed. Japan's militarism was a subject that was always coming to the fore, and as constantly being explained away. In November 1920 we find the Premier, Mr. Hara, leading the chorus with the announcement that militarism was already extinct, knowing when he said it that he had to face a bigger defence budget than ever when the Diet met, and that fortifications were being built apace in the Luchu and Bonin Islands. During the Peers' debates in the next session of the Diet we find Mr. Nakashoji complaining that Japan was constantly condemned abroad as a militarist State and Baron Fujimura declaring that Japan had got a very bad name through her aggressive policy. One of the features of this period was the purchase on a large scale of various stores such as would be required in time of war. Purchases were made by wealthy concerns at the behest of the Government and facilities for these purchases were given in the way of credits extended by "semi-official" banks. These actions led to complications that were not destined to be straightened out for many years.

XXI

THE HUNCHUN RISING

So much bitterness of feeling had grown up in Korea that it was not to be cured by kindness. The military men, Terauchi and Hasegawa, who had been in charge, had no other idea than to enforce obedience and to prevent open expressions of discontent. No newspapers, of course, were permitted to exist unless they were either in the direct pay of the Government-General or completely subservient to it. The Tokyo Government was anxious that Koreans should be loyal and contented, but had very little idea how such an aim was to be achieved. Besides appointing Admiral Viscount Saito as a milder type of Governor-General, they issued an imperial proclamation that henceforth there should be no distinction between Koreans and Japanese—a promise that was for many reasons possible to fulfil only to a very limited degree, and which, under the policy adopted, could not be entirely fulfilled until the Koreans had become entirely indistinguishable from the Japanese. The process of assimilation, however, showed no signs of becoming popular, though the younger folk were ready enough to learn Japanese because of the advantages accruing from such knowledge, and some of the more mature were gratified at the abolition of the former iniquitous law which compelled all Korean business companies to have a Japanese director whose privileged position gave him practical control. No item in the administration had encountered so much criticism as the control of the people in the country districts by gendarmes, and charges were made in the Diet that these men were not only petty tyrants of the worst kind, but habitually ravished Korean women. Their abolition was promised, but as they were merely labelled policemen instead of gendarmes, the difference was not commensurate with the need. General

Akaike, who was in command of this force, was of the school of Terauchi and Hasegawa, but lacking in such liberality as these greater men possessed. In spite of the fact that more than half the trouble in Korea had been caused by Japanese policemen and gendarmes continually interfering with the people, nagging at them and telling them what they must and must not do—all for their own good, no doubt—General Akaike made plans for an ideal policing of the peninsula, with three policemen in every village. He took occasion in December 1919 to denounce Christians as disloyal and rebellious, which also showed a lack of understanding of the best methods of pacification. When there was so much alarm in Japan itself about "dangerous thought," it was natural that there should not be less in Korea, and on March 1, 1920, lest there should be a recrudescence of the *Mansei* disturbances by way of celebrating their anniversary, three thousand precautionary arrests were made.

No expedition was shown in disposing of the persons arrested in the *Mansei* riots. Though the floggings which had sometimes ended fatally had been explained as being in accordance with ancient Korean custom and necessary owing to lack of prison accommodation, there was very little hurry to relieve the prisons of those who had found accommodation there. From time to time news was heard of trials of the *Mansei* rioters. Six months after the disturbances, for instance, 239 Koreans were sentenced by the Seoul District Court to terms of imprisonment ranging from six months to two years. Others were less fortunate. On March 25, 1920, over a year after the disturbances, a batch of three hundred had only just finished the ordeal of inquiry before the "preliminary judge," and been committed for trial; and it was not until July of the same year that Sun Ping-hsi, leader of a sect known as followers of the Heavenly Path, and equally under suspicion with the Christians, was put on trial. These trials dragged out interminably, possibly with some deterrent effect, but certainly without any promotion of confidence or affection.

Governor-General Saito and his Civil Administrator, Dr. Midzuno, were not lacking in goodwill towards the inhabitants, but were not sufficiently well acquainted with the conditions in the peninsula even to know where to detect some maladministration of a particularly bad sort that still continued. The powers of the police were in no way curtailed, but rather increased, and, with a lack of any sense of justice, they evicted a large number of Koreans from farmlands which in some cases their families had occupied for centuries.

These evicted families generally migrated across the border to Chientao, where there was room for them to settle so long as they were prepared to do some of the hardest kind of pioneer work, and they naturally became some of the most recalcitrant of the ever-increasing colony of Koreans who regarded Japan as their enemy. The later emigrants kept in touch with the malcontents at home, and the Japanese authorities regarded their activities, which were said to include the formation of assassination clubs, with nervous apprehension. Raids from across the border were frequently reported, and in May 1920 General Chang Tso-lin, the dictator of Mukden, stationed some cavalry in the border districts to keep the Koreans in order.

The Japanese method of dealing with these emigrants showed no scrupulous care for Chinese sovereignty. The establishment of Japanese consultates in these remote places was regular and reasonable, but the consulates were well supplied with armed police whose constabulary duties resembled those of the police in foreign concessions rather than those of a mere consular guard. They took charge on market days and acted generally as though they were on their own soil. The Chinese were long-suffering, but were sometimes moved to protest, the arrest of some Koreans who had become Chinese subjects being a matter that could hardly pass unnoticed. The Japanese Consul's reply, however, was that he did not recognise the naturalisation of Koreans. The Mixed Court (an organisation for dealing with offenders enjoying extraterritorial rights) was ignored, and Koreans were dealt with by the Japanese.

There were alarms and excursions in Korea itself, and demands for coercion. A conspiracy to blow up buildings was reported from the south and more border raids in the north. *Mansei* riots broke out at Wonsan on September 23rd; information was brought to the authorities of a huge revolutionary conspiracy, and arrests were effected in Mukden itself. One of the reasons for not withdrawing from Siberia had been the need for guarding the Korean border, and it was true that some of the wildest of the Koreans had gone into Siberia in search of liberty and the opportunity for revenge. Japanese soldiers patrolled the border from Possiet Bay to Manchuria, and everybody travelling there had to carry a Japanese passport. A vigorous hunt was also carried on in Chientao for recalcitrant Koreans in spite of Chinese protests. Although General Akaike had declared that a year's rigorous measures had brought disturbances to an end, October 2, 1920, witnessed a rising much more serious than anything that had happened the previous year in Korea. A mob attacked the Japanese consulate at Hunchun, in Chientao, and burnt it. Ten Japanese were killed in the affray. Fanciful details were given. There was a reluctance to admit that such vigorous action could be taken by mere Koreans. The attackers were described as bandits under Russian command, and the brutality of their actions, it was declared, proved that they were under Bolshevik influence. The assailants fled north after their raid.

No time was lost in making reprisals. Japanese troops were sent from the Korean border, and some landed in Possiet Bay and approached from that side. An official report stated that there were about a thousand rebellious Koreans in Hunchun and that Colonel Yamada had pursued the raiders but had not succeeded in catching them. Vengeance soon fell on less evasive foes. On October 30th thirty Koreans were shot in a school, in which they had taken refuge, and the school was burnt. A report issued by the Japanese

Foreign Office stated that on October 26th twenty of the "enemy" were killed, one mission school, one native school, and ten houses destroyed. Reprisals of this sort continued vigorously. Arrests were made wholesale; to be suspected was sufficient reason for being executed, and there was no squeamishness. Churches and schools, which the Koreans had built, spending on them sums which represented great self-sacrifice on the part of people so poor, were the special targets of the troops and were wantonly destroyed. On November 15th the military posted up notices in Hunchun expressing regret that so much damage had been necessary, and advising Koreans to be loyal henceforward. But on the 21st damage was going on as savagely as ever. Four thousand dead and a thousand houses destroyed was the Chinese Governor's estimate of the measures taken for the subduing of the malcontent Koreans, whose number was estimated by the Japanese at a thousand.

The Chinese authorities protested against the dispatch of troops into Chinese territory and against the excesses committed, but there was an outcry from the Japanese in the neighbourhood for permanent occupation, and as an example of the need the case was cited of the survivors at Shogando, one of the first villages to be disciplined, presenting a memorial of thanks to Colonel Oki, saying that since March 1919 they had been continually terrorised by lawless bands.

Admiral Viscount Saito at this time was on a visit to Japan, and at a banquet in Osaka said that it was to be regretted that Korea had been disturbed by world forces. Strong repressive measures were needed against the independence movement, he said, and a strict control over the malcontents. He hoped that quiet would soon be restored, but deplored the lack of understanding prevalent among the Koreans. Sincerity and unflinching energy must be shown in Japan's task, and infinite friendship and sympathy extended to the Koreans.

On another occasion Admiral Saito expressed the opinion

that the action taken by the troops in Chientao compared favourably with that of the "Black and Tans" in Ireland, and this method of explanation was improved upon by Colonel Midzumachi, who lectured some foreign missionaries in Chientao in reply to their protests. He reminded them of General Dyer's massacre of Indians at Amritsar, and said that the Japanese soldiers had taken care not to kill innocent people as Dyer had done. He also told them that it would only make things even if, as a retaliation for missionaries encouraging Koreans, Japanese Buddhists encouraged Indians. Shortly afterwards this same Colonel made a more friendly advance, inviting some of the missionaries to dinner; and immediately after he expressed the opinion to a journalist interviewing him on behalf of the *Asahi* that the missionaries were a low class of people and spread anti-Japanese propaganda.

Echoes of the Chientao excesses were heard in the House of Commons, but the only protests heard in Japan were against the folly of Colonel Midzumachi in speaking as he did. But the Colonel's manner was symptomatic of the times and even of the public temper, which had become curiously sensitive and at the same time aggressive. Major Okamura, who accompanied Midzumachi, showed even less discretion, and informed the *Jiji* that the missionaries were responsible for instigating the whole trouble.

It may be appropriate here to draw attention to the position of the Press in Japan with regard to public events, since in any democratic country the Press is expected to have a considerable influence on the course of policy, or at any rate to indicate the trend of public thought. Perhaps the Press in Japan did not differ greatly from that of any other country in taking it for granted that any sign of rebellion in a remote place was due entirely to moral perversity on the part of the rebels and that in any diplomatic dispute the other party must be in the wrong. It displayed a surprising lack of interest, however, and a recklessness almost as surprising in giving currency to fanciful tales. A curious sheet was the official paper, in English, published in Seoul, the Korean capital. Its mission was to inform foreign residents and tourists of the aims and progress of Japanese rule, and it defended every action of the authorities. When, however, the methods of Generals Terauchi and Hasegawa culminated so disastrously, the editor proclaimed that he was ashamed of having supported such men, but he relapsed into patriotic uncriticalness as soon as trouble broke out again. The Chientao incident ended in the increase of garrisons in the north and the migration of many Koreans farther into the Chinese interior. As usual, the Koreans seeking to avoid Japanese rule became the vanguard of penetration: the process still continues.

Viscount Kato, who had been Foreign Minister and was later to become Premier, expressed the opinion that all the trouble in Korea was due to the reaction caused through too much liberality after the Terauchi régime. When the Diet met at the beginning of 1921, Viscount Uchida, the Foreign Minister, announced the withdrawal of the Japanese troops from Chinese territory, and a partial concentration of the Siberian expeditionary forces in the Vladivostok neighbourhood, where they would serve to protect the Korean border—mainly by keeping control over the recalcitrant Koreans in Russian territory.

To Mr. Kiyose, a member of the small Kokuminto, or Nationalist party, alone belongs the honour of having, in the Diet, denounced the cruelties with which the rising in Chientao was suppressed.

A curious offshoot of the Korean troubles, and interesting mainly as bearing on a disputed question in international law, was the arrest in July 1920 of Mr. G. L. Shaw, a British merchant in Antung, the Chinese city at the mouth of the Yalu. Mr. Shaw was agent for a line of British steamers trading from Shanghai, and he always refused to allow the Japanese police from New Wiju, on the Korean side, to search his ships and examine his passengers. Nor was this the only offence he had caused. It was owing to his activity that the Japanese had been compelled to place a swing section in the Yalu bridge, at great extra cost, but to the salvation of the Chinese junk traffic on the river. And he had been instrumental in exposing an opium scandal in which Japanese officials were involved. One day in July 1920, as he was on his way to visit Japan, he was arrested at the frontier. His arrest was kept absolutely secret for over a month, during which time, as well as afterwards, his incarceration was accompanied by every circumstance of hardship and indignity. After some months he was released on bail, and compensation was offered on condition that he went away and gave the judicial authorities an opportunity to save face by saying that he had evaded. This he refused to do. No formal charge was ever brought in open court, but the police officials freely told interviewers that he had been assisting Korean conspirators and supplying them with weapons. Apart from the unimportant detail that the charges were untrue, the prosecution was of a nature which the best precedents in international law united in condemning. The Japanese Government had acted on the advice of a distinguished international lawyer whose weakness was a penchant for defending weak cases with extraordinary ingenuity. It turned out that the prosecution of a foreigner for a political offence committed abroad is not among the powers of a sovereign State. In this case the misapprehension arose out of the inability of Japanese officials to understand that Chinese sovereignty had to be recognised. Mr. Shaw had done no more than refuse to permit a totally unwarranted invasion of his own and China's rights by Japanese authority. This, of course, hindered the hunt for Korean malcontents, and here, as at Hunchun, in the case of the missionaries, this was regarded by the Japanese officials as hostile action against Japan. They even complained bitterly that the Chinese authorities were lax in their duty of "controlling" Korean malcontents.

There are two points that may be noted in connection with this case: first, that while it was freely reported in the

Japanese Press, and invariably with the plain declaration that Shaw was guilty, the effect of the arrangement by which a semi-official news agency in Japan was given the agency for Reuter was that the news was not telegraphed abroad until the correspondent in Peking learned of it. This was typical of the effect that the bargain made with Reuter had upon the news. The second point was that when an inquiry was addressed to Mr. Murayama, Acting Chief of Police in Korea, as to when Mr. Shaw would be charged and with what offence, he replied that under Japanese law the preliminary examination frequently took more than a year. That was only too true, and he might have added that during the preliminary examination the accused was unable to see his friends or even consult with his lawyer.

XXII

A STRANGE RELIGION

In the early summer of 1920 a religion called Omotokyo began to attract a great deal of attention. The Japanese have often been compared with the Athenians, and the comparison extends to a predilection for running after new things, especially new religions. We find in the same year an endeavour to popularise Seizaho, or a "Method of Quiet Sitting," an offspring of the Zen meditation, which was itself a rather distant derivative of the Indian *yoga*. There were a number of popular religions, the existence of which never seemed to arouse any hostility on the part of the older establishments, which, indeed, never lacked generous support. The best known of these faiths was Tenrikyo, a quietistic Neo-Shinto sect, founded by a farmer's wife and boasting over a million followers. Of somewhat similar origin was Omotokyo, but of different character. There is a quiet, sleepy town called Ayabe in the western part of Kyoto prefecture, the centre of a sericultural district, surrounded by hills. In modern times it has come into note as the home of Omotokyo, the junction of two not very important railways and the site of one of Japan's largest filatures, where several thousand girls reel silk. Here in 1836 was born the foundress of Omotokyo. In 1855 she married a dissolute carpenter named Deguchi, who made her the mother of eight children before his excesses killed him. For many years thereafter she toiled early and late, now rearing silkworms, now picking rags and wastepaper. Except the two youngest daughters, the children showed no gratitude for such devotion, but deserted her as soon as they could look after themselves. It was not until 1892 that she got religion, suddenly declaring herself possessed of a god and saying that she would build a temple for all the world at Ayabe.

She was apparently quite mad, and was even imprisoned for arson but liberated because the court found her to be insane. Her insanity proved to be more remunerative than a lifetime of toil. Followers gathered round and took care of her. One of her favourite occupations from this time till her death in 1918 was the making of *Ofudesaki,* or "honourable writings," with a writing-brush. The papers on which this entirely illiterate woman made these strange figures were carefully preserved, and expounders of the faith have traced in them fanciful resemblances to Chinese characters and equally fanciful interpretations of these decipherments.

Two men became the instruments of propagating the faith. An uncouth peasant, a religious enthusiast, but credited with a full share of bucolic cunning, married a daughter of Deguchi Nao, being adopted into the family and taking her name. This Deguchi Wanisaburo succeeded her as the prophet of the faith, but the St. Paul of the new religion was Asano Wasaburo, a distinguished lawyer. He was the chief interpreter of the writings, and made an attempt to raise Shinto from the very narrow localism in which it had always been set to the status of a faith universal.

Between 1915 and 1920 astonishing progress was made. On a low hill beside the railway at Ayabe a splendid temple arose, and near it was a still larger devotional hall, where Deguchi Wanisaburo directed the exercises under the influence of which enthusiastic followers would become possessed.[1] Long boarding-houses were erected for the accommodation of disciples who came from all parts of the country, and who after a course of instruction went out as propagandists. The sect also published a number of books and periodicals.

It might have been supposed that a faith so magnifying the glory of the gods of Japan would have found official

[1] On this subject of induced "possession," Percival Lowell's *Occult Japan* may be consulted. He wrote before Omotokyo became popular, but he describes similar religious techniques, Omotokyo being chiefly remarkable for the cultivation of "mass possession," a phenomenon which was one of the causes of official disapproval.

favour, especially under a Home Minister of the character of Mr. Tokonami. In September 1920, at the annual conference of prefectural governors in Tokyo, in which the Government maintained a faint echo of the compulsory visits of the feudal daimyo, Mr. Tokonami held forth on the beautiful custom of worshipping and revering the gods, which was the foundation of national morality, and which he was about to reinforce by increased subventions to the shrines and to the priests. At the moment when this edifying oration was delivered, Dr. Aoki was in serious trouble for having told his countrymen bluntly that this divine descent business made Japan the laughing-stock of the world. But Dr. Aoki's scepticism, shared overtly or covertly by the majority of the educated men of Japan, was less perturbing to the authorities than the fanatical belief in the gods that developed among the followers of the Omotokyo faith. A report had already been issued in July that Omotokyo had been prohibited in Formosa, and at the end of August it was rumoured that the authorities had determined to stamp out the religion in Japan.

These warnings had no effect; the devotees were apparently carried away by their enthusiasm. They arranged pilgrimages, and as a counterblast the more orthodox type of pilgrimage—always very popular in Japan—was officially encouraged. But Omotokyo monopolised attention. The white-clad pilgrim, often begging his way from shrine to shrine, was too common a sight to attract any attention at all; but the long-haired, unkempt Puritan enthusiasts of Omotokyo, who affected the horse as a means of dignified locomotion, were a novelty that caused some excitement wherever they went. Apocalyptic prophecies about the destruction of all the world except Ayabe, which was to be the centre of a universe governed in a new way, were regarded as derogatory to the Government, which was the proper guardian of the divine and imperial traditions. There was worse to come. So long as the interpreted "honourable writings" merely said that foreign countries were inhabited by beasts and ruled by demons, nobody was offended. Such beliefs are a stimulus to patriotic feeling in any country, but when the wild and whirling words published as the inspiration of Deguchi Nao included denunciations of "those on high" who were maintained by demons and oppressed the toilers, Bolshevism itself could hardly be more dangerous. Dr. Anesaki, Professor of Religions, whose lectures on Buddhism had been very popular in America among frivolous people who longed to be thought earnest and broadminded, expressed the opinion that cults like Omotokyo sprang up only through the neglect of religion.

Mr. Asano Wasaburo was nothing if not militant. He said that Omotokyo was slandered—as indeed it was, for as the agitation grew, men of Belial were not lacking who made the most outrageous allegations about the dealings of the devotees with demons and their stores of arms. Mr. Asano declared that he was going to purchase the *Taisho Nichi Nichi*—a daily newspaper in Osaka which had won much popularity but had been unable to survive the first year, which modern newspapers find so strenuous—and fight the Home Office or any other enemy. This, a little later, was actually done.

A number of retired military and naval officers had become Omotokyo devotees, and the cult, while ultra-patriotic, failed to regard the Government and general personnel of official control as being the best possible. It was believed to have reforming and possibly revolutionary tendencies. One of the retired military devotees was arrested at the end of August, but after that there was a lull in the agitation, and it was not till the middle of May 1921 that it became known that the two leaders, Deguchi and Asano, as well as some of their chief helpers, had been arrested on February 12th—a striking example of the extraordinary powers of the Japanese police who could thus contrive the disappearance of men so much in the public eye and yet ensure that not a word should be published about the matter.

This caused a sudden revival of interest, and the constitutional right to religious freedom was discussed. Mr. Awaya, head of the Bureau of Religions in the Home Office, expressed the official opinion that Omotokyo was not a religion. The Government, he said, was anxious to encourage new religions. This, no doubt, was perfectly true, religion being officially regarded as an excellent thing so long as it kept the thoughts of its professors occupied and diverted their minds from politics. But a religion which assumed an exclusive and political aspect was a very different thing, as the early Christians found amidst the all-embracing toleration of Rome. Perhaps some historic parallel was in Mr. Awaya's mind, for he added that the authorities also remembered that no religion had ever grown up without meeting persecution in its early days. The remark suggested that a little persecution was to be applied out of pure benevolence in order to make Omotokyo a real religion.

Martyrdom, however, was not to be the portion of the devotees. The first business taken in hand after the arrests was the destruction of the tomb of the foundress. Its "impropriety" had been the subject of much indignation, and consisted in the fact that it bore a close resemblance to the tomb of the Meiji Tenno. Looking across the valley from the hill on which the ornate temple stood, the beholder could not be unimpressed by the sight of the vast tumulus and its simple but dignified surroundings. The implied pretension that this demented peasant was the equal of the descendant of the Sun Goddess caused some real indignation. The foundress's daughter, wife of Deguchi Wanisaburo, now under arrest, protested that the Omotokyo adherents could not destroy that which had been raised in honour of the giver of their religion, but that if the authorities wished to destroy it they must do so by the agency of others. This they did, and they also destroyed the gorgeous temple, 3,500 reservists being mobilised to assist and to see that no resistance was offered. But the prayer-hall—a barnlike structure with a decoration of patriotic colour-prints—was allowed to remain, and worship was not subject to any interference.

The trial, when it came, was on a charge of *lèse-majesté*, certain passages in the Omotokyo publications, turgid in phrase but obscure in meaning, being held to refer in a derogatory manner to the Imperial Family. The accused were sentenced, and were released on bail pending the appeals. Stories were circulated about the connection of Omotokyo with the Chinese Red Swastika Society and the Korean Heavenly Path. During one term on bail Deguchi went off to Mongolia, supposedly on a religious mission, but came back and surrendered himself to the court. The case dragged on from futility to futility for six long years, and the religion lost its grip. Long-haired propagandists and their horses were no more seen, but the sect continued to propagandise. It issued a little magazine in Esperanto, which put the police to the trouble of learning that synthetic tongue.

XXIII

MORPHIA REPLACES OPIUM

For many years opium has been not only a drug, but a political issue, and a somewhat ambiguous part which Japan played in the business in the early days of Taisho has to be recounted. Much has been said regarding the trade in opium between India and China, the best apology for which was that both in bulk and in quality the Indian opium imported into China compared with the home-grown product much as the champagne imported into England compared with the beer brewed there. It was recognised, however, that the opium, whether Indian or Chinese, was more harmful than beer or champagne, but the British Government, which derived large revenues from the sale of opium, was disinclined to suppress the trade for the benefit of the Chinese growers. The awakening in China which led to the revolution of 1911 had warranted the hope that China would make a real effort to suppress the cultivation of the poppy, and the Government of India undertook to extinguish its opium export to China by regular stages spread over a decade. The successful achievement of the revolution, culminating in the abdication of the Manchus on February 12, 1912, gave an added strength to the movement, and the abolition of poppy cultivation in China was so successful that for some time the Government of India gained by its bargain, owing to the rapid rise in price.

The danger that opium, which was comparatively harmless to the temperate majority of its users, would be replaced by more harmful alkaloids was foreseen from the beginning, but China had an efficient Customs service, and there was a strict ban on the import of such drugs. Being contraband, these drugs could not, of course, be entered on any bills of lading for goods consigned to China. So far as other countries were concerned, however, morphia, heroin, and cocaine were ordinary articles of commerce, and their consignment was perfectly legal. It became known that the British manufacturing chemists were exporting large quantities of morphia and heroin to Japan, where, in 1917, the import returns showed that 600,000 ounces of morphia were received. Drug habits were almost unknown in Japan, and the legitimate medical use of the drug did not account for the use of more than 30,000 ounces. None whatever appeared on the export returns. That it went to China was, however, notorious. It was even known which were its principal ports of entry. It went in over the Korean border at Antung; at Dairen, whence the South Manchuria Railway formed a convenient means of distribution; and at Tsingtau, whence the railway to Tsinan was also serviceable. It reached the actual consumer through a multitude of minor channels, but almost conspicuously by means of countless little Japanese medicine shops established on Chinese territory, which were protected from search by extraterritorial rights.

The British Government recognised its responsibility in the matter, and made an arrangement that the export of no opium drugs should be permitted to Japan except with a certificate from a Japanese consul that they were required for medical use in Japan. Such certificates were in practice never issued, but no restrictions were imposed upon imports into Japan; American manufacturing chemists were as ready to supply the goods as the British had been, and in 1920 the import rose to 800,000 ounces.

Nor was this all. In Korea for some time past the poppy had been cultivated extensively, and now in Japan hundreds of fields were to be seen. The excellence of Japanese cultivation was manifest in the magnificent plants nearly six feet high, with great white flowers like peonies. In Formosa both poppy and coca were very successfully grown, and Japan became the largest buyer of coca leaves from the Dutch Indies.

To put an ironical climax to this monstrous development, Mr. Uchida Ryohei, a patriot of whom mention has already been made, produced several numbers of a monthly *Asian Review*, the chief object of which appeared to be to tell the English in a near approach to their own language what he thought of them. Mr. Uchida being particularly interested in China, and most commonly referred to as head of the China *ronin*, might be presumed to be acquainted with the facts, but his most vigorous attacks on Britain were inspired by indignation at the part played by her in the debauching of China with noxious drugs.

The scandal was by this time so intolerable that some real steps had to be taken. Poppies disappeared from the fields south of Kyoto, and the import returns dropped heavily. A local British paper disclosed the fact, however, that large imports were still coming to Kobe but that only small quantities appeared on the official returns, whereupon the official explanation was given that the goods referred to were transhipment merchandise, and thereafter morphia as an article of import disappeared from the Kobe returns, being merged into the heterogeneous trifles collectively designated "Others."

In due course at Geneva the Japanese delegate, Mr. Sugimura Yotaro, was congratulated on the frankness of his statement of facts and the fervency of his promises that something would be done: "We are a nation of samurai: with us honour is more important than anything else." A year later Mr. Hoshi Hajime, Japan's greatest manufacturing chemist and a pioneer in the extraction of alkaloids, was fined 1,000,000 *yen* for illicit deals in opium—a sentence which was duly reversed on appeal. The gesture was made: there was no need for vindictiveness. Nor was there need for more than a gesture: "business as usual" was the order of the day.

XXIV

THE ANGLO-JAPANESE ALLIANCE

WHETHER the Anglo-Japanese Alliance put on Japan the obligation of participating in the Great War is arguable. For some days Japan maintained a neutral position, and offered Germany terms which would have ensured the maintenance of neutrality. Had Germany accepted these terms and continued to threaten British interests in Asia, it is difficult to see how Japan could have kept faith with both countries. But Germany sent no reply to the Japanese Note, and Japan came into the war "in accordance with the terms of the Anglo-Japanese Alliance." The historic importance of this Alliance to Japan could hardly be exaggerated. It encouraged Japan to go to war with Russia in 1904, and ensured freedom from intervention during that contest. It furnished her with a pretext, which otherwise it would have been difficult to find, for capturing Kiaochau and the Pacific Islands. It also launched her on that career of expansion and militarism which caused other countries, including the British Dominions, to regard her with fear and suspicion.

As soon as the Treaty of Versailles was signed, in 1919, the question of the renewal of the Alliance, which still had more than two years to run, began to be discussed. Successive waves of advocacy of renewal passed over the Japanese Press, presumably in response to official hints that a renewal of the Alliance was desirable. It was noted often that, while the Japanese Press was very independent in its criticism of home affairs, there was often a strange unanimity regarding foreign relations, while Japanese diplomatists abroad would sometimes enforce their arguments by references to the uncontrollable force of public opinion as represented in the Press. At this time, when a chorus of propaganda for renewal was in full blast, there was great ado about what was guardedly referred to as a "grave diplomatic blunder," and the Press was forbidden to mention it, while even in the Diet it was referred to only obliquely, though in terms of horror and reprobation. It appeared that, in a little journal circulated privately among members of the Foreign Office staff, there had appeared a story that King George had jokingly asked the Japanese delegates to Versailles, when they visited London, "whether old Wilson's long speeches had not sent them to sleep." Only on an announcement being made that the British Government attached no importance to the matter, and did not desire that anybody should get into trouble for it, were the perturbations quieted.

Hardly regarded in Japan, though of far more importance in the discussion of the renewal of the Alliance, was the request made by the Chinese Minister in London to the British Foreign Office that, in the event of the renewal of the Alliance, there should be no mention in the new agreement of the "integrity of China." The most obtuse mind could not fail to understand the implications of this request. The first Alliance had undertaken to preserve the integrity of Korea, which had subsequently been annexed by Japan; the Alliance still in force undertook to preserve the integrity of China, and had been instrumental in deterring other Powers from protesting against grave infringements of that integrity. This polite request was therefore more damning than the most voluminous indictment. A couple of months afterwards a Chinese in Tokyo flung a bomb into the Foreign Office, a method of expressing disapproval which, however reprehensible morally, has frequently proved more effective than the most powerful logic.

The most effective obstacle to the renewal of the Alliance, however, was the feeling against Japan that was fomenting in America. Both Chinese and Koreans had poured out their troubles into sympathetic ears, and there was in California a considerable access of racial antagonism. To be sure, the least reputable elements of the community were the best haters of the heathen, and found their virtues a great deal more reprehensible than their vices. Baron Shidehara, the Minister to Washington, used all his influence with Mr. Colby, the Secretary of State, to get discriminating legislation sidetracked, and Viscount Kaneko, an old Harvard scholar, was appointed to go on a special mission for the cultivation of good feeling. It was always found much easier to evoke self-satisfaction than to convert hostile critics. Viscount Goto, for example, wrote an article in the *Diplomatic Review* in which he pointed out how much more peaceful and unmilitary the Japanese always were than the Aryans. There had been civil wars, it was true, and there were the continental adventures of the Empress Jingo and of Hideyoshi, but even Hideyoshi was mild compared with Aryan conquerors. Another Japanese writer of the time, even more intoxicated with words and even less disposed to compare them with the facts, declared that the Alliance must be renewed because it had kept the peace of the Far East for the past twenty years. Marquis Okuma, also accustomed to utter panegyrics on Japan's innate pacifism, made belligerent speeches about the Californians. Feelings were further exacerbated by the endeavour made, through the Jones Shipping Act, to injure Japanese shipping on the Pacific for the benefit of the new American ships, and this led to some foolish local retaliation in the way of giving American ships the worst berths in Japanese harbours, and of arrogant behaviour of minor officials dealing with American ships—trifling matters, but very helpful in creating ill-feeling. At the opening of the Diet in January 1921, Viscount Uchida, the Foreign Minister, announced that the Anglo-Japanese Alliance would be renewed, with due consideration for the need of making it consistent with the Covenant of the League of Nations, should there be found to be any discrepancy. He expressed regret at the same time that the new Californian land law operated even more severely in respect of Japanese than did the law of 1913.

Naturally every incident tended to exacerbate feeling. In Vladivostok an American Lieutenant from the U.S.S.

Albany was shot dead by a Japanese sentry, but that was adequately explained by saying that the sentry mistook him for a Russian! In the Ginza—Tokyo's principal shopping street—a young European lady was attacked by a patriot because he thought she was an American! American spies were seen on all hands by the patriotic eye of faith. American and Japanese bluejackets came to blows in Shanghai. And the Foreign Office, always cautious and astute, hired as "adviser" an agent of the American Associated Press who had done not a little to awaken Americans to a knowledge of Japan's policy in China. The Foreign Office also engineered a satisfactory solution of the discussion over the small island of Yap, important only as a cable station in mid-Pacific and claimed outright by Japanese patriots as "mandated" under the Versailles Treaty. The general unrest greatly encouraged the militarists, and enabled them to lay out vast sums on the improvement of the army and navy. Moreover, they could point to the indubitable fact that the principal belligerent Powers had gone far ahead of Japan during the Great War in the development of scientific warfare. But if the militarists gained this point, they lost in another direction. They desired a renewal of the Anglo-Japanese Alliance, but the more militant Japan became, the stronger was the opposition to the Alliance. Racial prejudice was imported more and more into world politics, and the fear of a militant Japan intensified the prejudices against Japanese immigration both in the United States and the British Dominions, while the demand for racial equality preferred at Versailles was recognised as a bid for the right of immigration and increased the prejudice against an Alliance which might compel Britain to adopt a passive policy even if she did not actively support it. Even in England, though the Foreign Office desired renewal and did its utmost to prevent the news of the bitter hostility manifested at the Imperial Conference in the summer of 1921 from leaking out, the Alliance was far less popular than it had been, mainly owing to the Twenty-one Demands and to the secret agreement regarding Shantung. American hostility also had a far-reaching effect, and it was felt that American friendship was of more importance than a military alliance with Japan. China, of course, resented the idea of renewal, and not only did she remind both parties that an Alliance guaranteeing her integrity was equivalent to an agreement to monopolise spoliation, but popular demonstrations against renewal were arranged in Shanghai and elsewhere. Canada's attitude was an echo of America's, and the Australian Press, which had, under pressure, refrained for a long time from any criticism of Japan, relieved its feelings with expressions of dislike. The Premier, Mr. Hughes, had himself been critical, and was angrily referred to by Viscount Kato as a "peasant." It was represented to him that it was to his interest to support the renewal of the Alliance, whereupon his ill-considered advocacy only increased its unpopularity, and his suggestion that America should participate was so obviously impracticable that it only discredited its utterer. Another wave of inspired enthusiasm that passed over the Japanese Press failed to evoke any sympathetic response abroad.

The situation was very disquieting, but a diversion came from without. On July 4th, Lord Lee of Fareham, First Lord of the Admiralty, addressed to President Harding a request that he should call a Naval Conference at Washington, since the dangers of the situation in the Pacific did not admit of inaction. Pourparlers having already been made, the President immediately responded. Lord Curzon, the British Foreign Secretary, who was beginning to be dismayed by the increasing opposition to a renewal of the Alliance, and who realised that it could only be renewed if the Conference proved a fiasco, and perhaps not even then, pointed out that, since no notice of termination had been given by either party, the Alliance would remain in force for another year. A Note had already been sent to the League of Nations promising that on renewal the treaty would, if it were found necessary to do so, be revised in order that its terms should not conflict with those of the Covenant.

The indications were too plain to ignore. It was recognised that the end of the Alliance was inevitable. Japan could not refuse to participate in the Conference, since this would have been regarded as evidence of ill will and bellicose disposition; but the general reception of the proposal was decidedly cool. China now began to see distinct hopes of reward for having held out for an unconditional withdrawal from Shantung. Whether the Chinese situation would be discussed was still uncertain, and Japan did everything that was possible to keep it out; but it was confidently predicted that if China did succeed in dragging her relations with Japan before the Conference, she would be punished for having refused Japan's eminently reasonable offers.

Admiral Kato Tomosaburo, Minister for the Navy, was appointed head of the Japanese delegation, subsequently to be joined by Prince Tokugawa, in an ornamental capacity. Early preparations for a start were made, and one of the first Japanese arrivals in Washington was General Banzai, a Japanese adviser to President Hsu, who was evidently there in Japan's interests rather than China's.

Some endeavour was made, of course, to come to an agreement with China which would prevent China's case from coming before the Conference; but it was recognised that the case was almost hopeless. Mr. Obata, the Minister to Peking, after having apparently become more tractable, paid a visit to Tokyo, from which he returned more arrogant than ever, and on a draft of the Chinese proposals being presented to him, he handed it back, after the most cursory possible glance, saying that it was quite unacceptable. On the eve of the Washington Conference discussions between China and Japan had sunk to the level of accusations of untruthfulness as to what had been said and what had not. In Washington there was the greatest emulation between Japanese and Chinese delegates, and political propaganda was never such a fine art in all previous history. The

Japanese seemed to be inspired by a touching belief that there is nothing either good or bad, but talking makes it so. And even in the art of talking they were hopelessly outclassed by the Chinese delegates, who, moreover, had some impressive facts to lay before the Conference, and who, after long reluctance to offer Japan terms for an evacuation which they wished to be unconditional, freely published to Washington and the world what China was prepared to offer by way of settlement. It was not surprising that Okuma, that Old Man Eloquent, with the prospect of his statesmanship encountering such unpleasant publicity, furiously denounced the whole Washington conception.

Meanwhile the main purpose of the Conference—a reduction in naval power—was not lost sight of: it could hardly be, since Japan made immense efforts to get discussion confined to this subject; and, since reductions would inevitably be made on a basis of existing facts, naval shipbuilding and the fortification of the Bonin Islands were pushed on with feverish haste. The Conference was destined to have extremely important effects; but before discussing them we must glance back for a space at other developments in Japan.

XXV

THE PATRIOTIC CULT

In the web of the national life there are many threads, each of which forms a story in itself, and which, in a philosophic history, would be dealt with separately. Time, too, sweeps away a multitude of matters which were thought important in their day. It is usual to believe that it is the unessential which disappears, but it is quite possible that time is arbitrary and haphazard, and that trivial things sometimes remain while creative facts pass into oblivion. A chronicle like this must contain many things which the future historian will ignore, and among them facts may be dismissed in a word which later generations will regard as landmarks of history. But the daffodil still blooms when the empire has passed away and is forgotten, and who is to say which is the more important?

Nor are the main threads of the web of history separate and distinct, as the historian makes them appear. A nation, especially a centralised and insular one like the Japanese, is affected throughout in an infinitely complicated way by events, and even though an attempt at relating these events with some regard to chronology may result only in an amorphous conglomerate, that is a less misleading interpretation than would be the presumptuous attempt to play the part of Time and decide what should be included and what should be dismissed.

The courtesy visits of princes are in Europe reckoned as of little moment, and of use mainly as a popular spectacle. To the Japanese the visit of the Crown Prince to Europe in 1921 was a much more important matter. So far as is known, it was the first time a member of the Ruling House had ever been abroad, unless we are to accept the historical myth of the Empress Jingo who conquered Korea. It was a reminder of Japan's isolation, which had not been cast off so entirely as outward appearances suggested. Indeed, there was a remarkable mental reaction. The men who had made an eclectic study of foreign institutions and modelled a new Japan had passed away, and many of their successors had an inherited fear and suspicion of all that was foreign, against which they naturally erected a rampart of national egotism. Even a man like Mr. Hara Takashi, Japan's first commoner Premier, journalist and politician, bold and unscrupulous, an adept in every trick that has discredited parliamentary democracy all over the world, had an insular dread of what was foreign, a reactionary's fear of reform. Almost his last utterance was a lecture to a conference of bankers on the danger of "imported ideas," the irony of the situation lying in the fact that the bankers were assembled, at Mr. Hara's own instance, for the discussion of a plan to amalgamate the agricultural banks and bring agriculture into complete economic servitude to finance on the most approved Western model. About the same time, Mr. Ozaki Yukio, the protagonist of manhood suffrage, but now almost completely dissociated from party politics, lectured his countrymen severely on the theme that they had learnt much of what was evil from Europe and had, with this new equipment, retreated mentally into the mediæval Tokugawa days. He even had the rare discrimination and the rarer courage to denounce the worship of the State which had been substituted for feudal loyalty, and which had resulted in the glorification of patriotic crime and inhibited any criticism of national wrongdoing. A Japanese Warren Hastings, he said, would be quite secure from impeachment.

It was, then, with more significance than usually attaches to such matters, that the Crown Prince's visit to Europe was arranged. He was already accustomed to acting for the invalid Emperor, almost his first public act of this sort being to receive Sir Charles Eliot, the newly arrived British Ambassador, on April 6, 1920. It was a year later that he set out on his visit to England, where he arrived on May 7,

1921. His setting out took place amidst "a sordid struggle on the steps of the Throne," as critics correctly described it. A suitable marriage had been arranged for the Crown Prince, but it did not suit the Choshu Clan, and an endeavour was made to change the plans. Much has been written on the subject of "clan government" in Japan. In the previous reign the two powerful clans of Choshu and Satsuma monopolised power and competed between themselves. As time went on, though nothing was more frequent than denunciations of the "clans," the growing influence of the new capitalist class was making great encroachments on their prestige. Nominally Choshu and Satsuma controlled the army and the navy respectively, and Marshal Prince Yamagata was the State oracle without whose word no important step could be taken. Little, of course, is known of the details of the intrigue over the imperial betrothal, for all public discussion was prohibited, and it was, like so many other things that crop up from time to time, referred to as "the grave affair." Endeavours were made to break off the match on the ground that the health of the bride-elect was not good, but nothing worse than an allegation of colour-blindness was ever suggested. It is incomprehensible why Yamagata, who was all-powerful, ever allowed the struggle to take place. The bride's family were supposed to have Satsuma affiliations, but the two bodies, like the Genji and Heike, in Japan's "wars of the roses," had gradually lost their family aspect and were on the point of dissolution, being held together more by mercenary motives than by feudal loyalty. Yamagata got the worst of the struggle, and the original plans held good. In spite of Press embargoes, such an affair could not be entirely hidden, and clan prestige received a fatal blow.

The Prince was, of course, received with honour in Europe, and many new precedents were created there in the way of increased liberty of movement, such as visiting the theatre—a thing which had never been done in Japan. And when he returned there was a brief season of confirming these democratic precedents. The cinematographers were permitted to direct their machines towards the imperial movements; the Prince appeared in "plus fours," and even swam in public. A month after his return the Imperial Household Department issued a frank statement of the Emperor's condition of health, from which it was clear that he would never emerge from the retirement which he had entered nearly two years before. The Crown Prince was shortly afterwards appointed Regent.

From this time the Regent was the cynosure of the patriotic cult, of which Mr. Tokonami, the Home Minister, was the most earnest promoter. Following precedent, but carrying the movement further, Mr. Tokonami had brought into a standardised form and placed under official supervision the Young Men's Associations of the villages and smaller towns. Individualism is not strong in Japan, and associations exist for all purposes; hence the young men, from the time of leaving the primary school until the age for military service, were generally in an association which helped at fires, festivals, and other public functions. At Yoyogi, in a suburb of Tokyo, a shrine dedicated to the Emperor Meiji, a museum of imperial relics, and other memorial buildings were constructed, in vast grounds beautifully laid out. This memorial to the Great Emperor, whose posthumous deification exceeded that of all his ancestors, was brought to the notice of his subjects in the remotest parts in various ways, notably by its being made the subject of the annual Court Poetical Contest at the new year of 1921—a contest open to all subjects, who compete in their tens of thousands. Mr. Tokonami conceived the idea of building a Young Men's Hall at Yoyogi, a scheme of which the Crown Prince became patron, in accordance with the Home Minister's idea that the young men of the Empire should look to the Regent as a personal leader in their devotion to the Imperial House. Yoyogi was to be a Mecca to which every youth in the Empire should make a pilgrimage the Young Men's Hall providing accommodation for them.

As in all such projects, the cost was enormous in proportion to the result, and when the Home Minister proposed that the Young Men's Associations should pay for it, each association being informed of the amount that it was expected to contribute, there was a storm of protest. It was, perhaps, Mr. Tokonami's only weakness that he often failed to understand that his plans for promoting patriotic fervour might not in others' eyes be clothed in such bright and attractive hues as in his own. It was remarked about this time, in connection with a great and long-established municipal scandal in Tokyo, that no funds had been more shamelessly embezzled than those allotted to the construction of a road to the Meiji Shrine, patriotic pilgrims being left to flounder through a quagmire. But human nature in Japan is not peculiar in failing to subordinate love of cash to love of country.

XXVI

THE GREAT DOCKYARD STRIKES

It is necessary to give some further consideration to the development of political consciousness among the working class. In 1921 there was a sufficient revival of trade to arouse evanescent hopes that perhaps the outlook was more hopeful than it had seemed, but strikes after the slump of 1920 took on a different aspect. They were not merely "prosperity strikes," but were associated with discharges of hands and reductions of pay. Naturally, too, they were associated with the study of the Socialist and Labour movements in Europe, and to be a Socialist was to be in constant danger of arrest and imprisonment. Some of the Socialists, Osugi Sakae setting the example, would refuse to stand up in court to hear their sentence. The outraged dignity of the court officials and their inability to make a man stand when he is determined not to do so made good copy for newspaper reporters, but though the demonstration was almost a childish one, it made a far-reaching impression as a demonstration of the impotence of authority when a man is bold enough to challenge it.

Nowhere was organised discontent more in evidence than in the great Government or "semi-official" concerns. At Yawata Ironworks, before the general slump had overtaken the country—for iron and steel slumped on Armistice Day —there was a strike in which 15,000 men walked out. Kokusuikai leaders rushed down to Kyushu to mediate, and were threatened with a thrashing by the strikers. The strike lasted only a week, the men having no funds, and the management, glad of the excuse, "victimised" on a large scale by discharging the more active of the strikers. The rebuffed braves of the Kokusuikai made their way back to Tokyo, where some of their number showed their true mettle by pommelling Mr. Ozaki Yukio, a solitary and elderly liberal statesman being easier game. Not that these heroes were always ready to tackle even one man. Mr. Miki, a famous political heckler, declared that the Kokusuikai were a pack of *gorotsuki* (ruffians), and when called upon to apologise, said that he had not meant all of them, but could name some who were *gorotsuki*. The apology was accepted! But they thrashed him a few months after at Otsu—apparently to prove that he was right. Mr. Ozaki's offence, of course, was his vigorous advocacy of manhood suffrage, a reform which, as already mentioned, was highly alarming to Mr. Hara. The Government was even accused of the Machiavellian method of discrediting the movement by organising the most disreputable of the community into suffrage processions. When some genuine suffragists were arrested in October 1920, the procurator conducting the case in the Tokyo court used every contemptuous epithet he could muster to describe them, his choicest being "dung worms." The Government might easily have demonstrated that the nation was not interested in the suffrage. It had reduced the taxpaying qualification to 3 *yen* a year. With the great rise in wages many working men were fully qualified to pay this amount of tax, but few indeed were keen enough politicians to go out and meet the tax-collector in order to get the vote, and though the taxes were very high the collection was seldom efficient enough to make them voters against their will. Besides, there was a more serious development. The cry was freely taken up —a mere echo of Russia, of course, but all the more alarming for that—that parliamentary institutions were out of date; the Diet was manifestly a corrupt debating society and impotent for reform. The effect of these ideas was to be seen later. Meanwhile there were plenty of preliminary alarms caused by the actions of men still in the beginnings of a Labour movement and troubled rather about household economics than about Marxian doctrines. Tramway strikes in Tokyo in 1920 caused much alarm, especially because the operation of this network of communication had become necessary to the civic life of the capital, the cars being always overcrowded to an incredible degree. Even the makers of comic picture post-cards found it difficult to exaggerate the crush.

The prospect of reductions in work making it inevitable that hands should be discharged brought about agitations for "discharge money," which Labour leaders endeavoured to make into a regular system. Naturally no uniformity could be attained. In some cases, where a certain loss of business was anticipated by the employers, extremely generous treatment was accorded; for instance, the Asahi Glass Co., at Amagasaki, discharged its men with handsome allowances as trade declined, the last thirty-one, all that were left when the works finally closed in November 1921, receiving between them 34,226 *yen*. In other cases, employers continued working at a loss until there was nothing left.

Socialists and all kinds of radical thinkers were continually arrested, but without the slightest effect on the growth of the movement. Extremists, of course, had to be treated severely, and in December 1920 one, Ito Isaburo, was sentenced to five years' imprisonment for being in possession of a bomb supposed to be meant for the Premier. But even so foul a conspiracy does not make it easy to understand the state of nervousness which, in the same week when this sentence was given, prompted the police to prohibit a play on *The Death of Ii Taro*, which was to have been performed at a mission college for young ladies, and to close an exhibition of *hokku*, held for advertising purposes at Mr. Hoshi's drug store in Tokyo, because it was discovered that twenty-nine of the verses were written by Socialists. Even less comprehensible was a raid on Kelly & Walsh's bookshop in Yokohama, in which 150 copies of the New York *Nation* were seized.

But lest they be charged with depriving themselves of knowledge of what the people were really thinking, the authorities took steps to find out. The Labour Section of the Social Bureau of the Tokyo Municipality circulated a

THE GREAT DOCKYARD STRIKES

questionnaire among a thousand workers when Ito Isaburo was being tried. The questions were somewhat academic, asking them what they thought of capitalism, whether they believed in trade unions, and so forth. It was noted with regret, mingled with satisfaction at the frankness shown, that many replied to the question, "Do you put self or the State first?" by writing "Self," while still more replied "None" to the question "In what Gods do you believe?"

In spite of half their leaders being continually in prison, the Socialists inaugurated a union, in order to give weight to their efforts, on December 9, 1920, though hardly had the meeting been opened when the police ordered it to disperse. The Socialists met again next night at the Young Men's Christian Association hall, at Kanda, in Tokyo. A gang of patriotic ruffians called the Kokoku Isshinkai attended and assaulted the Socialists. So outrageous was their behaviour that the police had to arrest some of them, but on Mr. Sakai raising a shout of "Banzai," they turned their attention to the Socialists again, of whom they arrested seventy-five, including Sakai and Osugi. The Kokoku Isshinkai (which was believed to consist of the super-patriots of the Kokusuikai) received sufficient encouragement to continue its activities for some time. Soon the members were distributing handbills inviting the reader to "Kill the Socialist Traitors." At the Tokiwagi Club on January 21, 1921, a Socialist meeting was broken up by the violence of these reactionaries. Labour had adopted May Day for demonstrating its solidarity in 1920. Labour Day in 1921, after a year of mental ferment, was signalised by severe collisions with the police in Tokyo and Osaka, and by less serious disturbances in several other towns. On May 9th the Socialists' Union called another general meeting, which was broken up by the police, and on May 28th the Government proscribed the Union, to which Sakai replied that they could not proscribe ideas. A few days later the Kyoto procurator was demanding eighteen months' imprisonment for Mr. Arahata, another Socialist leader, for unlawfully parading the street.

In all social affairs the go-between, or mediator, is far more prominent than in any Western country. In all sorts of compromise it is much easier to give way at secondhand than it is to do so face to face after having announced unalterable decisions. The intermediary takes credit for having persuaded each side to abate its adamantine demands, and in the last resort he appeals to each side to save him from the everlasting disgrace of not having been able to bring them together. Though sometimes strenuous, the position is honourable, and the natural desire to have a hand in other people's business makes it popular. The intermediary, indeed, is inclined to give himself airs. It is natural, therefore, that there was some competition for the privilege of settling strikes, but, the conditions being new, the results were not always happy.

One of the most unfortunate examples was the strike at the Fuji Mill, where 1,600 women and 400 men had stopped work. The strikers appealed to the Roshi Kyochokai, or Capital and Labour Harmonisation Society, to settle their quarrel. It was the first time that the workers had sought the help of this highly capitalised organisation, the offspring of Viscount Shibusawa's benevolent but not very perspicacious spirit, but unfortunately Mr. Wada Toyoji, the President of the Mill, was also a director of the Kyochokai, which therefore did nothing. The Yuaikai, which at this period was the most powerful body assisting Labour, addressed an open letter to the Kyochokai, which caused that concern a loss of face from which it never recovered.

The Kokusuikai, which had a tradition of mediation and of prestige among the lower classes, continually tried to make itself the arbiter of trade disputes; but it found conditions very different from those of old Yedo, where there had been no police and where the troops of coolies were not at all like the artisans of the twentieth century. In the case of a strike in the Osaka Electric Light Works in May 1921 the Kokusuikai offered to mediate, and were much disgusted at finding the Yuaikai already performing that office, or at least giving aid and counsel to the strikers. The Kokusuikai offered their services to the directors, but were told that the Chief of Police had already been so kind as to take the matter in hand. The braves were highly insulted, but were assured that only the Chief of Police, and not the Yuaikai, would mediate, and with this they had to be content. They had better fortune in a dispute in the Kawasaki Ironworks, in which their mediation was accepted.

But more serious troubles in the Labour world were developing, and the measures taken to curb them only inflamed popular feeling. At the beginning of July there were some dismissals in the great Dockyards at Kobe, which were the signal for the greatest strike yet seen in Japan. It began with a strike among the electrical workers in the Kawasaki Dockyard, and an incident at the outset inflamed feeling. A group of strikers were discussing the situation in the street when a gang of hired bullies, dressed in kimono, their sleeves tied back with blue *tasuki*, suddenly appeared and made a brutal attack on the strikers, who, being unprepared, suffered many injuries before they could get together for retaliation, which, of course, the blue *tasuki* men did not wait for. The strike quickly spread to the whole yard, and simultaneously to the Mitsubishi yard, whose workers showed more disposition to violence than the Kawasaki men, beginning their demonstration by smashing windows. On July 8th there was a demonstration, numbering 25,000, at Okurayama Park, and the next day 30,000 gathered at Egeyama, closely adjoining Okurayama. There were processions and meetings, the men parading the streets, mostly wearing straw hats and carrying folding fans, for the weather was getting very hot. It was impossible to keep the peace absolutely unbroken, and there were some scrimmages on the 12th. The Mitsubishi yard declared a ten-day lock-out on half-pay; and the Mitsubishi men, though more inclined to violence than the Kawasaki, were less insistent in demands. The Kawasaki men presented demands which included a syndicalist control of the workshops. The strike spread, involving the Kobe

Steelworks, the Dunlop Rubber Factory, the Formosan Co., and others, but these, though not inconsiderable concerns, were far smaller than the Dockyards, and were chiefly dangerous as adding to the possibilities of violence. The authorities took up a position of neutrality, which, from the strikers' point of view, was in itself a victory for them in principle, as strikes could be practically prohibited under the police regulations. But Governor Ariyoshi, of Hyogo prefecture, denounced the attempt to import syndicalism into Japanese factory management, and the profession of neutrality did not prevent the police from prohibiting songs and processions. With a strong enough force processions may be prevented, but it is difficult to prevent people from singing, and at a meeting in the big public hall in Osaka on the 19th the police were dismayed by their own impotence in the face of a mighty volume of sound from two thousand throats singing "Hurrah! the Revolution is approaching."

The principal leaders and counsellors of the strikers were Suzuki Bunji the lawyer, who from the beginning had done much to guide the Labour movement, a man of sound judgment and strong character and of orthodox non-revolutionary Socialist views, and Kagawa Toyohiko, the Christian social worker, who had tried, not unsuccessfully, to live in the Kobe slums in accordance with the principles of the Sermon on the Mount, and had gained the whole-hearted confidence of the poor.

The Kawasaki yard remained open for some time, but it dismissed the men who were prominent in pressing the workers' claims, and on the 14th also declared a lock-out. The same day troops were brought in from Himeji, the nearest garrison town (except Osaka), at the request of the Governor. It was recognised that there were special dangers in this procedure. Much indignation had already been expressed at the War Office on its own initiative dispatching gendarmes to Kobe, on the plea that the Dockyards contained much army and navy property, and though it was highly improbable that the soldiers would refuse to obey whatever orders they received, the clandestine distribution of "dangerous" literature among them had made the authorities extremely nervous. The men were accordingly hidden away in the port quarantine station and were not seen in the streets.

With a general lock-out and no apparent prospect of coming to an agreement, it was evident to the strike leaders that they had a very difficult task, for they were anxious to give no excuse for violence on the part of authority. They accordingly organised baseball matches, athletic meetings, picnics in the hills, and swimming meetings, but the police followed them round, broke up the crowds, and ordered them to disperse. The action was very provocative, but the leaders held the men well in check. It was felt that public sympathy, of which they were already assured of a large portion, was a valuable asset, and as a means both of evoking it and of turning it to account the strikers applied for hawkers' licences. These were refused, but some six thousand nevertheless became pedlars and so helped to maintain themselves.

There were some scrimmages outside the Dockyards which, from time to time, some of the strikers tried to enter; the police arrested at their houses, generally in the "small hours" of the morning, men whom they had marked as defiant; and the company served notices of dismissal on active members of the Yuaikai and other men who took a leading part in the movement. Meetings were under the most oppressive restrictions, always with police on the platform ready and only too willing to stop speeches. One of the curious incidents of the strike was a brief address to a group of strikers delivered in a Buddhist temple by the Hon. Bertrand Russell.

Both sides issued manifestos. That of the Kawasaki yard, issued in the names of 17,000 employees, declared that without syndicalist control of the shops permanent industrial peace was impossible—an argument which gained some strength from the fact that the supervision of skilled labour was notoriously the least satisfactory feature of Japanese industrial organisation. The management of the yard issued a counter-manifesto, in which it showed so complete an inability to comprehend the significance of the movement that it offered inducements for the secret delation of "intimidators." But in adopting the idea that strikers would never demonstrate unless they were misled or intimidated by evilly disposed persons, Japanese capitalists were only demonstrating how greatly they resembled capitalists in all countries, though at the moment Mr. Matsukata Kojiro, the President of the Kawasaki Dockyard, who was in Europe attracting great attention by his lavish purchases of pictures, was informing Press interviewers that Capitalism, as understood in Europe, was unknown in Japan. And indeed, Japanese employers often deceived themselves very thoroughly with the idea that, though they felt no particular obligations towards their workpeople, their employees were attached to them by a feudal loyalty. The destruction of this idea was at least achieved in July 1921, even if the strike was in other respects a failure. To the two manifestos mentioned, Kagawa added his own, briefest but most potent.

The situation was daily becoming more and more strained, and 30,000 idle men, prevented from meeting or holding processions, were developing a dangerous temper. As a means of keeping up their spirits and providing them with occupation, Kagawa proposed visits to the principal Shinto shrines in the city. To formal Christians this seemed a strange proceeding for the devotee of the Sermon on the Mount, but Kagawa was not a formal Christian, and the authorities could hardly object to the visiting of shrines, since it was always extolled officially as an act of loyalty and was practically compulsory on all scholars and soldiers. It was an ingenious expedient, but it proved ineffectual. As the crowd, less orderly than in a regular procession, passed along a street near the Dockyard, there arose a cry "To the yard!" Straightway the crowd turned in that direction, becoming more and more turbulent. The police on guard at the yard drew their swords, and resisted the attempt to enter the gates, one striker being killed by a sword-thrust through the body, and twenty others injured by cuts. It checked the rush, but added a degree of indignation and bitterness hitherto unfelt. The next day shrine-visiting was renewed, and the Labour Song sung by 10,000 at the gate of the Nanko shrine—one of the holy places of official patriotism. After this the men refused all offers of mediation, and it was observed that the Kyochokai—the Capital and Labour Harmonisation Society—did not even try to mediate: its capital was ten millions, but its prestige was nought. Kagawa bitterly denounced the police for their murderous methods, and was arrested for doing so. The men held out as long as they could, but they had no funds, and at length, on August 9th, they issued a combined manifesto calling on all the strikers to return to work. Kagawa was thereupon released. It was the end of any idea that the relation of Capital to Labour was a continuation of the feudal tradition, though the shibboleth was still occasionally repeated. In the next session of the Imperial Diet there was some demand for putting Labour Unions on a legal footing, with both sanctions and penalties, as there had also been in the previous session, but since the one object considered in all such reforms was the conservation of the power of the police in case of emergencies, little progress was made. Similarly, there had been for some time past proposals for the abolition of the policeman's sword. The tendency to draw the weapon when the crowd became recalcitrant was never so disastrously shown as during the Dockyard strike, but prolonged discussions only resulted in shortening the weapon by a couple of inches.

XXVII

A CROP OF SCANDALS

THE year 1921 was remarkable, among other things, for its crop of scandals, though it must be confessed that many of those which gained publicity in that year were of a quite respectable antiquity. From time to time the deliberate progress of the Kitahama Bank trial was reported. The directors of this Osaka bank had made away with nearly all the money, and, after ten years, the case was still proceeding. Neither the offence nor the delay, however, was specially remarkable, and it is as a matter of curiosity rather than importance to record that the procurator of the court summoned a broker and sharply rebuked him for extolling the character of one of the directors who was under trial, for, in contrast with this praise, which was doubtless inappropriate, was the fact that no newspaper ever appears to have got into trouble for assuming the guilt of an accused person while the case was still *sub judice*.

It was in 1921, as already recorded, that the Yawata trials, begun three years before, concluded. Sentences were pronounced at the end of 1920 on the high officials of Kyoto who had been arrested two and a half years before on charges of land jobbery, and their appeals dragged on for many months longer. Nothing came of the indignation of the Tokyo Barristers' Association who had made vigorous representations regarding the torture of some of the accused by the procurator in order to extract from them missing links in the chain of evidence. The barristers were promised that there would be a departmental inquiry. It was afterwards reported that Procurator Ichimatsu had resigned and intended to take up the practice of law, but in reality he was promoted to the Court of Cassation.

The tendency to slackness, characteristic of bureaucracy

everywhere, was specially pronounced in Japan, and put a premium on dishonesty. In 1921 the posts and telegraphs, whose breakdown affected the general public more directly than the evidences of similar incompetence in other Departments, were still wallowing in the slough, from which the Government attempted to raise them by doubling the foreign postal rates, not daring to charge a higher tariff on domestic mails so abominably handled. Such slackness naturally provided opportunities for dishonesty. Petty frauds were numerous, and where a man of ingenuity and enterprise found scope for defalcation the results were amazing. The postmaster at Takaradzuka, an amusement resort near Osaka, ranking only as a village, found that it was perfectly easy to indent for large quantities of postage and revenue stamps and to dispose of them by private trade all over the country, without having to account for them. He was on the point of becoming a millionaire when he had the misfortune to attract attention to his wealth, which led to an exposure of his methods and to punishment in due course. Similarly, a single clerk in the Kokura Municipality, near the Yawata Steelworks, was discovered by chance when his defalcations had reached 200,000 *yen*. These were prominent but not isolated cases. The Tokyo Municipal scandals were notorious. Taxes were very high, but public works were incredibly neglected. Peculation was shameless and justice was flouted. To the fact that their dishonesty was a matter of common knowledge the corrupt officials seemed to be indifferent, their only mark of respect for public opinion lying in their bribery of the journalists to keep their unsavoury doings out of the newspapers. Members of the Diet thundered against this inconceivable corruption, and at last Viscount Goto undertook the office of Mayor on the understanding that he should cleanse the Augean stables. The Viscount was a man of extraordinary ability, but it was remarked that though early in life he had been a struggling doctor, and had given up this unremunerative profession for an official career, which, successful as it had been, was never lavishly paid, he was nevertheless at this date a millionaire. However, this was not considered any disqualification for his new task, but quite the contrary.

In connection with the Tokyo Municipal Scandal, a development in the evolution of judicial ideas was noted. In comparison with British or American cases, criminal trials in Japan were remarkable for the lack of witnesses. In the Korean Conspiracy, as we have seen, no witnesses were called, the conspirators being incriminated by nothing but their own confessions. In the Kyoto scandal (see p. 174), similarly, the accused were required to furnish the evidence against themselves. There was an old Chinese rule that until a man confessed he could not be sentenced, and the Chinese tradition hung heavier over Japan's judicial system than over any other Government Department. As time went on it became increasingly common for men who had confessed to repudiate their confessions in open court and to declare that they were extorted; and procurators frequently lost their tempers and tried to bully prisoners into a retreat from this stand. In the Tokyo Municipal Scandal two Tokyo barristers, Kishi Seiichi and Sasaki Toichiro, incurred the deep resentment of judicial circles by instructing their clients to hold out at the preliminary examination and confess nothing. They were plainly told that they were enemies of justice and unworthy of their profession. Actually, however, they were inaugurating a better system of the administration of justice.

The great scandal of the period was that concerned with the Kwantung administration, the name of Dr. Koga being most intimately associated with it. It was by no means the first scandal in which he had figured prominently, but in the others the prosecution had failed to secure a conviction. In this one also he was destined only to lose his official post, and it is not a little remarkable that a man with such a record, when he was actually under examination, was quoted by a Japanese newspaper as a reliable authority on the guilt of Mr. G. L. Shaw, which he declared was indubitable.

The ramifications of the case were extraordinary, and the preliminary examinations lasted over a year, during which time it was found advisable to dismiss Dr. Koga from his post of Director of the Colonisation Bureau and to search the house of Koga's associates, including the Marquis Inoué. The names of distinguished men were involved in the scandal. Procurator-General Hiranuma, long before the preliminary examination was finished, ascribed the whole disgraceful business to the degeneracy of the upper classes. All kinds of corruption were disclosed. The South Manchuria Railway in one case bought a coal-mine from a member of the Diet (of the Government party, naturally) at a very high price. Enormous sums were paid for the privilege of selling opium to the Chinese. Brokers interested in the creation of an Exchange at Dairen facilitated the process with a gift of 100,000 *yen*. Every sort of bribery and graft seemed to centre round the Kwantung and South Manchuria Railway administration, and the farther the inquiry went the more deeply was the Tokyo Government itself implicated. It was the first Government really based on a political party—the Seiyukai—and the party had to obtain funds. Some of the evidence pointed to the Dairen Opium Bureau being its principal means of support. Procurator Yasuoka, of the Port Arthur court, in the course of the trial, when a discussion regarding the calling of witnesses sprang up, bluntly declared that Mr. Hara, the Premier, would be the best witness to call. Application was made for calling Governor-General Yamagata as a witness for the defence, but the court decided against such a step. It was declared that Mr. Oka, the Chief of the Metropolitan Police, had conspired with Koga to destroy evidence, but naturally this charge was not investigated. Koga had been Chief of the Metropolitan Police himself, and he was a faithful henchman of the Seiyukai, whose president, Mr. Hara, would never let a friend down. There was one Nakano with whom Koga had been involved in a scandal in the Metropolitan Police days, and Nakano was the principal accused in the opium scandal. He seems to have become alarmed at the turn things were taking, and inclined to turn informer. He declared that Dr. Koga and he agreed that the opium profits must be used for public purposes, but Koga emphatically denied this apparently obvious sentiment. Perhaps the context gave a special meaning to public purposes, making it synonymous with the Seiyukai funds.

It took a year to bring the case into court and another year to dispose of it, but the procurator only gathered energy. He brought the case to a close with a speech that lasted throughout three sweltering days in July 1922. He reviewed Koga's wealth, his unsatisfactory explanation of its acquirement; Nakano, he said, had had two-thirds of the opium profits and Koga one-third. A dead man, Kambara, whom they had pretended was a madman, had really been their victim, the procurator declared, and had committed suicide through the shame in which they involved him. The Japanese reporter who described the scene in court said that from being nonchalant, Koga's face turned black with rage as denunciations fell from the procurator's lips in interminable succession and with devastating force. That this terrific onslaught was unexpected the reporter clearly showed by his remark that the accused were utterly astonished and confused, feeling that they had quite lost face, such injuries did the procurator heap on their heads and with such inconsiderateness did he insist upon imprisonment when they had only expected a fine.

However, they did not lose the sympathy of the court, which imposed trifling sentences on three of the accused and acquitted the other nine, including Koga, for whom the procurator had demanded two years' imprisonment.

There were other charges, however, and the court declared that the receipt of a thousand shares in the Dairen Exchange as a reward for consenting to its establishment was bribery, and must be punished with six months' imprisonment—with stay of execution.

So justice was content with a gentle gesture of disapproval.

The foreigner who records such things as these must expect to be charged with racial prejudice unless he forthwith explains them away; and it is true that they stand in need of much explanation. Japan was faced with many difficulties in the bringing in of a new order. She lacked men who combined wealth and public spirit to lead her on the new democratic path. She even had to create, since that was also lacking, a mercantile aristocracy to carry on her new commercial relations. Few politicians could exist without aid from wealthy business houses; few business houses were so happily circumstanced as to feel no need whatever of Government aid or helpful legislation. Thus a vicious circle of mutual aid was created, which easily degenerated into the most shameless jobbery and corruption. Party funds always needed replenishing, and every business needed safeguarding. The statesmen who received subsidies from private sources had to replenish those sources from the public purse.

As an example of the sort of demands made on the Government may be mentioned the Imperial Silk Co., created with a capital of 50,000,000 *yen* to rescue from the consequences of their own rashness the men who had speculated in the silk boom. Its doings aroused a great deal of criticism, and there were some stormy meetings; but though some excitement and alarm were caused by the failure of the Mogi silk firm and of the Morioka Bank which financed it, a general bankruptcy was averted. Brokers were enabled to carry their stocks and adjust their contracts with the filatures. It was the humble farmer and silk-reeler who paid the damage, the farmer being ordered to cut down production by half till the market was eased. Government intervention to save banks and large concerns from bankruptcy was frequently invoked, the usual form of relief being a loan from the Post Office Savings Bank deposits at 2 or 3 per cent. The authorities dreaded a panic above all things, and would even issue to the Press orders prohibiting the mention of runs on banks.

It was a period when the sense of responsibility appeared to be lost. Losses had to be averted and money had to be made, and no expedient seemed to come amiss. Contracts for Bradford goods to the extent of 60,000,000 *yen* were repudiated. Adjustments in the cotton trade were on a far larger scale, and were as little concerned with honour. It is pleasant to record that the flame of patriotism shone brightly in this turmoil of irresponsible evasion: the Osaka Hosiery Export Association circularised everybody within their reach ordering them to assist in the boycott of an obscure Levantine firm domiciled in Japan which had failed to take delivery of goods ordered.

Abroad it was the same. An international readjustment with China was looming in the near distance, but the extension of the Japanese Salt Monopoly to Kiaochau was hit upon as a convenient means of increasing revenue, if only for a season. Mukden was compelled to honour depreciated Chinese notes at full value for the benefit of Japanese trade, and on the Dairen Exchange, brought into the world by such venal midwives as Koga & Co., an enforced gold currency put upon the Chinese merchants the responsibility of meeting the embarrassments caused by the extraordinary decline in silver, while Mr. Hayakawa, the President of the South Manchuria Railway, preached the gospel of more friendship and cordiality towards Japan's Chinese neighbours.

Clouds were gathering round the Bank of Formosa—a semi-official concern which had to lend money to the Government's friends. It was also bitten by the mania for speculation and had financed Japanese plantations in Malaya and Borneo. An enforced stringency now compelled it to cut off supplies from these dependents, though they were among the best worth saving of the bank's debtors. Capitalistic penetration abroad had to be curtailed; but as the subject of a first-class scandal the bank's time had not yet come.

As contributory to the crop of scandals which so distinguished the Era of Great Righteousness must be accounted the universal demoralisation brought about by the Great

War. A foreign scandal that extended to Japanese shores was the failure of the Banque Industrielle de Chine, which had offices in Yokohama. This concern went to the length, when failure was inevitable, of circulating puffs regarding its prosperity, and, with a frugality that it had not practised in any other direction, it sought free publicity for these puffs in the Press. The Japanese duly noted the attempt which was made by the French Government to compel the Chinese Government to make good the losses brought about by the dishonesty of the directors in Paris.

Amidst the orgy of unscrupulousness the records of the time show instances of an exaggerated sense of duty and responsibility, such as the suicide of Captain Kimura, in charge of the telephone service for the autumn manœuvres in Kyushu, who by taking his life showed his sense of responsibility when the telephones refused to function. It was found afterwards that mischievous urchins had cut the wires in play.

XXVIII

THE MURDER OF THE PREMIER

TOWARDS the end of 1921 there were two very notable murders. On September 28th Yasuda Zenjiro was stabbed to death, his murderer afterwards committing suicide. Yasuda was reported to be Japan's richest man. He had started in a humble way, but showed a genius for banking and devoted his whole energies to the accumulation of wealth. He was reputed to be a very hard man, and though he enjoyed the respect which outstanding success always wins, it would be untrue to say that his death caused any deep mourning. He never contributed to charities, but was lavish in promoting public works. The murderer was a comparatively young man who had been a bandit in Manchuria, and he appeared to have had some grudge, direct or indirect, against the aged banker. In almost any circumstances suicide after murder leaves, in Japan, a credit balance in favour of the murderer. It shows that he was in earnest and deemed it a cause in which it was well to sacrifice his own life. The obscure murderer was far more honoured at his funeral than was the great banker. The funeral of the murderer was indeed a remarkable one. It was attended by large bodies of *soshi*, or professional bullies, and of Labour leaders. For the murderer was a "China ronin" and a stout fellow generally, who was supposed to have avenged a wrong at the cost of his own life; and while the Labour leaders did not preach, or even countenance, murder, they took no trouble to disguise their satisfaction at the cutting-off of a man who represented Capitalism in its worst phase. Generally the bullies and the Labour men were sundered by a hatred that nothing could bridge, but on this occasion they joined in a public demonstration of sympathy with a murderer. It was a portent so alarming that men of the ruling classes who had always considered the story of the Forty-seven Ronin excellent mental fare for the lower orders, found themselves constrained to denounce this adulation of an assassin, and over two hundred men of wealth applied to the Metropolitan Police Bureau for special protection.

Exactly five weeks after Yasuda's murder a much greater man fell under the assassin's knife. On November 4, 1921, Hara Takashi, the Premier, was to take the night train for Kyoto on a speech-making trip. As usual on such an occasion, there was a crowd of admirers ready to shout "Banzai" as the train steamed out. As Hara, closely followed by his private secretary, Mr. Yamada, passed through the crowd a young man pressed forward and drove a dagger through his back. The Premier collapsed without a sound into the arms of the horrified bystanders and the murderer stood by without attempting to escape. The police took him in charge before the astonished crowd could take the summary vengeance that in another moment would probably have been his lot.

The murderer proved to be a railway employee of lower grade with a turn for politics. His immediate superior was the assistant station-master at the small station of Otsuka, who had often listened to Nakaoka Konichi's crude diatribes. The young man echoed the sentiments which Japanese statesmen are so fond of uttering about the degeneracy and corruption of the age, and he told the assistant station-master that he seriously considered committing *harakiri* in order to draw public attention to these current evils. In this he would have had some great exemplars, one of the greatest being General Nogi, only nine years before. But his audience was sceptical and more than a little bored with the young man's humourless self-importance. "A lot of people talk about *harakiri*," he said, " but precious few of them do it."

Now the Japanese are great punsters; it may be said without exaggeration that in their poetry an allusive pun takes as important a place as the simile and figure of speech do in English. The similarity of Hara, the Premier's name (though written with another character), and *hara*, the belly, seems to have passed through Nakaoka's weak mind. "I will not cut *hara*?" he said. "You shall see." The assistant station-master laughed and thought no more of the matter, till, a few days later, he heard of the tragedy. Nakaoka seems to have had no particular animus against Hara beyond the fact that he was the foremost man in a State in which there was something rotten. So it is possible that Hara died for no better reason than that he was the subject of a foolish pun. Moralists, however, among his own countrymen pointed out that he died by the sort of weapon that he was very fond of handling: in short, "those who take the sword shall perish by the sword." He was the *otokodate*—the stout fellow—supreme in politics, which he managed in gangster fashion; and he was a patron and employer of *soshi*, despicable and cowardly ruffians, of whom he generally had a bodyguard somewhere near. Terrorisation of individuals by gangs of these brutes was a political method that Hara regarded with benignant approval, and it was the mark of the *soshi* that he swaggered insufferably and boasted of his patriotism. It was one of the most hopeful signs for the country that, though members of the ruling class were overawed easily enough by these ruffians, the vanguard of the Labour movement, though they suffered at their hands, were never afraid of them.

Hara, a journalist-politician of humble origin, had demonstrated that in modern Japan it was possible for a commoner to attain the highest position in the State; but his instincts were far from democratic. He did, it is true, increase the electorate slightly, so that three millions out of a population of fifty-six millions were qualified to vote, but he opposed all further extensions of the franchise. In statecraft he had no principles but opportunism. That, under his régime, Japan's war profits were squandered recklessly on the army and navy indicated nothing beyond the fact that the country was under militarist control which had the wisdom to keep in the background and make the civilian members of the Government speak for it. But the country was full of money, and incredible sums were wasted no less mischievously than if they had been spent on armaments. It would be difficult to find an example of splendid opportunities so grievously wasted as in Japan under the rule of her Great Commoner.

As for Nakaoka Konichi, his life was probably saved by the bandit who murdered Yasuda. Admiration for the shedding of blood had been sedulously cultivated in story and drama, in art and the cinematograph. Even the primers upon which the minds of school children were nourished were of the same character, and in the Diet in 1921 Mr. Ando Masazumi declared that the Japanese school books were full of nothing but bloodshed. The authorities were reaping what they had sown, but the ruling class still thought it better to run the risk of individual assassination than to be collectively overthrown by any revolutionary movement. So "dangerous thinkers" were persecuted more vigorously than ever, while the gangs devoted to law and order and to patriotism were still encouraged. The murder of Hara was the signal for drag-net operations in which leaders of the Rodo Sodomei, or Federation of Labour (formerly known as the Yuaikai), were secretly arrested. But the appearance of bullies and Labour leaders together at the funeral of Yasuda's murderer had caused the gravest misgivings, so the precaution was taken of avoiding any opportunity for Nakaoka to enjoy the apotheosis which was the due of the disinterested murderer, and he was kept in the obscurity of prison instead of dying gloriously on the scaffold.

Hara distrusted new movements even among the gangsters who were such useful instruments in the game of politics as he played it. He was not greatly enamoured of the Kokusuikai, the new patriots patronised by his colleague, Mr. Tokonami, and he advised one of their deputations which waited on him to demonstrate their patriotism and capacity for leadership by organising parties of emigrants and going to Korea. The proposal was received with complete frigidity, which was fortunate, for only too many men of that type had already made Japan's name stink in Korea, and one can contemplate only with astonishment a statesman who knew how disastrous the presence of such men had already proved in the annexed territory, and who yet proposed to a body of men whom he did not care to deal with that they should continue the work of making Japan thoroughly hated by her new subjects.

Under the unfortunate working of party politics, however, the gangs of bullies and ruffians, though they professed a scorn of politics, began to assume political affiliations. The old-fashioned *soshi* was not to be identified with the Kokusuikai, and looked rather askance at this new body. Hence the *soshi* tended to gather under the banner of the Seiyukai, the patronage of whose leader was sure, while the Kokusuikai, despite the rather half-hearted patronage of the Home Minister, tended to range themselves with the Kenseikai. This was particularly noticeable at a stormy meeting of the shareholders of the Nippon Yusen Kaisha at Tokyo in June 1921, when the political grouping was emphatically Soshi and Seiyukai versus Kokusuikai and Kenseikai. Happily this political development did not fulfil the promise of its youth. None of the gangs had the physical courage or the mental capacity to oppose the Labour movement, so they utterly failed in the chief purpose for which exalted patronage was extended to them, most specifically in the case of the Kokusuikai. But this body, though its heart failed it when it was required to oppose the Labour men, still tried to dabble in high finance. A year after the packing of the Nippon Yusen Kaisha by bullies, the *Kokumin* complained that this had become a regular thing and that the company could not call a meeting without its being subject to the noisy coercion of these ruffians; invited in the first place as partisans, they remained as blackmailers, and the *Kokumin* said that it cost many thousand *yen* a year to buy them off. The occasion for this complaint was interesting. The domination of the meetings by bullies had begun to compromise the dignity of the Imperial House. It had been one of the important factors in the process of modernising Japan that the Imperial Household, the wealthiest family in the country, invested largely in such new ventures as the Nippon Yusen Kaisha. Invaluable as this was at the beginning, it began to prove a source of embarrassment, as it was felt that where the Household Department was concerned discussion was apt to be burked. Fortunately the Department always conducted its transactions with great circumspection.

Another instance in which the Kokusuikai displayed a taste for high finance rather than Labour politics was the case of one Ishii, the King of Bankrupts. Ishii was a great speculator on the rice market; but his speciality was the flotation of new companies. His method was simple, but ingenious. Members of his family and employees in his office became the shareholders in these companies, and the non-existent property of the company was pledged with the Osaka banks for large loans. By this means, combined with his unfortunate lack of judgment in regard to market fluctuations, he incurred liabilities which exceeded his assets by something near 70,000,000 *yen*. Naturally this caused much excitement in Osaka, but the ease with which Ishii had committed his crimes contrasted strikingly with the difficulty of bringing him to justice. Month after month went by without his even being declared bankrupt, the authorities being obsessed by their dread of a panic and believing that if they did nothing, nothing could happen. The Kokusuikai leaders, always on the look-out for some means to increase their prestige, offered to arbitrate in the case, and, so as to increase confidence, they gave voluntary assurances in advance that they would not compel the bankers by force to accept their decision. The bankers, however, could not be inspired with confidence; they waited instead with patience on the dilatoriness of the courts, which, a couple of months later, accepted the creditors' petition and declared Ishii bankrupt. Very little was recovered from the wreck, but Ishii, after his blaze of publicity, sank into the obscurity of prison for a term.

One outcome of this exposure was the collapse of the

Sekizen Bank, followed by runs on a number of banks which lasted for a fortnight. Again, however, the authorities decided that it was best to preserve the façade of solvency, however dubious might be the ways of the financial labyrinth behind it. Accordingly the Bank of Japan came to the rescue, and the crisis was again averted.

While patriotic societies under exalted patronage failed to inspire confidence, a society far more formidable came unaided into existence. The Eta became class-conscious, and resented the humiliations which they had accepted for hundreds of years as the will of Heaven. Their official name, Shinheimin, possessed no magic power to elevate their status. Conscription and compulsory schooling only emphasised their ostracism instead of obliterating it. Education, refinement, and wealth did not enable their Eta possessors to attain a better social position. A typical incident of the time was the acceptance of a young man with every qualification for employment at the central post office in Kyoto, an acceptance which was withdrawn when it was discovered that he was an Eta, the reason given being that not only would his employment cause trouble in the staff, but would be uncomfortable for the young man himself. Official advocacy of a more liberal attitude had no effect, and the class-conscious Eta at last took the matter into their own hands, calling themselves the Suiheisha, or Equality Society, and adopting a militant programme. There was a little fillip to the academic advocacy of reform. Prefectural Governors were lectured, on their annual visits to the capital, on the desirability of uplift in the Eta villages. The Hara Ministry proposed a plan for emigrating the Eta to the still sparsely populated northern island, the Hokkaido. The Eta, however, made no response. They organised themselves to fight their own battles, and received their baptism of fire on March 18, 1923, in a three-days' battle with patriotic ruffians in the neighbourhood of Nara, after which they were left in peace. Caste, however, is stronger than law, and the utmost that could be achieved was to make officials and soldiers careful.

XXIX

THE WASHINGTON CONFERENCE

Some important international conferences have now to be considered, taking place respectively at Dairen, Washington, and Changchun. The Dairen Conference began before that at Washington, but though it lasted longer, it came to nought; yet it served the purpose of keeping Siberia out of the Washington Conference. Some delegates of the Far Eastern Republic appeared at Washington and made their statement, but did not succeed in making their representations the subject of debate.

No better tribute could be paid to faith in the potency of public opinion in a democratic country than the tremendous efforts on the part of both Japanese and Chinese delegates, in the weeks immediately preceding the Washington Conference, to make a good impression. Both then and during the Conference an amount of interest was worked up which to-day is inconceivable. The record of the debates and arguments, then of such lively interest, would now be quite unreadable.

The interest of the Conference from the Japanese point of view was, of course, of a very different nature from that of the other participants. It was with a certain relief that Japan looked forward to a halt in the feverish preparations for war, and before the Conference began, Admiral Baron Kato Tomosaburo announced that Japan had never entertained the idea of maintaining a navy equal to that of Britain or America. And the naval question was intimately connected with the Shantung settlement in the Treaty of Versailles. Concerning that settlement Mr. Borah had said in the Senate in August 1919: "It will dishonour and degrade any people who seek to uphold it. War will inevitably follow as the result of an attempt to perpetuate it." It was to stave off this war that the Powers met at Washington.

China had determined to set her case forth before the whole world, and rejected Mr. Obata's attempt to offer better terms and settle the matter in Peking. A week later (November 12, 1921) President Harding formally opened the Conference. At first everybody's breath was taken away by the boldness of the proposals for naval reduction made by Mr. C. E. Hughes. A show of enthusiastic acceptance was followed by the protracted chicanery which still left unlimited competition in the smaller craft and the murderous submarine. The professional combatants saved their jobs and their influence in the counsels of their respective countries. Steps were taken in Japan to assure the public that, whatever might appear on the surface, nothing was really being sacrificed. Though fervent in their offers, the Japanese delegates insisted on the retention of the new naval monster, the *Mutsu*; and perhaps more remarkable still was that the launching of the battleship *Kaga* on November 17th and of the *Tosa* on December 18th were made patriotic fête days in a manner unprecedented in naval launchings. Nor were these giant hulls launched in vain: they were not fitted with 16-inch guns, as had been their original plan, but became aircraft carriers.

We need not linger over the details of tonnage and other arbitrary limitations by which the cost, at any rate, of making war was reduced. As if not to be behindhand, the Japanese military authorities proposed reducing the size of the standing army so as to be able to spend the money saved thereby on superior equipment. One of the Washington treaties placed a limit on fortifications in the Pacific, in an equally definite manner, by ruling that islands within certain lines of latitude and longitude should not have any increase of fortification. The limit included Hong-Kong and Formosa, but not Hawaii—which became the subject of much patriotic indignation. The whole business assumed an aspect of ridicule by a tremendous argument arising in Washington as to whether "Japan's island possessions" included Japan herself! A great deal of discussion was also wasted over whether the Bonin Islands were an integral part of Japan—a point that did not matter greatly, seeing that Japan had just completed their fortification with feverish haste, and would not be likely for many years to have any occasion for still further strengthening them; but it was observed that the *Japan Times*, a paper in receipt of Government subsidies in order to enable it to give the world correct information about Japan, took occasion to declare that the islands were not fortified. It may have been ignorance: few people in Japan knew that they were.

What Japan most feared of the Conference was that it would develop into an arraignment of herself at the bar of international opinion in regard to her treatment of China; but though the Shantung question could be kept off the agenda of the plenary Conference, its discussion could not be avoided. The Earl of Balfour and Mr. C. E. Hughes, the chief British and American representatives, proposed the way out—that the discussions should take place between the Chinese and Japanese delegations, in the presence of British and American observers. Many telegrams passed between Washington and Tokyo, and thirty-six sittings were held, before the Shantung treaty was signed. It was felt in Japan as a defeat and a humiliation, but the actual withdrawal from Shantung was leisurely, and, in the end, Japan still retained large gains, for though China again became mistress of her own house, large Japanese interests, commercial, financial, and industrial, remained.

Regarding Siberia, that was successfully kept out of the Conference. Japan was actually negotiating with the Chita Government in a Conference at Dairen. But Mr. Hughes did not leave the matter entirely alone. The American Secretary of State had an invincible objection to the Bolsheviks, but he did not regard this as any excuse for invasions of Russian territory or violations of Russian sovereignty. It is seldom indeed that the Government of one sovereign State addresses the Goverment of another friendly sovereign State in terms so sharp as those of the Note of May 31, 1921, when the

United States said: "The Government of the United States can neither now nor hereafter recognise as valid any claims or titles arising out of the present occupation and control, and it cannot acquiesce in any action taken by the Government of Japan which might impair existing treaty rights or the political or territorial integrity of Russia."

On January 24, 1922, Mr. Hughes tackled the Japanese delegation at Washington, reminding them once more of the Japanese promise to withdraw from the Maritime Province and Saghalien and of their undertaking to respect the integrity of Russia and not to intervene in its domestic affairs—an undertaking which, he supposed, applied to the Siberian fisheries also. He pointed out that the Americans had withdrawn in the spring of 1920, nearly two years before, and that he could not help thinking that the latest limit of the occupation should have been the day that the last of the Czechs withdrew. He expressed sympathy with Japan in the unfortunate affair at Nikolaevsk, but he regretted the punitive occupation, and disapproved of vicarious punishment.

The delegates assured him that his confidence was not misplaced, and that the Dairen Conference was progressing hopefully.

It was difficult to put a good face on all this, but, after all, this publicity given to matters in which the Foreign Office had kept its counsel discreetly showed where the trouble lay. The aged Viscount Shibusawa, always busy on goodwill propaganda, was in America, as disarmingly candid as ever. He deplored with his American friends the Twenty-one Demands, which were contrary to all samurai tradition and utterly distasteful to Japanese sentiment; but he failed to explain why neither he nor any of his countrymen discovered this until it became apparent that old Okuma had overreached himself. The conscience of some of Japan's best men had, however, revolted at the Siberian business, and Mr. Hughes's admonitions filled them with a sense of shame.

Yet, from another point of view, Japan had won no small victory. She had established a principle which she had long sought to establish, that in matters affecting China and Japan there should be no interference of third parties, but settlement between Japan and China alone. Still more important, the fixing of the naval ratios at five for Britain, five for America, and three for Japan, gave Japan the hegemony of north-east Asia; and, taking the lessons of the war into consideration, this meant that whatever Japan did in this region not even Britain and America would combine to prevent her by force. There was nothing to fear either from Hong-Kong or Manila; the only shadow of doubt was as to whether it would not have been still safer to include Hawaii and Singapore in the area of restricted fortification.

The man who would have been most bitterly disappointed at the Shantung settlement died while the Conference was in progress. The Marquis Okuma's active eighty-three years came to an end on January 9, 1922. He was a man of unfailing buoyancy and great popularity. Neither democratic nor liberal by nature, he promoted liberalism and democracy because he saw that they were winning horses, and he had no respect whatever for that mediæval tradition in which he had been reared. He had enormous courage and of scruple none whatever; he scoffed at the Genro, and defied the whole bureaucracy. He attacked Inoué bitterly for upholding and being upheld by the Mitsui firm; but his own connections with the Mitsubishi were just as intimate. His wealth was believed to have had its origin in army contracts in the Satsuma rebellion. With it he founded Waseda University, which had the reputation of turning out politicians rather than scholars. He was intensely vain and talkative, monopolised conversation, and loved to convey the impression that he was a living cyclopædia of all knowledge. He affected a detestation of the Chinese ideographs, and never wrote a line; he was entirely reckless in utterance because he was always ready to deny what he had said. His performances in regard to China brought discredit and suspicion on Japan, but he lost none of his personal popularity, and 200,000 people attended his funeral.

A month later died Prince Yamagata, also a survival from the days of the Shogunate, one of the makers of New Japan, and since the assassination of Ito the authority without whose sanction no important decision could be made. He, like Okuma, was connected with the Satsuma rebellion. Saigo, the famous rebel leader, had been his friend, and he washed the severed head of his defeated foe ceremoniously according to the usage of the past. Age made him cautiously conservative where his own initiative was concerned, though hardly able to resist so headlong a man as his contemporary Okuma, but he retained some vigour of mind and interest in affairs to the last. With him, for all practical purposes, the council of Elder Statesmen became extinct. Saionji continued to live, but was no longer interested in statecraft. The death of Yamagata was the end of an epoch.

XXX

SITTING TIGHT IN SIBERIA

It is time that we turned our attention again towards Siberia, where the adventure of rescuing the Czechs was still dragging on, and was destined to last exactly as long as the Great War itself had done. Preparations were made for the exploitation of the resources of North Saghalien, chiefly timber and petroleum, workmen and plant being sent for this purpose, and it was stated that three and a half million *yen* was to be spent on public buildings in Decastri on the mainland, which pointed to an expectation that the occupation was permanent. Elsewhere the Japanese found it increasingly impossible to make any headway. Brutal Cossack officers were ready to set up as robber barons so long as they could depend on Japanese bayonets to protect them from the vengeance of their victims, but beyond this the restoration of conditions such as the "true Russians" really wanted made no progress whatever. It was impossible to carry on a Japanese administration anywhere. The language difficulty was great, and no Russians, whatever their political complexion, were willing to act as intermediaries in getting Japanese orders carried out. On the other hand, it was necessary to have some sort of relations with the Japanese, and this could only be effected by obtaining a recognition which was still denied to Moscow. A Conference was arranged to be held at Nikolsk-Ussurisk on April 1st in order to organise a united Government for Eastern Siberia, but the Japanese, hearing of this, performed the *coup* already described, by which all attempts at self-government were crushed simultaneously from Vladivostok to Blagoveschensk, in every town along the railway. The movement was immediately taken up in Verkne-Udinsk, where the Far Eastern Republic was proclaimed on April 6th, under the leadership of Alexander Krasnoschekoff, the master-mind of East Siberian politics, whom, earlier in the intervention, a Japanese regiment had for three months hunted through the forests like a wild beast. A Conference was called at Verkhne-Udinsk, and there was some fierce debate. The only subject on which all were agreed was that the Japanese must be got rid of, and those who had suffered most by the intervention were the strongest advocates of declaring unity with Moscow and defying them. The longer they debated, the more attractive did this desperate but unmistakable expression of their hatred appear. The situation was saved by the receipt on May 11th of a telegram from General Oi, in command at Vladivostok, congratulating the new republic on its formation and promising that the Japanese would evacuate as soon as a stable government was formed. It was not till five days later that a telegram arrived from Mr. Chicherin, the People's Commissary for Foreign Affairs in Moscow, recognising the Far Eastern Republic as a separate and independent State.

This was a sad blow to the brave Semenoff, who, after a desperate appeal to the Crown Prince of Japan "in the name of the martyrs of Nikolaevsk," risked his life in an aeroplane and fled from Chita at the beginning of July, leaving his followers to look after themselves. He had offered his services to the Far Eastern Republic as Commander-in-Chief, and the manner in which the offer was received confirmed his conviction that should he fall into the new republicans' hands they would show no gratitude for the patriotic sacrifices that he had made. He and the remnants of General Kappel's Cossacks were transported across Manchuria by the Japanese, whose use of the Chinese Eastern Railway for such purposes elicited more American criticism. There were nearly a thousand Japanese in Chita, who fled in August, after their desertion by Semenoff. It is significant that over half of them were women. They were said to have lost three hundred million roubles by this withdrawal of support, but as at this time a thousand-rouble stamp was required for a letter, the figures were not impressive. The refugees had served as an excuse for the military operations, but were mostly there because of the military operations that protected them. They distributed themselves between Vladivostok, Changchun, and other remaining military centres.

Some efforts were made to rekindle interest in the Siberian adventure, but General Ishimitsu complained that discipline had gone to the dogs in Siberia, and that even the idea of vengeance for Nikolaevsk failed to arouse any enthusiasm. A Nikolaevsk film was shown in Japan, but had no effect. When the Far Eastern Republic had been in existence five months, and the towns on the Amur railway showed plainly that nothing but Japanese compulsion could prevent them from adhering to it, a general evacuation began, Habarovsk being abandoned to its own devices on September 14th. There was a good deal of anxiety in Vladivostok lest Semenoff be let loose on the city, and though Kappelite and other "White Guards" were dumped there (in defiance of the promise given by General Takayanagi) and General Oi refused to disarm them because he "wanted to avoid a conflict," it was found advisable to shunt Semenoff about in safer places. In December he was in Port Arthur giving a banquet to upwards of a hundred of his Japanese fellow-soldiers glorious. Although General Oi had congratulated the Far Eastern Republic on its birth, he withdrew his forces with deep misgivings, and warned the Russians that Japan would never tolerate Bolshevik neighbours. General Takayanagi, a week or two afterwards, explained that General Oi did not mean that quite literally, but he warned the people of Vladivostok that commerce with the Reds would inevitably involve them in war. Mr. Obata, in Peking, before the year was out, warned the Chinese Government to be circumspect, because Japan would never recognise the Far Eastern Republic. In spite of General Takayanagi's warnings, Vladivostok on December 3rd, after some debate in the Assembly, formally acknowledged the legislative power of the Chita Government, whereupon the *Vladivo Nippo*, the Japanese military organ in Vladivostok, denounced Chita as a body with which nobody could have any dealings. A few months earlier (August 27, 1920) this mouthpiece of the Japanese military occupation had attracted some attention by its venomous valedictory to the Czech-Slovaks. The last transport was just sailing—two years after their "rescue," and the *Vladivo Nippo* expressed the joy that all high-minded men felt in their departure. They were base hucksters who made war for their own profit, who had no ideals, who had sold Kolchak, and much more to the like effect.

At the same time it was stated that the Swedish Red Cross had reported to Geneva that there were 200,000 of the German and Austrian prisoners of war still in Siberia, living in the most terrible conditions, practically nothing having been done as yet beyond the efforts of small European Red Cross parties to relieve them. No Japanese ships could be spared (though many were available for charter), and the Japanese Red Cross did nothing. Equally indifferent was the Japanese Y.M.C.A., which, a few months later, received an imperial gift of 10,000 *yen*; General Tachibana, who succeeded to General Oi as Commander of the Expeditionary Forces, reporting that the services of the Y.M.C.A. were essential to the military expedition, and that it must not be withdrawn! It was remarked, however, that, though it seemed so impossible to relieve the prisoners, large sums were spent on the entertainment of foreign delegates to an International Sunday School Conference in Tokyo and on a party of visiting Congress-men. Not long after the Swedish report, it was stated that the League of Nations had hired two ships "in the face of enormous difficulties" for the repatriation of the prisoners. In April 1921 it was reported that there were only about 20,000 prisoners left to repatriate. The Red Cross report to the Council of the League of Nations a year earlier, which declared that none of the prisoners could survive another winter, was thus proved inaccurate. This was the last that was heard of the

"German Front in the East," which, with the rescue of the Czechs, was the reason for launching the expedition.[1] But it was more than two years after the *Vladivo Nippo's* valedictory curse on the Czechs that the adventure came to an end.

Certain changes in personnel took place in the leadership of the expedition. General Oi, as already mentioned, was succeeded by General Tachibana; a little later General Takayanagi, the mouthpiece of the General Staff, was "put on the waiting list," nominally because he had given to a geisha some of the cigarettes sent by the Emperor to the officers of the Expeditionary Force. The real reason was never disclosed; after six months the gallant General was back in Siberia as hopeful of favourable developments as ever. The civilian part of the Government was tired of the campaign, and would have been glad enough to withdraw, but the military men insisted on deriving an advantage from the Nikolaevsk disaster, though Tanaka was derided in the Diet. However, though the members were ready enough to sneer, they did not attempt to take action in the only practicable way. Baron Sakamoto, it is true, complained that the naval expenditure had increased fivefold in five years; Mr. Hashimoto pointed out that though the budget had swollen to the formerly inconceivable amount of fifteen hundred million *yen*, no new undertakings for the public benefit were included; and Dr. Wakayami described the budget as being "all for war and nothing for welfare." These were the only dissentients, and there was no direct demand for withdrawal from Siberia. The *Asahi*, however, whose proprietor, as already related, was beaten by a gang of

---

[1] Not quite the last. The "twenty thousand" was merely an official guess—the expression of a hope that this bothersome business was as good as over. An unofficial but more reliable investigation showed that in August 1921 there were still fifty thousand. This, however, did not render any the less ridiculous the statement in the previous April by an American propagandist kept in Shanghai in the Japanese interest, who informed the world in his most emphatic manner that the mobilisation then being made in Urga by Baron Ungern was really a German menace!

patriotic bullies for his opposition to the intervention, declared that there was a strong movement for withdrawal. There may have been a desire, but there was no visible movement.

Such a desire was faintly manifested at the Colonial Conference in May, at which various high officials met in order, as it seemed, to discuss Siberian affairs, and as the Conference was a novel one, its title appeared rather inappropriate. Prominent at the Conference were General Tanaka, Minister for War, and General Tachibana, Commander-in-Chief of the Expeditionary Forces. A good deal had been said, especially in regard to Siberia, about Japan's "dual diplomacy," it being apparent that the Foreign Office often failed to say the last word in foreign affairs, especially as regards north-eastern Asia. To an interviewer on this occasion General Tachibana stoutly denied that there was any such thing as dual diplomacy. The War Office, he said, scrupulously refrained from any interference in foreign affairs—except when the interests of the Empire imperatively demanded it. The military still refused to budge from the Maritime Province at the Colonial Conference, and, as if to show that they were right, there was a Kappelite revolution in Vladivostok immediately after, and yet another Government was set up. One Merkuloff rose to the top, and his success was considered so promising that there were congratulations at the Russian Embassy at Tokyo, still feebly functioning.

Merkuloff proved to be more stable than any previous administrator. He did not dabble with Chita and Communist politics, and the Japanese armed his police for him. He was the most successful of the various administrators at putting a Russian façade on the Japanese military occupation. The civil administration, it is true, extended little beyond parading the streets with armed police, and Merkuloff was always begging for loans. He apparently maintained himself by selling the stores which it was the function of the Expeditionary Force to save from the hands of the Bolsheviks, and an Osaka gentleman of the name of Shima, who had already been criticised for "making undue profits by monopolistic dealings" on the Osaka exchange, was interested in a bank scheme for lending Merkuloff 5,000,000 *yen*, the main difficulty being that the lenders wanted to have the stores and realise on them before they would venture to lend in such a dubious quarter.

Baron Ungern, one of the more capable and most barbarous of the Cossack chiefs, in the spring of 1921 organised a forlorn hope at Urga. Japanese military officers assisted him in this task, and he set out to make a last attempt to destroy the Bolsheviks. But he was defeated at Kiakta, and was captured and shot at Chita on September 20th. This was the end of any attempt to turn back the tide of Bolshevism. It was also the end of Semenoff, who visited Japan and was the subject of many stories about difficulties with the loot that he brought as baggage. As it had been his own favourite strategy to sit astride the railway and rob every train that passed, it was only fair that he should suffer in his turn. The Kappelites in Vladivostok tried to overthrow the Merkuloff régime that they had set up, and were encouraged to take the field once or twice in order to demonstrate the necessity of the Japanese occupation continuing; but their heart was not in their job, and, after Ungern's execution, the Whites ceased to exist in Siberia except as parasites of the Japanese troops.

The position of the Japanese grew more and more uncomfortable. They could maintain a military force, but that was all they could do. Antonoff, who had been turned out of Vladivostok by the Kappelite *coup*, came back as agent of the Chita Government (head of the Maritime Province Board of Directors of the Far Eastern Republic, to be more precise), and, free of administrative responsibility, lashed the Japanese unsparingly with his criticism. That in itself they cared for little enough, but besides the humiliating notice to quit received from the United States, there was the still more undesirable publicity created by parliamentary committees waiting on Baron Hayashi, the Ambassador in London, asking him what Japan was doing in Siberia. All that Baron Hayashi could answer was that the Far Eastern Republic was making good progress, and that Japan would be glad to evacuate as soon as possible.

XXXI

THE END OF THE SIBERIAN ADVENTURE

WITH a view to arranging terms for this evacuation, a Conference between delegates of the Japanese Government and the Far Eastern Republic met at the Yamato Hotel in Dairen on August 26, 1921, Mr. Matsushima, who had been in charge of civil affairs at Vladivostok, being the chief Japanese delegate, and Mr. Petroff representing Chita. Besides these there were Mr. Shimada, Consul-General in Harbin, and General Takayanagi, on the Japanese side, and (late in arrival owing to secret agents going through his baggage) Mr. Turin, the Chita representative in Peking. The Conference was a hopeless business from the beginning. The authority and recognition of the Far Eastern Republic were ambiguous. Chita, moreover, claimed no jurisdiction over the vast basin of the Lena in the north, while its authority in the Priamur and Kamchatka was hypothetical. From the beginning the question of the evacuation of Saghalien was insoluble. Constantly it was dropped, and minor questions were taken up, so that both sides should be able to report progress and the approach to a general agreement. The Japanese wanted a treaty before withdrawal, and the Russians wanted withdrawal before a treaty. The Japanese objected even to making withdrawal one of the conditions of the treaty; they had gone in for an altruistic purpose, and they would withdraw with equal goodwill; they would not make withdrawal a matter of price to be paid. The Russians pointed out that meanwhile Vladivostok and every place misruled by the Russian parasites of the Japanese military occupation were being ruined, and would continue to deteriorate up to the day of the withdrawal. They pointed out also that the abominable Merkuloff rule existing in Vladivostok at that moment owed its inception and continuance to Japan's violation of the agreement of April 29, 1920, which she had herself imposed. The Japanese, both civil and military, agreed at length on an unconditional promise to withdraw from the Far Eastern Republic's territory, but did not agree that Saghalien was included in this territory. They wanted Chita to guarantee the Japanese fishing stations in Kamchatka against the Communist or Partisan raids, insisting on the authority there which they denied in respect of Saghalien. The situation was not improved by the murder in November of Zeitlin, a Chita commissary in Vladivostok, who had been a member of the Antonoff Government expelled by the Kappelite *coup*. Krassin's vigorous protest to the Powers against the shipping of six hundred of Denikin's raiders to Vladivostok also made it difficult for Japan to maintain her attitude of disinterestedness, while it did not serve to shake the firmness of the Chita delegates.

The promise to evacuate Vladivostok and the Maritime Province seemed, at least, to be something definitely decided upon, until it appeared that the question whether the war stores, valued at 300,000,000 *yen*, the protection of which had been one of the reasons for the intervention, should be handed over to Whites or Reds at the time of the evacuation depended upon Chita's agreeing with Japan on other points. And when the Japanese delegates required the abolition of Communism in Eastern Siberia as one of their conditions, it became obvious that the negotiations had little hope of success. Nevertheless, the negotiations dragged on, and performed the function of preventing the Siberian question from being thrashed out at Washington. During its progress Mr. Akaike, the reactionary chief of police in Korea, whose actions did much to stultify the liberalising influence of Viscount Saito, let it be known that there were 200,000 recalcitrant Koreans in the Maritime Province. Statements of this sort were an effective counter to any demand for withdrawal, and it was indeed true that there was a wild and ragged company of half-starved enthusiasts for liberty living how they could and ready for mischief. In February 1922, after the Washington Conference had closed, the Kappelites took the field and tried to repeat the *coup* of April 1920; but though they received some backing from detachments of Japanese troops, their success lasted only until some Red soldiers arrived from Chita: they had no stomach left for anything like fighting. Mr. Agareff, Chairman of the Peking mission of the Far Eastern Republic, published an announcement regarding this new activity, pointing out that it was one of the innumerable perfidies of the Japanese military men. It was true, he said, that there were fifteen to twenty thousand of the "White Guards" in the Maritime Province, but they and their ruler Merkuloff would be scattered like chaff the day that the Japanese left. As for their present activities, he said, the Japanese had promised that there should be no White Guard activities after the Dairen Conference had met, and this was how they kept their word! Merkuloff found it expedient to resign on March 4th, and was succeeded by another puppet, Eremieff, the Mayor of Vladivostok. Criticism such as Agareff's was particularly galling, and any dealings with the Russians opened the door to it. Especially was this felt at the Genoa Conference, when Chicherin attacked Viscount Ishii with unrestrained bitterness, and the truth of the accusations only made them the more uncomfortable to listen to; hence, when Antonoff came to Japan on March 5th, to start a branch of the Russian official news agency, there was a campaign of calumny against him, and when he returned it was declared in all the newspapers that he had been deported. It emerged at this time also that there was a Japanese opium monopoly in Vladivostok, run on lines as vicious and dishonest as those on which the monopoly was run at Dairen. And Mr. Ozaki Yukio raised a great storm in the Diet by denouncing the whole Siberian business, which had wasted 600,000,000 *yen* and gained nothing but the distrust of the whole world.

But it was impossible to come to any agreement at Dairen with a Consul-General as nominal head of the delegation, and actually subservient to General Takayanagi, of the "great plans." It broke down finally on April 21st, exactly eight months after it had opened, having accomplished nothing—not even entirely stifling criticism at Washington. As the delegations withdrew the Far Eastern Republic was celebrating its second anniversary, and the Japanese troops, though supposed to be in occupation only of Vladivostok and Saghalien, were helping the Kappelites to shoot Bolsheviks 150 miles north of Vladivostok. Mr. Matsushima, on his return to Japan, declared that it was impossible now for Japan to withdraw her troops; but he, after all, was not a dictator of policy. Another gift was made to the Y.M.C.A. Just a year before 10,000 *yen* had been presented from the imperial purse on the general in command testifying that its services had become an indispensable auxiliary to military operations, and another two thousand was now granted to Mr. Saito Soichi, the General Secretary, for his war work in North Saghalien.[1]

One of the subjects of discussion at Dairen had been in regard to the Kamchatka fisheries, for which the Japanese fishing companies had tendered yearly to the Tsarist Government and the continuance of which was an economic necessity. There had been numerous reports of Bolshevik raids on the Japanese fishing stations and canneries, and Japanese warships had been sent for their protection. The Expeditionary Force had taken over the business of the yearly auction of fishing rights. On the Dairen Conference failing, the puppet Government in Vladivostok announced that the authority of Vladivostok extended over Kamchatka and that the auctions were about to be held. The fishing companies, however, refused to bid, and the military authorities extended the fishing licences and again took the

[1] It is only just to the Young Men's Christian Association to record that it did not always earn official approval. In China it was always regarded as a centre of evil propaganda against Japan. Early in 1923 the Soviet Government ordered the dissolution of the Y.M.C.A. in Chita because it was too religious and not in accord with the ideals of Communism; while in Seoul almost simultaneously the Japanese authorities closed the general Conference of Korean Y.M.C.A.'s because it was imbued with Communism.

money. But though the big fishing companies found the situation agreeable enough, the small traders were forced by circumstances into a far more liberal frame of mind, and many of them complained that military protection had ruined trade and left them no recourse but to return to Japan. The Tokyo Chamber of Commerce endorsed this view, but the War Office cared for none of these things. The Foreign Office advised the Japanese to stay, and the War Office advised them to go. Perhaps the War Office had the better reason, for it was carrying out its own plans, and under its auspices a new portent was arising. Ishii had retaliated on Chicherin by refusing to agree to the Far Eastern Republic's admission to the Non-Aggression Pact, and the inwardness of this refusal was immediately seen in a vigorous recruiting carried on among the "Whites" scattered through Manchuria. June 1st found two reactionary parties at daggers drawn in Vladivostok, only kept from fighting between themselves by fears of the Japanese disarming both sides. General Dietrichs, a Tsarist officer of high character who had been with the Czechs, reappeared at this moment. He made a show of being strictly constitutional, and maintained the recognition of Merkuloff until an "election" put him in charge and he was proclaimed Governor of Priamur.

Negotiations were begun for a new Conference, and as the question of Chita's jurisdiction in Saghalien and Kamchatka had blocked the way at Dairen, it was agreed that at the new Conference at Changchun (the point where the South Manchuria Railway and the Chinese Eastern Railway meet, being Japanese and Russian lines respectively, on Chinese territory), Soviet Russia as well as the Far Eastern Republic should be represented, so that the whole question might be settled. Mr. Adolf Joffe, the Soviet representative at Peking, who had experience of diplomacy without gloves at Brest-Litovsk, was appointed representative for Soviet Russia, with Mr. Janson as his chief assistant, and the Japanese were somewhat taken aback when they met at Changchun on September 3rd, by Joffe announcing that he and Janson were also first and second representatives for the Far Eastern Republic. There could be no valid objection, however, and the Conference began.

In the interim there had been a good deal of discussion about the arms and the promised withdrawal. It had been announced in July that the forces would be withdrawn from the Maritime Province by the end of October, whatever happened. This was followed by the statement by one Higuchi, one of the stormy petrels of the intervention, that whoever got the Vladivostok arms would be supreme in Eastern Siberia, and that the disposal of them depended on the result of the forthcoming Conference. They were, as a leading Japanese newspaper reiterated, Japan's trump card.

The Japanese, as well as the Russians, sent representatives of bigger calibre to Changchun, Mr. Matsudaira (destined later to be Ambassador to Washington) was chief delegate, but General Takayanagi was still there to represent the interests of the General Staff.

Mr. Joffe wasted little time. There was some manœuvring for position, concerning the dual representation, the question whether an agreement should be come to, as Japan wanted, with the Far Eastern Republic first and the Soviet afterwards, and whether the Japanese proposals at Dairen should be the "basis" of the discussions. What of the arms at Vladivostok? asked Joffe. That question, he was told, could only be settled after the other terms had been agreed upon. But what of the evacuation: was it irrevocable? Mr. Matsudaira replied that it was. Mr. Joffe then gathered up his papers and said that was all that was needed.

The Japanese delegates were now suppliants, praying him to continue, which he consented to do on the proposed "basis," conditionally on its being subject to revision. "And what are you doing with the arms?" he asked again. They would be delivered to a Russian Government, was the sinister reply. Joffe did not agree that arms which were supplied to Russia for fighting on the side of Japan in the Great War could be handed to the enemies of the Russian

THE END OF THE SIBERIAN ADVENTURE 275

Government, and he insisted on a definite reply. The matter was referred to Tokyo, and Viscount Uchida's reply came that they would be handed to the Government functioning in Vladivostok at the time of the withdrawal. Then, if there was bloodshed after withdrawal, Joffe said, Japan would be responsible—an argument that made little impression, since bloodshed was a familiar thing under the Intervention. And if Russia agreed, was Viscount Uchida ready to abandon his protégés? Of course not; an agreement between Reds and Whites would form part of the settlement.

The real crisis of the Conference was on September 19th, when Joffe demanded a date for the evacuation of Saghalien, and was told that that could only come after a treaty had been signed and satisfaction promised.

Joffe made no pretence to be suave. He told the Japanese delegates roundly that the Nikolaevsk affair that they made so much of was entirely the fault of the Japanese themselves. The arms that they were bargaining over, he told them, they were already selling to Marshal Chang Tso-lin and to Dietrichs, and he added contemptuously that their protégés would not be able to keep them long. They had promised to evacuate Siberia, and Saghalien was part of Siberia. Finally he wanted something definitely and truthfully: there had been too many falsehoods. The Conference was broken off, again with nothing accomplished, on September 25th. On September 26th General Dietrichs ordered a conscription of all able-bodied men for the White Guards.

Viscount Uchida, the Foreign Minister, in his official explanation of the rupture, dwelt vaguely on the impossibility of coming to a conclusion with Communists, owing to their fundamental heresies regarding the nature of property. Mr. Hanihara, Vice-Minister for Foreign Affairs, declared that Russia had proved herself faithless; but the Japanese Labour Unions passed resolutions demanding an unconditional withdrawal from all Siberia. For a little while the idea of a pure "White" buffer State was boosted. Dietrichs set out on a campaign of conquest; but the futility of supplying him with stolen arms was soon manifest, for his men had no taste for anything beyond easy murder and pillage. The peasants and a few Red Guards soon drove them flying back to the Japanese for shelter.

The irrevocable date for evacuation was rapidly approaching. The Foreign Office published a friendly declaration expressing the hope that trade would be resumed and would lead to happier relations with the Soviet, though in the negotiations there had been nothing more carefully avoided than any definite committal to recognition of the Soviet Government, to gain which, as they knew, was one of the more important objects of Joffe's appointment.

A diversion occurred in the interval before the troops left. The arms scandal could not be hidden. Indeed, it came almost to an open rupture between the Foreign Office and the General Staff. The General Staff had, ever since the unhappy business began four years earlier, played its own hand and pursued its own policy; and in the latter months it had descended to helping itself to the war stores in order to supply the discredited instruments of its policy. General Uehara, the Chief of the General Staff, declared in an interview that he had never acted except in obedience to the Cabinet Council—which was not to say that he had not overborne it. As for the arms story, he said, it was invented by Joffe and spread by fellows in the Foreign Office. That the story of the interview appeared in a Japanese newspaper was no reason for believing it, but it was in accordance with what was expected. General Yamanashi, the Minister for War, denied everything. However, the matter had to be cleared up, for nobody believed the denials. The General Staff found a scapegoat in a Major Hara, who undertook to monopolise the blame. His trial by court-martial began on October 14th at Kumamoto. He loyally took the responsibility for everything, and declared that none but himself knew of the movements of trainloads of munitions and of the long pretence of guarding warehouses that were already looted.

The farce gained the dignity of tragedy before it was

played out. Hara's wife took the accusations seriously, and, overcome with shame, flung herself overboard from the Fusan ferry. The news was kept from Hara until he had told his whole story in court—for the Staff were taking no risks—and it was to a man stricken with grief that the judgment of the court was delivered. The sentence was as farcical as the trial: Hara was condemned to serve eighteen months' imprisonment, but execution of sentence was postponed for two years—a form under which the accused escapes punishment altogether. The Chief Judge eulogised the prisoner: his acts, he said, had been inspired by the finest patriotism, and his acceptance of responsibility was an act of the noblest self-sacrifice. The officers of the garrison sobbed in chorus. The court pointed out that after the prescribed period of probation there would be a resumption of an honourable career. Mrs. Hara had served the General Staff well.

Dietrichs, defeated by the Reds but by no means downhearted, demanded the delivery of the Russian arms by October 15th. He also protested against the dismantling of the Vladivostok forts by the departing Japanese. He finally handed over his dictatorship of the imaginary buffer State to the Vladivostok municipal assembly, which declined to take delivery of the arms (of which vast quantities still remained). The Japanese completed their evacuation on October 26th, trying, till the last gang-plank was drawn up, to organise the Whites for another slap at the Reds. On the 28th Admiral Stark, with a fleet of a score of broken-down steamers, overcrowded with those who could not expect consideration from the Reds, followed the Japanese. Some refugees made their way overland from Possiet Bay to Hunchun, on the North Korean border. Some eight thousand were left stranded in Gensan, a port of north-east Korea. The inhabitants of Vladivostok hung out red flags to celebrate the absorption of the Maritime Province into the Far Eastern Republic, which itself not long after went into voluntary liquidation and merged itself into Soviet Russia.

So ended a four-years' campaign to save Siberia from Bolshevism. It cost 700,000,000 *yen*, thousands of lives, and infinite misery. It desolated, disorganised, demoralised, and ruined the whole country, and destroyed Japan's trade there, besides leaving a legacy of hatred. Before it was ended the Minister for War was openly derided in the Imperial Diet, and for years after it was ended the highest names in the army were besmirched with accusations of embezzlement of the money voted for the venture. It elicited sharp reproofs from America, humiliating criticisms from England, and accusations of falsehood from Moscow.

Stark's score of lame ducks, after receiving some charity in Shanghai, made their way to Manila, whence the victims of intervention dispersed. The eight thousand left in Gensan and as many more in the neighbourhood of Hunchun were abandoned to their fate. Winter found them unclad, without fuel, and starving. The General Staff did not lift a finger. The Japanese Red Cross, being a purely military organisation, did not feel called upon to do more than offer outdoor medical relief to a couple of hundred who had injuries. It was left to a few foreign missionaries and foreign business men in Korea to organise relief, which they did with the generous help of their fellows in Japan. The civil authorities in Korea belatedly lent a hand. In the end many of the refugees were drafted off to Mukden and Harbin, the military men still hoping to be able to use them against the Reds. Some took service under General Chang Tso-lin and the rest scattered among the open ports of China, men, women, and children dissipating the last remnants of any idea among the native population that the white people were superior beings.

XXXII

DISSENSIONS IN ALL QUARTERS

Viscount Takahashi, who succeeded Hara as Premier, proved less masterful and a less capable leader than his murdered predecessor. He even lost his nerve for spectacular finance when the situation really required boldness. It was a turbulent time. The demand for manhood suffrage was once more enjoying a great vogue, and appeared to have become a really popular aspiration. Huge processions were organised, and the Diet had to be protected against the demonstrations. In this session at the beginning of 1922, however, the scenes within the Diet were far more disorderly than any without. The Seiyukai had had an unprecedentedly long innings, and the political world felt the need of a change. There was no lack of excuses for turmoil. The Minister of Education, Mr. Nakahashi, was the butt of some virulent attacks because he had promised to raise some of the high schools to university status, but was denied the necessary funds by a Government which had suddenly become nervous about money matters. The South Manchuria scandals were the occasion for fierce vituperation. Mr. Suzuki Fujiya, a Kenseikai member, roundly accused a number of Seiyukai members of having received money from the corrupt Opium Monopoly at Dairen. "Bushido restrains me from naming them," he cried, "but it is not necessary. Look at them: they are white with fear!"

A serious constitutional defect was the subject of much discussion. *Iaku joso*, or the right of direct appeal to the Throne, was enjoyed not only by the Minister for War, but by the Chief of the General Staff. This privilege of the General Staff, combined with the rule that the Ministers of Defence must be officers of the highest rank on the active list, enabled the militarists to control policy, and they had not scrupled in the past to defy the Diet from behind the rampart of the irrevocable imperial sanction. The debates, however, even when concerned with serious matters, were conducted with little dignity. Flushed gentlemen, clad without in frock-coats but warmed within by too copious draughts of saké, roared and bellowed, and arguments frequently culminated in a rush for the rostrum, whence the speaker of the moment would be dragged into the midst of a free fight. At one sitting Bedlam was let loose when a live snake came flying down from the spectators' gallery and fell among the Seiyukai benches. When quiet was restored and the snake abolished, it was found to have been flung by one of the Seiyukai's own hired bullies, who, owing to the awkwardness of the missile, had failed to hurl it, as he had intended, into the midst of the Opposition.

Yet the Diet retained more good sense than a spectator of its uproariousness could have expected. There was at this time an acute fear on the part of the authorities of the communistic drift of opinion in the Labour ranks, where, indeed, it was a common cry that soviets were better than parliaments; yet the Government had not the courage to silence this cry by the gift of the vote. Each party had its own Suffrage Bill, but the Government circumvented them all, saying that it agreed in principle, but that the time was not ripe. Kagawa, who was secretary of the General Federation of Labour, openly dissociated himself from the extreme elements, but he proceeded to activities which were considered still more dangerous. He organised a federation of the four hundred existing agricultural societies into a Tenant Farmers' Union, and grave fears were expressed in the Diet as to the possible dangers of a body consisting of four million households and controlling the most vital industry in the country. There were continual prosecutions, including a haul of seventeen accused of corrupting the politics of the army —the most dreaded manifestation of all. Serious strikes and collisions with the police were common; and though unemployment did not exist on a large scale, the demonstrations of the unemployed were alarming. On March 17th great excitement was caused by an explosion near the "Double Bridge" entrance to the Imperial Palace. A man carrying a bomb dropped it and was blown to pieces. An explanation was published that he had done it deliberately by way of a demonstration. Such a story would not be acceptable in the West, but in Asia, especially in China and Japan, the idea was not a novel one, though the means adopted were unusual. The Government, hag-ridden by all these alarms, introduced a measure popularly known as the Dangerous Thoughts Bill. It included a fatuous provision for the punishment of persons for political offences committed abroad, by which it was hoped that international law might be overridden if another Shaw case occurred; but its chief objects were to increase the powers of the police, who already exercised almost unlimited rights of search, arrest, examination, and detention, and to make the definition of sedition so wide as to include anybody whom the police desired to prosecute. The Diet, though not excessively liberal, jibbed at a measure so reactionary, and the Government, dubious of support even in the well-disciplined ranks of the Seiyukai, let the session come to an end without taking a vote on the Bill.

The Government outlasted the session of the Diet, but not long. The Seiyukai, under Mr. Hara, had had the virtue of loyalty to its own members, but Viscount Takahashi was not of the same calibre: he trusted in agile and ingenious adjustments rather than in the solid phalanx into which Hara had organised his mercenaries. He tried to save the Government by making Jonahs of unpopular Ministers, and there were acidulated arguments over the *ichiren takusho shugi*, or "one go all go principle." Takahashi declared that he did not believe in any such theory, and invited two of his Ministers to resign. They refused flatly. The position was a difficult one, but Takahashi had learnt the art of being genial in the most adverse circumstances. He invited his colleagues to a Japanese dinner with *go* (Japanese chess) afterwards. All wore Japanese dress, and transported themselves in spirit back into the Middle Ages, and there was much mutual admiration. It was a brief respite: the amenities of Old Japan could not long avail in this troubled age: and the Cabinet resigned on June 6th.

During the last days of the Takahashi Ministry the Prince of Wales paid a visit to Japan, and during his month's stay from April 12th Japanese officialdom exercised in their highest degree those arts of lavish hospitality for which Japan was justly famous. The occasion was remarkable, apart from its picturesqueness, for the evidence it afforded of the growth in importance of the Japanese Press. Reporters were detailed in large numbers to "cover" the tour. Trouble began almost from the moment of the Prince's landing, the Press vigorously resenting the manner in which a Japanese aide-de-camp had refused to allow some reporters to approach the royal visitor. The newspapers overflowed with indignation when their reporters were not admitted to the little church in which the Prince and his entourage attended divine worship in Tokyo, though it was obvious that there was no room for them, and the Embassy was abused for its discourtesy to the Press. It has been remarked already that the Japanese attach none of the sacredness to foreign royalty that they emphasise in regard to the Imperial Family. This was seen in the continual encirclement of the Prince by men with cameras until His Royal Highness complained of it himself. The reporters held indignation meetings and threatened to boycott the visit. Their arrogance was incredible. At Kyoto, for instance, the local authorities treated them with the most sumptuous hospitality, but because the Governor put in an appearance for only a few minutes there was another indignation meeting. This was typical of the attitude of the parvenue Press, one of the greatest, and at the same time one of the least estimable of Japan's quasi-Occidental developments. A couple of the most prominent of the Tokyo papers had their revenge a few months later on the British Embassy for its lack of obsequiousness. They published articles, in which there was not a word of truth, about a policeman being assaulted by two members of the Embassy Staff, and proceeded to such embroidery as to declare that they had learnt, as the result of their inquiries, that the whole Staff, from the Ambassador to the youngest student-interpreter, were intoxicated nightly. It is only just to record that Japanese of distinction were equally liable to attacks as outrageous.

Admiral Kato Tomosaburo had made so good an impression at Washington that he was, after the usual consultations between Viscount Kiyoura and Prince Saionji and other prominent courtiers, recommended to the Throne as the next Premier, Viscount Uchida being his Minister for Foreign Affairs, and Dr. Midzuno, Saito's lieutenant in the administration of Korea, being given the Home Affairs portfolio. Dr. Midzuno was to hear something more of the Koreans. He had hardly been appointed when there was an outbreak of propaganda hostile to them. The *Hochi*, in an alarmist article, said that in Tokyo alone there were 5,500, of whom 2,000 were students, and that all alike were implacably hostile to Japan. Other papers took up the cry: there were 12,000 Koreans, it appeared, in the Osaka district, also of dubious loyalty. There was, in reality, nothing but sensation-mongering in this, but it was to bear terrible fruit later on. The Koreans were mainly brought into the country by labour contractors, and the Japanese, of whom there were a considerable number unemployed, looked askance at these men, working rather conspicuously on outdoor tasks, though the work was not such as the unemployed desired for themselves.

Japanese Labour men, indeed, took little or no notice of these Korean labourers: they had affairs of their own to look after. It was not till the summer of 1922 that the last was heard of the Kobe Dockyard strikes of a year before. Fifty-five of the strikers, who had been placed under arrest, were at last sentenced a year afterwards. They had counsel to represent them in abundance, but the law had the whip-hand of them, and counsel merely pleaded for clemency, which made an anti-climax to the strike, though it may have been fertile soil for dangerous thought.

The strikers were left to their fate, for nothing short of a revolution could help them. Labour politics continued to develop in their own way, and an association of business men, the Nippon Keizai Remmai, was formed, which was expected to have great influence as a conservative force, but of which little more was thereafter heard. Some agitation distinguished the appointment of a Labour representative for the International Labour Conference at Geneva. A kind of ballot had been devised, but the two who received the highest numbers of votes declined the honour—the second being Kagawa, who, though still closely connected with the organisation of Labour Unions, had abjured Labour politics. The third on the list, Mr. Tazawa Gisuke, accepted. He was a Director of the Kyochokai, or Harmony Society, and may be presumed to have received the official vote. His appointment was vigorously opposed by the Labour men, but without effect.

There were some strikes during the summer, but though ill-feeling increased, poverty made the strikers more amenable than before. The Kokusuikai continued its efforts to mediate, and took in hand the personal chastisement of the Sawata Alloy Co.'s employees in Kyoto, which resulted in complaints that the police had witnessed the assaults and had not attempted to prevent them. But strikes were incidental and ineffective so long as Labour was only partially organised. The endeavour to form a single big union, however, only showed how divergent feelings were. The chief unions met at the Tennoji Hall, Osaka, on September 30, 1922, to form a single body under the name of the Nippon Rodo Kumiai Sorengo. It was not a successful meeting. The police, who were in attendance to prevent the utterance of dangerous thoughts, found that they were needed to keep order, though their procedure in arresting prominent men only caused more uproar. There was an adjournment for negotiation, and the meeting reopened in the afternoon, but with no better success. The Rodo Sodomei (originally the Yuaikai) advocated centralisation, which the Kumiai Domeikai stubbornly opposed. The two parties nearly came to blows, and might actually have broken the peace but for the police, who made more arrests.

The delegates met again on October 2nd, when a leader named Tsukamoto spoke for two hours on brotherly love and unity, his two hundred hearers sobbing like children; but such luxuriating in emotion does not imply change of opinion, and the One Big Union was not successful. Viscount Takahashi had remarked that, in the control of Socialists, Japan might learn much from America—and this at a time when the American prisons were full and the Industrial Workers of the World were being hunted down. The Japanese authorities certainly favoured the American idea of trade unionism—each concern with its own union, so that it should be entirely ineffective in any struggle with the employers, who, of course, were free to combine to any extent they desired.

A few days after these Osaka meetings the Nippon Rodo Sodomei celebrated the eleventh anniversary of the inauguration of the Yuaikai. In spite of the disappointments through which they had just passed, they had reason to congratulate themselves on the growth and vigour of their society, and especially on the development of ideas and independence of thought which it had undergone. The doings of the Kokosuikai were denounced, and the police stopped the big speech of Suzuki Bunji, the president of the union, and this in spite of a declaration that the Sodomei believed that ideas would prevail over violence. Violence, it was evident, was not yet out of business.

The next month (November 23rd) the Nomin Remmei, or Farmers' Union, was inaugurated. The preposterous Kokusuikai was used in an attempt to suppress it. There was widespread resentment at the greed of the landlords. Some tenant farmers refused to pay rent and abandoned their farms. Some tried refusing payment and staying on the land.

With these the Kokusuikai gangs dealt, the farmers submitting, though not without loud complaint. It was not that the farmers had less physical courage than the townsmen, but they dreaded the official power which they believed lay behind these blackguards.

XXXIII

THE OLD AND THE NEW

The Washington Conference did nothing to ameliorate relations between China and Japan; but the story of the manifold intrigues that centred on the Japanese Legation in Peking is the story of China rather than of Japan. All the Powers professed that they desired to see a strong, prosperous, and united China, and they conspired with one venal general after another, keeping the country in a continual state of war. Dr. Sun Yat-sen in the South could never refrain from coquetting with Japan. At one time Japanese agents tried to induce him to make a declaration that he did not regard Manchuria and Mongolia as an integral part of China, holding out the hope that if he made this declaration Japan would recognise the claims of the Canton Government to be the legitimate Government of the Chinese Republic. The result was that Sun Yat-sen, indignant at such a proposal, entered into an "unholy alliance" with Marshal Chang Tso-lin, the Manchurian dictator; both were advancing on Peking, and the generals of both were bribed to let them down. Japan gained infinite discredit by her dealings with a corrupt gang called the Anfu Club, who were prepared to betray their country in every way for personal gain. Overreaching themselves, they took refuge in the Japanese Legation, which not only protected them, but smuggled them out to resume their malign activities from a safe place. "Incidents," of course, were numerous, and Mr. Obata, the Minister, always enforced the rule that the Japanese version was true and the Chinese version ridiculous. It was not till December 17, 1922, that the Japanese garrison left Tsingtau in fulfilment of the undertaking made nearly a year before at Washington. Centralised Government was by this time so disintegrated that Britain, who was supposed to abandon Wei-hai-wei at the same time, never did so, for lack, as officially explained, of a responsible person or body to receive it. Certain it is that Tsingtau, already deteriorated in upkeep in Japanese hands, sank into sad neglect when the Japanese administration was abolished. Except for a voice here and there, feebly advocating a more friendly attitude, there was an almost unrelieved advocacy of strong measures towards China. The Chinese students had naturally become intensely political, and Japanese critics denounced "government by schoolboys." Viscount Kato never lost an opportunity of showing that he was completely unrepentant regarding the Twenty-one Demands, and continually denounced the Government for not taking a still stronger and still more provocative line in China. Even the exponents of Japanese liberalism were hardly distinguishable from the Jingoes on Chinese questions. Baron Sakatani, who had succeeded the bellicose Okuma as President of the Japan Peace Society, denounced the conciliatory policy towards China, though no such policy was visible. Japanese liberalism at this time, however, was of a peculiar quality. The same statesman, at the beginning of 1923, asked in the Diet for assurances that there should not be, in the new College of Literature and Science, a perpetuation of "the old evil of the predominance of knowledge"—for the East had its war between religion and science as well as the West. General Yamanashi, the Minister for War, then actively engaged in making military drill and instruction a part of the middle school curriculum, endorsed Baron Sakatani, deploring the decline in the spiritual outlook and the growth of materialism, which had resulted in fewer applications for entrance to the Military Academy. The Minister for Education apologetically remarked that efficient teaching was hardly possible without some knowledge of mundane things. But General Yamanashi was not satisfied. Not only was there a lack of eagerness for the army as a career, but the conscripts were often recalcitrant—a dreadful development which the Minister for War ascribed to the "progress of thought." Mr. Tokutomi, Japan's most eminent publicist, developed the theme that conscription should be the key-note of national policy, for Japan, without this moulding to pattern, became a slave to foreign propaganda. The official solicitude for the spiritual outlook was exhibited in the canonisation of the mediæval Buddhist reformer Nichiren, under the name of Rissho Daishi—a very recalcitrant person and a "dangerous thinker" in his time, who spent a large part of his life in banishment on one of the more distant islands. But it is a world-wide phenomenon for the heretic and seditionist of one age to become the fortress of the reactionaries of the next.

A phenomenon of this time which caused growing concern was the discovery that Japan, from being a country of comparatively low prices and wages, had become one of the dearest in the world. Western Europe, from the time when the gold of the Incas first began to flow into Spain, had had continual additions to its gold supply, and this possession of an abundance of the currency metals gave to Europe a tremendous advantage in commercial dealings with Asia. The process of levelling up is a very gradual one, but in Japan it was done suddenly, by the wealth which flowed in as a result of the war. The sudden cessation of the war and the resumption of manufacture in Europe found Japan wealthy, eager to adopt new amenities of life, and best able to get them by purchase. A high protective tariff was little restraint on purchase abroad, though it enabled many new industries to come into existence in which prices and wages alike were on a high scale. Bankers and Finance Ministers were alarmed at the prospect of all Japan's war wealth disappearing in the purchase of foreign goods which people had hitherto done without well enough. An official committee was appointed to decide on means for lowering prices, but as it was not allowed to recommend either the abolition of protection or the removal of the embargo on the export of gold, it got little further than a plan for the improvement of the transport and handling of goods, especially foodstuffs. As a means of preventing the nation from spending its gold, the embargo on its export was illusory. With a practically inconvertible paper currency inflated in accordance with the needs of the increased population and the increased rapidity of commercial turnover, the Yokohama Specie Bank, which was the dispenser of foreign exchange, really offered a premium on imports by maintaining the rate near the value at which it had been fixed when Japan had a free gold market. This, combined with the fact that Japan still had a long way to go in mechanical modernisation, ensured an excess of imports year by year which economists deplored, feeling that the country was a natural spendthrift on the road to ruin. There was some outward evidence on which to base jeremiads. Nothing was more frequently deplored than the "double life" led by increasing numbers of Japanese, who built Japanese houses with a European annexe, indulged in frequent "foreign" meals, and kept two complete outfits of clothes, the Oriental and the Occidental. Another real handicap in Japan's commercial readjustment was that while labour was still not highly paid, it being only in a few industries that wages were on a European level, it was at a low standard of efficiency, and, in the piping times of the war, had lost all discipline. Inefficiency and slackness, however, were more characteristic of the administration and offices of Japanese factories than among the workmen, so that the frequent expositions of the theme that Japan's economic salvation lay in the reduction of wages only increased ill-feeling without contributing to the solution of the problem.

Another effort was made during the Kato Tomosaburo Government's spell of office to settle the Saghalien problem. Adolf Joffe, who had conducted the negotiations at Dairen, was already a sick man before they ended, being attacked by the severe neuritis which was to make the rest of his life a martyrdom. Being ordered by his doctors to a warmer climate, he proposed going to Hong-Kong, but the authorities there expressed alarm, so Viscount Goto, who possessed a great *flair* in such matters, and who had always expressed contempt of his countrymen's Bolshephobia, invited the Russian official to Japan. For weeks Joffe lay ill at the hot-spring resort of Atami, and, getting no better there, removed to Tokyo, taking up his quarters with his family and two secretaries, in the Seiyoken Hotel. Here, after communications with Moscow and long preliminary conversations, negotiations were begun with Mr. Kawakami, who had been Minister to Poland, as Japan's representative. This conference, like the others, was foredoomed to failure. Mr. Kawakami's method was to keep repeating the Japanese version of the "seven hundred cruelly massacred by the Red troops at Nikolaevsk," and whenever Mr. Joffe pointed out that the facts and the significance of the incident were different, Mr. Kawakami repeated it all over again. This method would have worn down the endurance of any invalid lacking the invincible determination of Joffe. Nor was this all that he had to endure. From the time that he landed he was surrounded by spies and pestered by journalists. When the negotiations began, a *communiqué* was prepared daily for the Press, and he complained that much besides appeared in the Japanese newspapers, including distorted versions of the conversations. The journalists who sat outside his bedroom door called themselves (since two or three could never be gathered together in Japan without forming a society) the Russo-Japanese Press Association; and, because they considered that Joffe was not sufficiently obsequious to them, several of them published at great length utterly untrue stories, asserting that Mrs. Joffe and one of the secretaries were lovers and went out in motor-cars by night in pursuit of their amours, these slanders being accompanied by editorial disquisitions on the superiority of Japanese to Russian morals. Joffe was furious and demanded apologies. The offence was merely repeated. He then told the Russo-Japanese Press Association that unless it expelled from its circle the representatives of the papers that had slandered his wife he would not allow any more *communiqués* to be issued. They replied that they could not go against their own people in a matter that concerned a foreigner. The *Mainichi*, which had not participated in the slanders, editorially lectured the Russian envoy on the impossibility of his negotiations succeeding if by his lack of complaisance he antagonised the whole Press, and the gang outside the bedroom door sent him a round-robin ultimatum. The negotiations making no progress whatever, Joffe was at length recalled to Moscow, and it was not till January 1925 that a settlement was arranged through Mr. Karahan, the Soviet Ambassador at Peking.

In chronicling events still recent, an immense number of incidents interesting in themselves but external to the story of the nation have to be passed by, but here and there some incident that fits into no historic sequence must be rescued as illustrative of the fashions and ideas of the age. Such a one was the sensation of the early summer of 1923. At Karuizawa, a summer resort in the mountains a hundred miles inland from Tokyo, a caretaker had just been cleaning out one of the cottages for the occupation of its owner, in the first week of July, and he proceeded to another cottage in the neighbourhood to see if it needed similar attention. When he opened the door, he encountered a dreadful stench, and he found two bodies hanging from a beam. They were in an advanced stage of decomposition, having been there, as was later discovered, for a month. The bodies proved to be those of Arishima Takero, a famous novelist, philosopher, and scholar, and Hatano Akiko, a literary lady married to the director of a fire insurance company. Letters left behind showed that it was a *shinju*, or love suicide. The affair piqued the curiosity of the public. *Shinju* was common enough. Such cases averaged, the year round, about one a fortnight. Generally it was the desperate act of young people whom circumstance prevented from marrying, and it had a rational inspiration in the vulgar belief that lovers who left the world together in this manner would be able to enjoy one another's society in another world. But here was the case of a man of forty-five and a woman of thirty, who could not possibly entertain such superstitions. Arishima, moreover, was the exponent of a far higher philosophy and had the reputation of being something of an ascetic. He had owned some six hundred acres in the Hokkaido which, a few months before, he had presented to his farming tenants, having first organised them into a co-operative union; still more recently he had similarly abandoned a house with large grounds in Tokyo, worth half a million *yen*, devoting them to the amelioration of the poor. They were not previously known to be lovers; and had they been, the case was not beyond possibility of arrangement, the lady being childless and divorce easy. But for some reason they chose the exit usually made by the young, ignorant, and poor. Every publicist in Japan expressed his opinion about it, and such is the force of example that in the next three weeks there were as many *shinju* and other suicides as would usually be recorded in six months.

This story of Arishima and his end was symptomatic of the modernisation of Japan. He had taken up an art new to Japanese literature; he lectured on the prominent authors of Europe; he cultivated a rationalistic philosophy—and he ended like the hero of some fond tale of mediæval Japan. In such manner ancient feelings still underlay a country that had been greatly transformed outwardly. For Japan was no longer mediæval and Oriental in aspect. There were parts of the great warren of Tokyo, indeed, where low wooden houses ran in lines that bore little trace of foreign influence. The Imperial Palace itself, surrounded by cyclopean walls going down to a stagnant moat, would have looked ancient but for the motor-cars running through the grounds; but all about it were great blocks of modern buildings seven and eight stories high, and life poured through with a swiftness unknown to former ages. Yokohama, the port of the capital, was a modern town, with its docks and wharves, the well-built offices on the old Foreign Settlement, and the Bluff, where most of the foreign merchants lived, hardly conveying a reminder of the East. War prosperity had wrought great changes. In every large town handsome buildings of a type previously unknown had sprung up. Electric tramways and railways and a rapid increase in motor vehicles were speeding up life in a degree undreamt of. Only seven years earlier if a motorist ventured out of the towns he might run for hundreds of miles without meeting another car. Everywhere he stopped he would be surrounded by a curious crowd. By 1923 there was a remarkable change. Every corner of Japan was now visited by cars; the old village omnibus with its rickety frame and starved horse had nearly disappeared, and villages formerly isolated were now brought into touch with city life by motor-car services. In the poorest hamlet the people were now familiar with ice and electric fans, and amateur economists preached against the luxurious tendencies of the age.

There were problems, of course, but nothing serious. Baron Kato Tomosaburo, Japan's "big navy" admiral, who had won much fame as a pacifist at Washington, died at the end of July, and his Cabinet, which had not been a success, resigned. After the usual conferences between elderly courtiers, Admiral Count Yamamoto, who had not proved a very distinguished Premier, was again nominated for office. The old courtiers were terribly afraid of appointing any man young enough to be in danger of absorbing a new idea. A "transcendent" or non-party Ministry was nominated, and the country, rushing headlong forward on its new activities, showed no particular interest in this mediæval group called to rule over it.

XXXIV

THE GREAT EARTHQUAKE

But there was a rude check to these abundant energies. At noon on Saturday, September 1st, a violent earthquake shook Japan in the very heart of its activities. It was a brilliant summer's day, with a high wind blowing, and everybody busy with their affairs, when, without warning, the earth shook, filling everybody's heart with terror. There was a rush for the street, where, the earth continuing to vibrate with sickening persistence, people watched as tiles showered from the roofs, buildings crashed, and cries for help and screams of pain and fear rose on all hands. After minutes that held an eternity of anguish, the convulsion abated. People began to look into the damage and see what they could save. Most of the large modern buildings at least had stood, though some collapsed. Earthquakes, after all, were common enough. There had been a couple of bad ones the previous year, one on the day the Prince of Wales left killing several people; and there had been a severe shake at Nagasaki the previous November. One never gets used to earthquakes; each is more alarming than the last; but familiarity brings the idea of surveying the damage and putting things straight. The water-mains, of course, were broken, but some ice-cream and bottled drinks remained; and their vendors were soon doing business again on Tokyo's main streets, for it was a hot day and there was a haze of dust. But one thing they had overlooked: in every house there had been a fire cooking the mid-day meal. Soon from a hundred wrecked buildings the flames began to creep and crackle. There was no hope of help from the fire brigade. People hurriedly gathered whatever they could carry and began to trek for safety. The big buildings that had seemed like havens of refuge became roaring furnaces; the flimsy Japanese houses went up in instant flame. Wider every moment grew the conflagration, and the people knew not where to go, flames appearing on every hand. Many stacked their belongings on the bridges, thinking the fire would spare them, but flying embers set fire to them, and their owners often jumped into the canals and were drowned. In the poorest part of the city there lay a great vacant lot, the site of a former military clothing factory. Here, the refugees felt, they would surely be safe. No flames could assail them there; and in they trooped, carrying their scanty belongings. Over thirty thousand crowded in, cumbering the ground with their chattels. The place was full, and then the inevitable happened. Fire was all round them in a densely built area, and the flying sparks set the bundles alight. Soon the whole densely crowded space was a furnace. Few, if any, escaped from their fiery prison. The whole unhappy company were burnt to death with the fuel that they had supplied for their own burning.

At the Yoshiwara, the famous licensed brothel quarter, there were terrible scenes. The brothel-keepers barred the doors to prevent their slaves escaping. Some were crushed in the fall of the houses, some were burnt alive when the fire came. By the time the survivors could escape there was no exit. They plunged into an ornamental pond, hoping to live thus till the fire passed, but only to perish still more miserably than their sisters.

Nearly two-thirds of Tokyo was wiped out in this great conflagration, and the people in Karuizawa, a hundred miles away, where the earthquake was severe but not disastrous, saw the whole sky aglow all night with the burning of the capital.

And yet Tokyo experienced by no means the worst of the shock. It was on the northern edge of the devastated area. For sixty miles south the railway track was destroyed, while Tokyo had an outlet only seven miles to the north, whence, for the next three weeks, every train that left was incredibly crowded, hundreds sitting on the roofs. Of thickly populated areas Yokohama was the chief sufferer. The earth's convulsions were frightful. Huge buildings at the instant of the quake poured down in a cataract of brick and stone. In the whole business area a Mitsui warehouse, the Young Men's Christian Association, a new and still unfinished telephone exchange, and perhaps a couple of others, remained standing. At the pier a great crowd was waiting to wave farewell to the passengers on the *Empress of Australia*, which was about to cast off and sail for Vancouver. At the first shock the solid stone wharf sank and left the people struggling in the water. They were all taken on board, and many more besides. Across the end of the same pier was the Messageries Maritimes steamer *André Lebon*, which also received many hundred refugees.

Fire broke out immediately in the ruins of Yokohama, the air was full of acrid dust, and the flames drove back rescuers who endeavoured to save people pinned under the wreckage. It was thought that at least some of the pleasant houses on the Bluff, sorely shaken, would be spared, but the violent wind carried the flames across extraordinary distances, and the heat was so fierce that living trees blazed like matchwood. Of a city of over half a million inhabitants nothing was saved. Where the quake failed to demolish the fire destroyed. The whole city, as the Mayor reported in a wireless appeal for help sent from one of the ships, was a sea of flame. Many were driven into the sea by the flames, and though the ships' boats worked valiantly, great numbers were drowned. The crowd who took refuge in the little park were all but stifled by the hot breath of the conflagration that swept over them; and those who trusted to the waters of the creek for safety perished by hundreds therein, their bodies blocking the waterway for weeks after. There were terrible incidents. At the Catholic school one nun and three or four girls escaped as the roof descended intact over the crumbling walls, and there they stood helpless while those within who had not been killed by the beams were burnt, calling to them for help.

At Yokosuka, the naval port near the entrance to Tokyo Bay, the shock was as severe as at Yokohama. Enormous stores of oil fuel for the warships broke their reservoirs and poured into the sea, covering the water with a thick layer for many miles. The town burnt, the very stones of the roads being calcined.

Over an enormous area it was the same story. The people in the summer resort of Miyanoshita, in the Hakone mountains, found themselves imprisoned by a landslip that blocked the road down to Odawara, and all night they saw the flames of the city of Odawara, while all about them boulders would hurtle down the steep hillsides at every after-tremor.

The civil authority broke down under the stress of this disaster, and the restoration of order and the possibility of communal life continuing were due to the army. Martial law was proclaimed in the Tokyo area, General Fukuda taking command. Splendid work was done for the relief of a situation that was unprecedented in nature and magnitude. The keeping of order, the rescue and care of the injured, the disposal of the dead, the distribution of food and water, the erection of shelter, the restoration of the means of communication—all had to be seen to in a devastated area that included the very nerve-centre of the Empire.

Anxiety was felt regarding the safety of the Imperial Family. The Emperor and Empress were at Nikko, where the earthquake was not sufficiently severe to do any great damage. The Prince Regent, however, was in Tokyo, and on the night of the 2nd the new Cabinet was duly installed by him in the grounds of the Akasaka Palace, with the embers of Tokyo still burning round them and the earth still trembling with the after-quakes. Several members of the collateral branches of the Imperial Family lost their lives; but of distinguished people in Tokyo at the time there were remarkably few who suffered, the poorer parts of the city being those most swept by the fire.

The people behaved magnificently, and there were heroic deeds without number. To most it seemed as though they must be in the centre of the disturbance, and they awaited help from without, rendering meanwhile all the aid they could to one another. The best as well as the worst of human behaviour in this time of stress came from the continued functioning of habit both in action and thought. At a time when every thought was needed for the relief of distress the official mind was particularly prone to find itself preoccupied with its habitual ideas in an exaggerated form. Before Dr. Midzuno, the former administrator in Korea, had had time to hand over the portfolio for Home Affairs a message was communicated to the police throughout Japan warning them against the malign activities of recalcitrant Koreans. This, with the previous sensation-mongering in the Press, led to terrible results. Rumours spread that the Koreans had been responsible for the fires, and a man-hunt started in which over four thousand were killed, as well as several hundred Chinese. The police in some cases assisted, but the better minds did what they could to protect these unfortunates and to give them safe-conduct out of the devastated area. When it was seen what a terrible mistake had been made, the official mind again functioned according to habit and prohibited all mention of Koreans in the newspapers all over the country, and even foreign telegrams were scrutinised and suppressed; while when accounts appeared in papers abroad the embassies immediately wrote denying that any such things had happened. Among the worst of the man-hunters were the Young Men's Associations, whose affiliation on official patriotic lines has already been referred to, and many subsequent trials were held, in which the offenders received formal sentences of imprisonment, with "stay of execution," so that nobody was punished at all.

Another example of this automatic functioning when the mind was paralysed by disaster was the strange action of the police in rushing round to arrest all known Socialists—so much had the idea taken root that whatever untoward things happened must be due to radical thinkers. In three days about 1,300 were arrested—an extraordinary feat of misapplied energy. A batch of nine were taken to the Kameido jail where they loudly sang the "Labour Song" and laughed when the police ordered them to be silent. The military were sent for, who, in the words of the officer's report on the subject, "stabbed them to death in accordance with Article 12 of the Garrison Regulations." It was not found advisable to allow this act to become known, however, and the bodies were disposed of secretly, so that it was not until October 10th that the news leaked out. No action was ever taken in the matter.

The strangest and most gruesome of the post-quake tragedies was the murder of Osugi Sakae. There was a story that at the time of the earthquake, when a crowd of working-class people were making towards the grounds of the Imperial Palace to escape the fire, and, having been diverted by the police, met the fire again and returned, battling with the police for admission, Osugi suddenly appeared among them and spoke fiery words, ending with "Remember Russia, and never lay down your arms!" This was afterwards denied, and the battle was minimised. There was a captain of the gendarmery, Amakasu by name, in charge of a section of the city, a fanatical patriot, obsessed by fear of "dangerous thought." He examined the lists of arrests made all over the city—for the drag-net was out systematically—and found that Osugi's name was not mentioned. With the aid of detectives he discovered him on September 15th, and arrested him, together with his wife and a seven-year-old nephew, who happened to be with her at the time. The three were taken to the Kojimachi gendarmery station and lodged in separate cells. The following day, soon after sunset, Captain Amakasu, accompanied by two non-commissioned officers, visited the prisoners. Entering Osugi's cell, he addressed a few words to him, and, getting behind him, suddenly locked his arm round his victim's throat, forced him down, and planted his knee in his back. In a few minutes the last convulsive movement had ceased: the murder had been accomplished without the shedding of blood and in perfect silence. Amakasu, with his two subordinates, proceeded to the next cell, where Noe was sitting. He asked her whether she thought soldiers absurd people, to which she smilingly replied that people had all sorts of opinions about all sorts of things. Amakasu, excited by the murder just committed, did not grip her with the same skill as he had used on her husband, and she twisted and gurgled horribly. It was ten minutes before she was dead. The child in the next room, hearing these strange sounds, screamed with terror: Amakasu soon put an end to that, with his two hands round the boy's throat.

No information regarding these murders was allowed to leak out for many days, but when it became known the military authorities tried the case by court-martial. Counsel, with a great part of the Press echoing him, dwelt on the patriotic nature of the crime. The murder of the child, however, was a difficult thing to swallow, and an extraordinary attempt was made in court to get Amakasu to deny it. There was a brief adjournment for his instruction, after which he said that he had no recollection of what happened. Somebody had done it, however, and the non-commissioned officers could not be persuaded to take the blame on any conditions. Amakasu received a sentence of ten years' imprisonment, which was rapidly whittled away on various pretexts, and the *Mainichi*, with the greatest circulation in Japan, said that Amakasu was regarded as a national hero.

Mention has already been made of two foreign passenger steamers in Yokohama harbour at the time of the earthquake. Both the *Empress of Australia* and the *André Lebon* narrowly escaped destruction with their crowds of refugees in the great patches of blazing petroleum which drifted over the harbour. Both the foreign and the Japanese ships in harbour did much rescue work, but they had different objectives. The first instinct of the foreign colony was to seek the water-front, where there were ships, and to proceed to Kobe, the dwelling-place of the only other foreign colony of any size in Japan. The Japanese had no such common purpose, and seldom wished to proceed to Kobe. The foreign ships therefore transferred to the Japanese ships many of the Japanese whom they had rescued, and the larger part of the company that they took to Kobe were members of the foreign colony, who were taken care of by their friends and fellow-Occidentals, who, both in work and gifts, showed splendid generosity. In the course of the rescue work some Japanese men, in their passion for self-preservation, began dragging women out of the boats, and were beaten off by the sailors. These facts had a strange sequel. Japanese newspapers, the *Osaka Mainichi*, its sister paper the *Tokyo Nichi Nichi*, and the *Kobe Yushin Nippo*, related how the foreign ships took only women on board, whom they took out to sea, ravished and flung overboard; and they also accused the foreign ships of caring only for foreigners and refusing to help the Japanese. It was the underlying racial prejudice coming to the surface in a time of excitement; but though the authorities took such care to prevent the facts of untoward happenings being published at home or abroad, they remained entirely indifferent to these slanders, and not a single Japanese writer expressed any disapprobation. In due course the embassies abroad published in the newspapers of the countries to which they were accredited statements of all that had been done for the foreign residents, crediting the Japanese authorities with everything, and not mentioning that the foreign colony had done anything to help themselves.

The doings of the Young Men's Associations have already been mentioned in relation to the Korean massacres. Their activities in other directions were more commendable. They organised relief squads and went about assisting many helpless people. In Tokyo, where martial law was most effective, the bands had little scope, but elsewhere they had a great deal of liberty. Their method was mainly to take from those who had and give to those who had not, and, while they afforded a certain amount of assistance, they were lawless and overbearing, and sometimes became indistinguishable from bandits. Many eventually became the subjects of prosecutions at law. Viscount Goto, now Home Minister, commended their activities in the Diet: but on the same occasion he denied that there had ever been any suppression of news concerning the Koreans.

Official statistics put the total number of dead and injured at 156,693, but the actual number must have been much larger. The generally accepted estimate of the loss in property was 550,000,000 sterling. One of the first questions raised concerned the recovery of insurance money. Much of the fire insurance was reinsured abroad, especially in England; and on September 11th Reuter's agency, the relations of which with the subsidised Japanese news service were extremely intimate, telegraphed abroad that the Japanese insurance companies were all going to pay claims in full. It was already well known in Japan that they could not pay even 10 per cent., but had the foreign companies responded it would have been easy and advantageous to make up the deficit with loans. None did respond; earthquake risks were definitely barred by the terms of all policies. There was so much agitation that the Government rashly promised that the Japanese companies should pay 10 per cent., but an investigation showed that they could not pay even half of this, and in the end the Government had to lend the necessary money for the "sympathy payments" to the insurance companies, who only accepted the loans on condition that they should not be compelled to carry them on their books as debts. This relief came very late, after the acutest need had passed.

Immediately after the earthquake there was a great flood of expression of sympathy from abroad, and large supplies of food and clothing were dispatched. Help was also rendered by the American and British naval squadrons. But none of this could really appreciably lighten the burden laid upon the Japanese authorities. The problem was an enormous one. Temporary provision had to be made, and then permanent reconstruction undertaken. A million and a half people had left the capital, and there was actually a shortage of labour. A Reconstruction Committee was formed which, dominated by Viscount Goto, who was prone to grandiose ideas, proposed to rebuild Tokyo on a magnificent scale regardless of cost. The plan appealed to the imagination, but the prospect of a vast foreign indebtedness appalled the authorities, and it was dropped, without their coming to the stage of facing what would have been the chief difficulty. Though Tokyo had appeared to be a vast warren with little organisation except the public services—a mere mass of gregariousness—nearly everybody had his own place, his own occupation, and even the smallest attempts to disregard the former plans were found very difficult. So Tokyo became a vast sea of wooden sheds with corrugated iron roofs, and attempts at town planning began from the basis of the capital that had existed on the eve of the fire—not as a New Jerusalem. One of Goto's plans was for the creation of a deep-water harbour at Tokyo at an initial cost of 350,000,000 *yen*. That dated from long before the earthquake, but had to be dropped with the rest of the megalomania. There were two reasons for this demand for a harbour at Tokyo: the first was that in Japan everything centralised in Tokyo. It was not only the political capital, but the centre of all culture and education, to a greater degree even than Paris centralised the activities of France. The other reason was that there was a feeling of hostility towards Yokohama. Fifty years before, the foreign trade of the country had been largely in the hands of the merchants on the old Foreign Settlement; but for many years their business had shown no increase, while the foreign commerce in Japanese hands had grown until the foreign merchants' share was inconsiderable. The European in Japan, however, was more conspicuous than he would be in the United States, small though his numbers were, and the mediæval tradition was carried on that he was an obnoxious invader of the sacred soil—a tradition which, of course, was streaked with kindlier and more rational senti-

THE GREAT EARTHQUAKE

ments. This led to plans being suggested, when the Tokyo harbour scheme fell through, for a port at Tsurumi or Omori—anywhere but Yokohama. The advocates of these schemes lost sight of the fact that Japanese interests in Yokohama were vast. For the resumption of the silk trade, Japan's most important export, which centred entirely on Yokohama, a new conditioning house was the first substantial building erected. The Yokohama authorities themselves had an idea of taking advantage of the occasion by way of buying up the few remaining perpetual leases, over which there were perennial taxation disputes, but this fell through. After grave neglect of Yokohama, as compared with the energy displayed by the Central Government in making a workable restoration of Tokyo, it was realised that unless the principal port were also restored the capital must languish, and inducements were offered to foreign traders to return.

A special session of the Diet was called on December 10th, when the dwindling of the big schemes was set forth. The Government's share in budgetting for reconstruction was reduced from 730,000,000 *yen* to 597,000,000, and again to 468,000,000. But the raising of a foreign loan was not accomplished under the Yamamoto régime at all. Kiyoura's nominee was not regarded as a political success, and the Yamamoto Cabinet resigned at the end of the year. The immediate cause of resignation was an outrage unprecedented in the modern annals of Japan. On his way to the Diet on December 27th the Prince Regent was fired at by a young man named Namba Daisuke, who had become imbued with the idea that regicide was a short cut to reform. His action, of course, was not only fatal to himself, but confirmed the authorities in their determination to root out all radical thought. It also had the effect of partially restoring the seclusion from which the Regent had emerged. The resignation of the Cabinet, according to Occidental standards, was absurd, but in Japan it was traditional that, whenever any grave mischance occurred, everybody whose virtue should have been sufficient to avert such an event should assume responsibility. Deplorable as the event was, the Yamamoto Cabinet was fortunate in being able to resign in circumstances that commanded sympathy rather than detestation.

XXXV

THE HIGHEST AND THE LOWEST IN THE LAND

NEVER was the lack of any constitutional machinery for advising the Emperor so keenly felt. Viscount Kiyoura, President of the Privy Council, tried to bridge over the difficulty. He visited the two aged invalids, Prince Matsukata and Prince Saionji, the last of the Genro, and was presumed to have discussed matters with them; under the eye of a crowd of watchful journalists he visited Count Makino, Minister of the Imperial Household, and Viscount Hirata, Keeper of the Privy Seal. But Kiyoura was hopelessly conservative; he dreaded men whose minds were not firmly rooted in mediævalism. In the end he advised the Emperor that he could find nobody but himself to make a Cabinet. Not that he aspired to office: he would greatly have preferred to be spared such responsibilities. Nor was his assumption of office popular, for though he enjoyed great prestige he commanded no confidence. He formed a Cabinet even more "transcendent" than Count Yamamoto's, being composed entirely of members of the House of Peers. Dr. Midzuno came back as Home Minister, in spite of the Korean tragedy, and General Akaike as head of the Metropolitan Police. Akaike was a great believer in police rule, and in the previous June had arrested all the more prominent Socialists. They were kept safe in prison throughout the horrors of the earthquake, and were still there. Akaike confessed that the chief difficulty concerning them was that they would confess nothing and that the police knew nothing.

It was not merely among liberal thinkers that the Kiyoura Cabinet was unpopular. Viscount Miura, still the oracle-in-chief, summoned to his house Viscount Takahashi, President of the Seiyukai (now suffering a split, Tokonami and others forming a schism called the Seiyuhonto), Viscount Kato, President of the Kenseikai, and Mr. Inukai, President of the Kokuminto (now dissolved into the Kakushin Club in order to await a favourable opportunity to join forces with one of the big parties), and exhorted them to destroy the Kiyoura Government. It was one of the strange anomalies of Japan that a man of such antecedents should be able to command the respect, and even the obedience, of men so much better than himself.

As might be expected, a Cabinet consisting entirely of Peers, and openly contemptuous of party obligations, found the Imperial Diet a very obstreperous body indeed. A train in which some political leaders were travelling was wrecked, and excitable members even accused the Government of having used this means to dispose of its enemies. On January 31st, there being a large number of hired bullies as well as members in the House, the Diet was dissolved amidst an uproar fit rather for pandemonium than for a legislative body. Twelve days afterwards the Premier, addressing the Gubernatorial Conference, expressed the opinion that the earthquake had had the good effect of steadying national thought, but that they could not rest on their oars, for the flood of deterioration was not easily to be stemmed.

The Premier spoke truly, though the truth was not as he conceived it. In his mind, no doubt, lurked the idea that the murders of Socialists and the multitudinous arrests after the earthquake had taught the "dangerous thinkers" a lesson. Those in a safe position themselves are prone to regard lawlessness on the part of the police as salutary. From quite another point of view, however, this terrible destruction in the heart of the Empire had had a very sobering effect. The feeling of pride and confidence engendered by war wealth had been expressed in multifarious activities, many of them of a beneficent character, but it had been accompanied by an arrogance and a recklessness which were doing Japan much more injury. Speaking generally, a moderation of view succeeded the shock of the earthquake, and nowhere was this more beneficently seen than in the more friendly attitude towards China that was adopted at this time.

In the reaction from the enthusiasm for Viscount Goto's big scheme for reconstruction there was an inclination to go to the other extreme, and the feasibility of doing without any foreign loan was discussed. Such vast purchases had to be made, however, that it was necessary to have funds to draw upon, so in February 1924 a loan was arranged in New York whereby Japan borrowed 150,000,000 dollars in New York and 25,000,000 sterling in London. The net rate was in the neighbourhood of 7 per cent., and, while it was appreciated that money borrowed in London was necessarily at a higher rate of interest than Britain was paying on war debts, the fact that the interest on the American share was a little higher than that on the British caused keen disappointment. It was a far higher rate than Japan had been asked to pay even when she staked her existence on the Russo-Japanese War, and there were some indignant remarks about its being a national disgrace.

It has already been related how the last serious "clan" intrigue made the betrothal of the Crown Prince a matter of public gossip and speculation in the year when he paid a visit to England. Although the original plan was adhered to, it was fully a year before it was made irrevocable by the imperial sanction, which was given on June 20, 1922, and it was not until January 26, 1924, that the wedding was celebrated. It was a comparatively simple affair, as was only meet in a ruined and impoverished city, but even so it was a great departure from tradition. The ceremony was held before the family shrine in the Imperial Palace, the bride and bridegroom in archaic dress. Afterwards came the great concession to modernism, when the wedded pair, in European dress, the Princess wearing a coronet, drove together to the Akasaka Palace, through streets lined with soldiers and with multitudes of school children, who now and then, also departing from tradition, which prescribed perfect silence, broke into cheers. There was something symbolical in thus leaving the Palace, itself an archaic structure rather like a Buddhist temple; in the grounds were assembled a crowd of the Court ladies, many in their ancient dress, with scarlet skirt and large stiff coiffure, and some in silk dresses of the simplest possible European type and no pretence to fashion —a strange company, the disappearing relic of ancient days. There were some buildings in the venerable grounds that had been ruined by the earthquake, and this added to the impression made by the driving away of the modern young couple to the frenchified palace at Akasaka, which had not suffered a crack.

Marriage in Japan had always been a family arrangement, with no occasion for either priest or registrar. Its legal sanctions were secured by a subsequent visit to the city or village administrative office, when the family registers were adjusted. During the Taisho era, however, shrine marriages became somewhat fashionable, in conscious imitation of the Western custom. There was a spontaneous division of function between the Shinto and Buddhist priesthood. Infants were presented at the shrine, and there was an increasing disposition to elicit the aid of the Shinto priests in making marriage more ceremonious. The Buddhist priests were content with the funerals, for which they were in unfailing demand.

While referring to a change in marriage customs indicative of a greater respect for womanhood, we may also consider a social reform for which the effort became conspicuous just at this time, as well as the opposition to that effort. A notorious feature of Japanese cities had been the quarter set apart for licensed prostitution, the most famous of all these being the Yoshiwara district in Tokyo. Family life and marriage were such humdrum affairs that all fond romance was illumined by the garish lights of the licensed quarter, and as the Japanese taste was always for the tale to go down in a sea of blood rather than end in the happy consummation, the circumstances afforded ample opportunity. The prostitutional art and literature of Japan form, indeed, a subject that merits encyclopædic treatment, but cannot be dealt with here. The usual pattern of the licensed quarters was a double row of very ornate houses, with the women all sitting in gorgeous dresses behind great bars, like a waxwork show in a wild-beasts' cage. The women were sold for a term of years, parents or guardians receiving the money. In explanation of commercial lapses it has often been affirmed that the idea of contract, in the sense of the Roman Law, was entirely foreign to Japan, yet the immoral contract was always maintained with the utmost rigidity, and extended on dishonest pretexts so long as the victim had any commercial value.

The system of licensing and inspection in Japan, as elsewhere, was defended on hygienic grounds, but the defence proved to be as fallacious as in other countries. Its real bulwarks were the revenue derived from it and its convenience to the police, whom it enabled to keep an eye on bad characters and to extract information about them from their paramours. The burglar and the embezzler alike were generally detected by the recklessness with which they spent their ill-gotten gains in the licensed quarters.

New ideas on the subject arose, and several societies, conspicuous among which was the Women's Society for the Reform of Manners, declared war on the system. For years they received little help from the Press, and even when the Press found the subject good for circulation the police remained hostile. The war boom in Japan shed some light on the economics of prostitution. Money was so easy to earn that the class of women who eked out existence by illicit prostitution declined, though there was no lack of daughters for sale, especially at the high prices that were offered. Certain reforms were instituted. In the cities on the route of the foreign tourist the cages were abolished and a row of photographs substituted. A law was also made that a woman might break her contract and leave the stews at any time; but this was futile, for the women had no liberty of movement and seldom dared ask for liberation. Their keepers, besides, always took care that they had large debts.

These debts were good in law, and until they were paid there was no liberty. Women escaping were taken back by the police; and should the money be raised for the liberation of a woman, it only served to buy another.

Nevertheless, public feeling began to manifest itself in a manner hostile to the system. It was noticed that the first buildings with any pretence to elegance that were erected in devastated Tokyo after the earthquake and fire were the brothels of Yoshiwara; but in March 1924 the Dai Nihon Brothel-keepers' Union issued a manifesto against the malign activities of the Women's Society for the Reform of manners, and held meetings at which they denounced the adoption of newfangled and imported ideas calculated to undermine the Empire. Members of the Society, of the Salvation Army, and other bodies which opposed the system were liable to being hustled and assaulted by gangs of bullies, and appeals to the police for protection were but coldly received. Later in the same year there was actually a strike of pimps. Where the cages were abolished men were allowed to sit before the brothels shouting to the passers-by. These took to mingling with the crowd for the more efficient performance of their tasks, and when this was prohibited the greatest indignation was expressed. It was the only way, they declared, to prevent the business falling into the hands of unlicensed pimps, and they declared a strike in order to demonstrate the seriousness with which they regarded the issue.

City expansion and the policy of providing licensed quarters for the increased population led to some strenuous fights and to some sordid scandals. In Osaka, in particular, they were hardly out of one scandal before they were into another. Everybody wanted a finger in this profitable business, and when a new licensed quarter was being promoted there was speculation in land and extensive bribery in the securing of sanction. Even Cabinet Ministers' names were besmirched with the dirty business, and party funds, as well as Government revenue, were replenished out of the slave trade. Happily there were valiant fighters against the system. One of these, Mrs. Yashima Kajiko, died in June 1925 at the age of ninety-three. She was the founder of the Women's Society for the Reform of Manners, and up to her last illness strove for the amelioration of her less fortunate sisters.

Before we leave this subject we may note a new development which found the police much sterner moralists. At the beginning of the reign the wearing by women of anything but Japanese dress was extremely rare, except at Court functions. The change in European fashions during the war brought about a great difference. Young women working in the cities in numbers and with a freedom hitherto unknown discovered economy as well as smartness and convenience in the short simple dress that had become fashionable; and when the European craze for dancing spread to Japan the new type of smart young woman was quite ready to adopt it. Dancing classes and dancing halls became numerous, naturally not without a certain amount of irregularity in their management. To prevent "deterioration in national morals" all sorts of restrictions were introduced, Tokyo leading the way with the prohibition of any dancing after ten o'clock at night. It was not merely an unreasoning conservatism which defended the geisha and the licensed prostitute and was shocked at the appearance of a class of young woman possessing greater freedom of manners than had been customary. The *hetairai* of the old school were completely subservient to the police. The modern girl was far more likely to be the active partner of a "dangerous thinker," and held the police in far less respect. There were even cases of bands of patriotic ruffians—always distinguished for their conservatism—invading private houses in Tokyo where dancing was going on, and ordering that it cease, as it was bad for public morals.

After the earthquake Mr. Cyrus Woods, the American Ambassador, had made great political capital out of American benevolence and friendship; but the glow of gratitude received its first chill when it was found that when it came to business on a large scale the New York money market wanted even better interest on its loans than London. Worse was to follow. Sympathy with the sufferers from the earthquake did not make them any more welcome as immigrants in the eyes of the exclusionists in America, and legislation was in progress for putting an end to all Oriental immigration. Such a measure was quite unnecessary, because the "Gentlemen's Agreement" that Japanese should not be allowed to emigrate to America had worked satisfactorily, and Mr. Hanihara, the Ambassador in Washington, in accordance with instructions from Tokyo protested against the bill which was, in April 1924, awaiting the verdict of the Senate, where it had many opponents. Mr. Hanihara's protest, however, only ensured the passage that it had been intended to prevent. Like most diplomatists, he was fond of abstract phrases, and informed the Washington Government that the consequences of passing the bill would be grave. The fact that this ambiguous phrase had been known to be used as a threat made it extremely annoying to the Senators, some of whom regarded it as a menace of war, and, within a week of the presentation of Mr. Hanihara's Note, the Senate passed the bill by 62 votes to 6. Apparently they were glad of an excuse for dealing drastically with a matter which only grew the more troublesome with the passage of years. Great indignation was expressed in Japan, for though it was recognised that the law made little practical difference, its passage was an indignity. Mr. Woods, who had revelled in adulation, resigned. Except in print and occasionally on the platform, an admirable moderation was shown in Japan. One patriot committed suicide in the compound of the American Embassy, and another hauled down Old Glory from the Embassy flagstaff and stole it. These were almost the only demonstrations of resentment.

Simultaneously with the passage of this bill, in connection with which so much offence was given by the refusal of

THE HIGHEST AND LOWEST IN THE LAND

naturalisation to Japanese, Mr. Funatsu, the Japanese Consul-General in Mukden, issued what amounted to a command to the Chinese authorities that they were not to grant naturalisation to Japanese immigrants, this being with special reference to the hundreds of thousands of Koreans now domiciled in China. Many of these men were disaffected, and the Japanese authorities desired to avail themselves of their extra-territorial rights so that they could arrest them at any time on Chinese soil. This unwise attempt to extend jurisdiction over China gave rise to complications which became more difficult with the passage of time.

XXXVI

A BETTER CHINESE POLICY

THE one good point about the Kiyoura Government was that it did not condescend to manipulate the general election which followed its dissolution of the Diet, but the results of that election demonstrated its unpopularity and the impossibility of continuing in office, so, on June 6, 1924, the Cabinet resigned. The split in the Seiyukai had brought about a curious grouping of the parties. The Kenseikai won 146 seats, the Seiyuhonto (schismatics from the Seiyukai) 120, and the Seiyukai 101. The Kakushin Club, not yet having formed any political affiliation, secured 30 seats; the Business Party, which alone had a definite platform, had 8, and there were 57 Independents. It was clearly time that the Kenseikai should have an innings, but even if the Independents were all purchased, it had no security. A curious compromise was effected, Viscount Takahashi (now a commoner again, having resigned his peerage) consenting to become Minister of Agriculture and Commerce, though he had lately been Premier, and Mr. Inukai, who had also held higher office, becoming Minister of Communications. Thus the acquiescence of the Seiyukai and Kakushin Club was secured, though the most important offices were held by Kenseikai men. The Home Minister was Mr. Wakatsuki, the Finance Minister Mr. Hamaguchi, and the Foreign Minister Baron Shidehara. It was often referred to as the Mitsubishi Government, Viscount Kato, the Premier, and Baron Shidehara both being closely connected by marrage with the house of Iwasaki, the controllers of the Mitsubishi firm.

It might have been supposed that it would be impossible for the unrepentant sponsor of the Twenty-one Demands ever to become Premier. In point of fact, his term of office witnessed the inauguration of the most liberal policy towards China that had been known for many years. Probably its inauguration was assisted by Kato being Premier, the "China ronin" and other Jingoes being satisfied that China would be kept in her place by such a man. Baron Shidehara was the author of this more liberal policy, and succeeded in creating a more friendly feeling than had existed since the Chinese revolution.

The new policy was not put into effect without opposition. There were objectors of all classes. At one time Barons Sakatani, Yabuki, Fujimura, and Oi, representing the Koseikai Club—one of the Peers' groups—waited on the Foreign Minister and demanded assurances that Japan's interests in China were being properly protected; at another time ten leading politicians of various parties visited him on a similar errand. Another Peers' "club," the Kenkyukai, requested the attendance of Mr. Debuchi, the Vice-Minister, and subjected him to a catechism; and hardly had they finished when a band of patriots, known as the Taisho Sekishin-dan, invaded the Foreign Office, and, on being informed that Baron Shidehara was absent, tried to reassure themselves on the China question by smashing the furniture and beating a secretary, Mr. Takahashi. This last exploit turned out to have been instigated by an *agent provocateur*, in the employ of the police, a conscientious and enterprising fellow who liked to give results.

Special interest was created in Chinese affairs by the visit to Japan in November 1924 of Dr. Sun Yat-sen—friendly once more. He had fled from a distracted Canton, where the factions had indulged in massacre, but was quite prepared to make a bid for power in Peking. During the few days that he stayed at the Oriental Hotel in Kobe he was visited by many important people from Tokyo, and when he left he was understood to have arrived at the correct idea regarding the difference between Japan's relations to Manchuria and her relations to China. Whether he had really embraced these ideas, and whether this new orthodoxy would have helped him to the presidential throne in Peking, was never known, for he arrived in China a sick man, and died without taking any further action in the affairs of his distracted country.

The general election was hardly over when an organised campaign for economy began, with the usual denunciations of the luxurious tendencies which were supposed to be demoralising the nation. "Lion" Hamaguchi, the Finance Minister, who had a reputation for honesty and courage, combed out the departmental budgets, but found, like his predecessors, that economy in spending is one of the most difficult of all achievements. But that was not the only plan he had in view. He made a much more spectacular show with a "Luxury Tariff," consisting of a miscellaneous list of articles, concerning many of which all that could be said by way of showing that they were luxuries was that Japan had done without them for centuries. A tax on people who aped Western manners was not altogether unpopular, but what really ensured the passage of the bill was the fact that fundamentally the tariff was in the nature of a special tax on the small foreign colony. Mr. Hamaguchi declared that the tariff would not in any event cause a general rise in prices, and would not even enhance the cost of Japanese substitutes for the goods which were to be taxed their full market value on entering the country. Though honest as a politician, he could not have been so simple an economist as to believe his own words. The revenue the tax brought in was negligible. The articles taxed made a very small figure on the national import list, and their decline deprived the tariff of value as a raiser of revenue; but prices of domestic products rose out of all proportion to the importance of the articles taxed. It created an opportunity of which Japanese manufacturers and dealers did not fail to avail themselves. Perhaps because they are by nature extravagant, the Japanese always hold up as an ideal the abjuring of luxuries, and this, together with the anti-foreign character of the tariff, enabled it to maintain its place, while the amount of controversy that it occasioned made it a useful camouflage of the complete failure that Hamaguchi experienced in his endeavour to cut down the expenditure of the army and navy. This failure was not altogether unnoticed, and a popular cartoonist represented him as a toothless lion (in reference to his nickname) trying in vain to crack that hard bone the defence budget.

Mr. Hamaguchi's immediate predecessor, Mr. Shoda, who had been responsible for the "national disgrace loans" and who had also been Finance Minister under Terauchi, when the Nishihara loans were lent to China, had expressed the opinion that the *yen* was too high, and that $42 per 100 *yen* would be appropriate, and would assist exports. His own efforts at checking the sale of foreign exchange were very half-hearted and timid. "Lion" Hamaguchi took a bolder line, and forbade the Yokohama Specie Bank to give bills on foreign banks. The price of the *yen* being this rendered purely a subject of speculation, it quickly sank until it reached $38\frac{1}{2}$ cents, which may have been good for exports, but so alarmed the authorities that steps were taken to force it up again. It was no time for such amateurish experiments, for the existing conditions were very serious. The false values of the boom were still being carried on the books of many a firm and many a bank undiminished. The sanctioning of credits through the Bank of Japan as an emergency measure after the earthquake had been taken advantage of none too scrupulously. The Bank of Formosa, for example, had discounted with the Bank of Japan the 80,000,000 *yen* or more that it held in bills against Suzuki & Co. without any possibility of repayment. Many such dubious commitments as these were as yet not generally known, but the *Chugai Shogyo*, a commercial paper in Tokyo, published mainly in the Mitsui interest, uttered a well-timed warning against the habit that the Government had adopted of helping shaky concerns to bolster themselves up with loans at low interest advanced from the deposits in the Post Office Savings Bank —a fund totalling at this time some 1,600,000,000 *yen*.

Mr. Hamaguchi did nothing to remedy this state of affairs, but confined himself to the preaching of thrift and a vain endeavour to practise it. His health suffered considerably, and the Finance Ministry was a grave of reputations, so he was glad enough later on to take the post of Home Minister, regarded as the most important in the Cabinet, since it conferred authority to direct the police and prescribe the thoughts of the people.

XXXVII

THREE REMARKABLE TRIALS

THERE were three remarkable trials held in the latter part of 1924. Namba Daisuke, the young man who had shot at the Prince Regent on his way to the Diet, made no attempt to escape, but was arrested on the spot. It was many months before he was brought to trial—months spent in trying to extract from him names of confederates or associates. Deplorable as was his action, he was a man of great firmness, and implicated nobody; but if he had a morbid sense of his own importance it received the fullest indulgence. The Supreme Court, with numerous judges on the bench, sat as a court of first instance to try him. The trial was held *in camera*, but, as was always the case, a good many details leaked out. The prisoner sat throughout his examination—a fashion which Osugi started, and which never failed to ruffle the dignity of the court. When sentence was pronounced, however, he stood up and shouted, "Banzai for the Proletariat!" Such was the accepted story; but the Department of Justice issued a statement, which alone was allowed to be published, to the effect that Namba heard the pronouncement in a humble attitude and expressed contrition for his deed and for the distress that it had occasioned to his family. Two days later—on November 15th—he was hanged, and for days after the Press gave prominence to morbid details about his last hours and the disposal of his body.

The second of these notable trials was that of a pirate named Etsure with thirty-six of his followers. This adventurer, early in 1922, set out for Kamchatka in a chartered steamer, on an expedition of plunder and massacre. Indignation at the Nikolaevsk massacre was the pirates' excuse for the wholesale murder in which they indulged whenever they met a Russian boat or a group of Russians whom it was safe to attack. Allegations were freely made that the expedition had the encouragement and assistance of the General Staff, and it was stated in the course of the trial that the pirates were supplied with arms from one of the Japanese military posts on the coast opposite North Saghalien. Some extraordinary scenes were witnessed in court, repentant pirates emotionally shedding tears, and Etsure roaring at them in his rage when they disclosed some altogether gratuitous atrocities. Etsure himself declared that his one object had been to add Kamchatka and Okhotsk to the Empire. Counsel, one after another, eloquently enlarged on the exalted motive, and the whole gang got off with sentences which indicated the attachment of a very small degree of importance to Russian lives. Regarded, as some of the pirates insisted that it was, as vengeance for the Nikolaevsk massacres, it was ample, and the Russians had it to their credit balance that they had executed the chief of their own murderers. However, it counted for nothing diplomatically. Japan executed none of hers. Mr. Yoshizawa in Peking was still arguing as to the degree of completeness with which North Saghalien was to be exploited as compensation for Nikolaevsk, and about the time of Etsure's sentence the negotiations suffered a temporary severance owing to Mr. Karahan not proving sufficiently "sincere"—so that the Japanese garrisons were left in Alexandrovsk and Decastri yet another winter. Repeated appeals by the pirates, with lessening of sentences, dragged on till 1926.

Commonplace as regards the charges made, the third trial was by far the most extraordinary in its procedure and significance. The trial was held in Formosa, eighteen Chinese Formosans being charged with seditious practices. The formation of political societies and the advocacy of governmental reform were strictly prohibited on the island, and these intellectuals had been guilty of both. Their activities, however, had been carried on far beyond the jurisdiction of the insular courts. The men charged had all been in Tokyo, where they had presented a petition to the Diet asking for the establishment of a Formosan legislature. Before taking this step they had sought the sanction of the Metropolitan Police, which had been readily granted. But no heed was paid to any questioning of the court's jurisdiction. The procurator, when demanding sentence, made a fantastic harangue. It embraced the whole of Europe and Asia; the British Government's difficulties with the Labour Party, the massacre at Amritsar by order of General Dyer, the successes and failures of the democratic system. That the activities of the accused were really harmful he hardly attempted to show; and though he dwelt with great emphasis on their disobedience to police regulations, he carefully avoided the question whether the Tokyo police were not fully capable of regulating the behaviour of Formosans visiting the capital.

The court, with an almost unprecedented assertion of independence, acquitted all the accused, but the procurator appealed against the sentence, and three months later a higher court sentenced the young politicals to terms of imprisonment extending up to four months and to fines up to 100 *yen*. The Supreme Court confirmed these sentences, which were partially remitted on May 10, 1925, on the auspicious occasion of the Emperor's "silver wedding." After it was all over the *Mainichi* and *Yamato* mildly criticised the unjustness of the sentences and the unwisdom of this sort of political persecution. There was no criticism in Formosa because the Press there was kept under complete control by the police.

Even such mild and belated protest, however, was a sign of a new awakening. Not a voice was ever raised in Japan against the "subjugation" of the aborigines in Formosa by dropping bombs on their villages and every year drawing the high-power electric cordon more narrowly round them; nor was there any criticism of the harsh rule of the Chinese Formosans. It was the same thing in Korea. Every report of the recalcitrancy of the Koreans was readily swallowed, but the method of rule was never questioned. Very rarely somebody would make a strong speech in the Diet, but the subject was never followed up. An inquiry was made in the Diet, for instance, at the time when the Supreme Court was considering the case of the Formosan intellectuals, and Mr. Goto, the Civil Administrator in Formosa, refused to reply on the ground that the case was *sub judice*. More rarely still, a critical article would appear in a newspaper; but there was no liberal Press to keep a constant eye on such questions. Democracy, indeed, was so new a thing that no idea of responsibility for the welfare of the new possessions ever crossed the public mind in Japan. The publicity given by foreign journalistic effort to the Korean "conspiracy" of 1911 resulted in the liberation of the accused, but subsequent "conspiracies" in both Korea and Formosa were tried *in camera*, and large numbers of men were sentenced to death or to imprisonment without anybody having an opportunity to judge the value of the evidence and without anybody expressing a wish to have such opportunity.

XXXVIII

POLICIES AT HOME AND ABROAD

WERE the secrecy of diplomacy to be abolished, as some enthusiastic reformers promised it would after the Great War, some interesting facts might be disclosed regarding the visit of Mr. Martial Merlin, the Governor of French Indo-China, to Japan in May 1924. He was received with royal honours, and no visiting sovereign could have been more obsequiously entertained. Much was rumoured about a commercial treaty which was to enable Japan to supply the French Indies with some goods in partial exchange for the rice that she purchased there. But French colonial policy is not easily modified, and four years later it was still pending, though another treaty had been concluded meanwhile. It was suspected, however, that more highly political questions were really at issue. A group in Paris had informed the world that they were the directors of the Russo-Asiatic Bank and therefore the shareholders of the Chinese Eastern Railway, and there was a good deal of speculation as to whether Mr. Merlin was really in Japan on the business of entering into an engagement that should console Japan for the lapse of the Anglo-Japanese Alliance and, in the accepted manner, guarantee the integrity and independence of North Manchuria. A much livelier attention was directed towards the question when Mr. Karahan, the Soviet Ambassador in Peking, closed a bargain whereby the Soviet Government secured the management of the railway, under a Chinese President. It was after this that Mr. Karahan's conversations were resumed with Mr. Yoshizawa, the Japanese Minister in Peking, and at last, on January 21, 1925, a treaty was signed settling the Saghalien question on the basis of Japan exploiting the oilfields and getting half the oil as her share. Thus was Nikolaevsk avenged, and the Japanese troops returned in the early summer following. Regular diplomatic relations were soon resumed, but it was to take over three years for the negotiators to conclude a Fisheries Convention.

Meanwhile, however, when it was clear that Mr. Merlin's visit could not help either Japan or France in regard to the Chinese Eastern Railway, Japan had arranged a railway deal with Marshal Chang Tso-lin, the dictator of Mukden. Opinions differed greatly as to whether Chang Tso-lin was a creature of Japan. As a bandit leader he had fought on the Japanese side in the Russo-Japanese War, and the one thing certain was that he had a profound distrust for Russians, Red or White. The South Manchuria Railway already had a branch line to Taonan, and it was arranged—since the Consortium precluded independent foreign railway enterprises in China—that Marshal Chang should himself build a line from Taonan to Angangchi, a point in the proximity of Tsitsihar, on the Chinese Eastern Railway. Chang, of course, had neither the money nor the engineers to build the line, so both were supplied by the South Manchuria Railway. Whether this was quite in the spirit of the Consortium agreement might be doubted, but the Consortium had been so entirely negative in its effects that a way round it was rather welcomed. It led to something like an open breach with Russia, however. This new interest of China in her own railways inspired the Chinese President of the Chinese Eastern Railway to be something more than a figurehead, and when the Soviet management dismissed the "White" Russian employees the President cancelled the notices of dismissal. The *Isvestia*, the Soviet official newspaper, saw in this an indication of Chang Tso-lin's hostility, and opined that this hostility was due to the help that Moscow had been giving to Feng Yu-Hsiang ("the Christian General") and the Canton faction, the Kuomintang; and it warned Chang that it would be the worse for him if he forgot that besides these foes in front he had Russia in his rear. Russia's major grievance, however, was that the Taonan-Angangchi line would deprive the Chinese Eastern of some of its trade, as well as give Japan a strategic railway which would enable her at any time to cut the Chinese Eastern at Tsitsihar. But the Soviet complaints were disregarded, as it was indisputable that, with Japan and Chang Tso-lin agreed to act together, it was impossible for Russia to do more than protest. The increasing population and productivity of Manchuria made railway construction an economic need. A stream of immigrants from misgoverned provinces in China had begun, and later increased to a flood; and Baron Shidehara laid down the policy that future railway building in Manchuria was to be both in name and in fact Chinese.

In home policy reaction was more in evidence than liberalism. In the Diet session of 1925, it is true, the Government at last brought in a Manhood Suffrage Bill, which was hailed everywhere as a great advance. Even the most cynical remarked that it would make the purchase of votes much more difficult than it had been hitherto. Apart from questions of corruption of this sort, critics of the parliamentary system had a striking example of the system's weakness. Japan by this time had some ten thousand miles of Government railways, and had come to a point where further construction, owing to the mountainous nature of the country, was so expensive that it could not be profitably undertaken. Dr. Sengoku, Minister of Railways, therefore put forward a policy of improving existing lines rather than extending the service, but he discovered that so many members of all parties had recommended themselves to the voters by their promises of local railways that he had the whole House against him, and had to modify his eminently sound policy.

One of the chief reactionaries of the day was Dr. Okada, the Minister of Education. He carried on unceasing war against dangerous thoughts among students, and, just as he thought it was rooted out, received the rude shock of discovering that there was a radical society so well organised that it had a branch in every high school in the country. Students were secretly arrested in scores and kept *incommu-*

nicado for months; all mention of the arrests was prohibited; all study of Socialism and other dangerous subjects was also forbidden, and professors and schoolmasters harbouring subversive thoughts were driven into resignation. It was impossible to lay down any law for the mental foot-binding of the universities, but instructions were given that while the individual was free to study what he chose, societies for the study of "dangerous thought" could not be permitted, and that the least indication of an intention to proceed from theory to practice would receive condign punishment. Spasmodic endeavours were made to prevent the importation of dangerous literature, and books with red covers were eyed with special suspicion by the police.

Among other prohibitions issued by Dr. Okada was one that students should not indulge in theatrical performances. The old-fashioned theatre had been a school of loyalty and bloodshed; but new ideas had wrought havoc. Rebellious students, in protest against Dr. Okada's prohibition, staged Strindberg's *The Father*, Ibsen's *Ghosts*, and Gorky's *In the Depths*. Those accustomed to the heroic drama, with its prolonged disembowellings, may have found these healthy and refreshing; but the older men found them disturbing; they were too provocative of thought. Happily for their peace of mind the old spirit was not extinct. A retired military officer, stumping the country in the interests of loyalty, reported that young women at one place where he spoke had expressed an earnest desire to be buried alive beneath the Meiji Shrine, in accordance with ancient use, to ensure by their sacrifice its lasting prosperity. There was some shedding of tears over the impossibility of such testimony in these days, but as a token of their desire for the larger sacrifice the maidens of the place cut off their hair, which was duly buried beneath the shrine.

The most notable reactionary measure was the passing of the Peace Preservation Bill, more commonly known as the Dangerous Thoughts Bill. It did not pass the Legislature unchallenged. Mr. Wakatsuki, the Home Minister, and Dr.

Ogawa, Minister of Justice, found it a hard task to convince many of the Representatives of its necessity. Ogawa, confronted with an accusation that the Dangerous Thoughts Bill was the price extorted by the mediæval Privy Council for its consent to the suffrage, hotly denied it. Indeed, there could be no doubt of Ogawa's personal taste for retrograde measures, for he was even then engaged in an attempt to make the procurators more powerful than ever by attaching special police to their offices. A more liberal member of the Kenseikai brought in a private bill to amend the law under which the police already enjoyed wide powers of summary jurisdiction, and Mr. Hara Sorejiro, of the Seiyuhonto, declared that a measure so unconstitutional, twenty years old as it was, ought to be abolished altogether. The spokesman of the Ministry of Justice, however, declared that the Government considered the law quite proper and had no intention of changing it.

The Dangerous Thoughts Bill was professedly aimed at the prevention of Bolshevik propaganda in Japan. Mr. Ozaki Yukio demanded an explanation of the need of such precautions now that Japan was in treaty relations with Russia. Mr. Aoki Seichi declared that that was the very cause that made it necessary. The bill provided that those who formed or who joined societies the object of which included the altering of the national constitution or the form of government, or the repudiation of the system of private ownership of property, should be subject to imprisonment not exceeding ten years,[1] with or without hard labour, while the penalty for instigation of such ideas was seven years of similar imprisonment. Mr. Hara Sorejiro asked why a measure for the general intimidation was needed when the law already provided sufficient punishment. Mr. Wakatsuki, the Home Minister, essaying to point out the mildness of the law, only succeeded in demonstrating its superfluousness when he said that "propaganda" was not mentioned because that

[1] When this book was in the press a still more drastic law was passed prescribing the death penalty.

was already sufficiently punishable under the Police Regulations and the Press Law. Few in the end had the courage to record an adverse vote, and when the bill came before the Peers, the Marquis Tokugawa alone spoke against it and refused it his countenance.

It had been the fashion for some time past to declare that militarism was extinct in Japan, and that the military men were discredited. Such an assumption was not at all disagreeable to the militarists themselves, as it diverted unwelcome attention from their doings. An unpleasant amount of attention, however, was concentrated on the completion of the army scheme for militarising the schools. To be sure, the most was made of the reduction of the standing army by four divisions, which had become necessary owing to the increasing cost of equipment; but advantage was taken of the occasion to distribute the spare officers among the schools, where they would, owing to their status, enjoy a much higher degree of independence in their relations with the principal than did the ordinary schoolmaster. There was, moreover, a special sum of 2,126,000 *yen* budgetted for the cost of the new military training. Some sharp criticism was heard, and none sharper than that from Mr. Ozaki Yukio. One of the consequences was that the Tekketsusha, or Blood and Iron Society, invaded Mr. Ozaki's house and made a disturbance therein, as well as scattering leaflets in all the neighbourhood denouncing the lack of patriotism of all who opposed the measure.

It was characteristic of this time of war on intellectuals that gangs of bullies, operating mainly in reactionary interests, behaved with intolerable arrogance and brutality. One gang, when the suffrage debate was in progress, invaded the mansion of Dr. Ichiki Kitakuro, Vice-President of the Privy Council, and smashed up the furniture. Other gangs visited Viscount Kato and Mr. Hamaguchi. On the occasion of a bill being introduced to enable foreigners to own land on illiberal conditions, the Government had to reassure the indignant patriots that the sacred soil of the Empire was in no danger. The Home Minister, Mr. Wakatsuki, publicly denounced this increase in the use of professional bullies, but while the intellectuals were vigorously pursued the ruffian gangs operated with impunity.

Nor was it only in respect of patriotic bullies that the law, so severe against reformers, was extremely lenient. It seemed almost that there was no other crime recognised except the questioning of authority. In illustration of this we may bestow a little attention on the case of Takata & Co., a great Osaka firm, agents for the Westinghouse and other engineering concerns and among the largest importers in the country. It came out during 1925 that the firm had been guilty of defalcations of a kind that shook to its foundations that mutual trust which is the essential lubricant of all great commerce. In Japan, as elsewhere, it was a common practice, when goods arrived before the bill of lading, for the importer to ask his bank for a letter of guarantee, under which it was customary for the ship to deliver the goods. Takata's, being in desperate need of money, and having enormous consignments arriving, resorted to an extraordinary method of gaining breathing-time. They asked the banks with which they dealt for letters of guarantee, mentioning small sums as the value of the most costly cargo. Having taken delivery they sold the goods and received payment. Such proceedings could not go on for long. The banks to whom the bills of lading were sent soon found an accumulation on their hands and made inquiries as to why they had not been applied for. How much of the money irregularly received was used to settle the other liabilities of the firm and how much was simply hidden away was never disclosed, but it was estimated that their liabilities were 50,000,000 *yen*, and that the assets were hardly worth dividing. The guaranteeing banks wanted to compromise—that is, to pass part of their liability on to the other banks and the shipping companies, and this question went on for years unsettled. A commercial swindle, on however large a scale, would not be worth recording unless it possessed some special characteristic. In this case, notwithstanding the seriousness of the offence and the large sums involved, nobody was ever prosecuted, and no suggestion was ever made that anybody should be prosecuted. Moreover, Takata & Co., "reconstituted," continued the same business under the same name, and with a "goodwill" not only undamaged, but actually enhanced in value owing to the new freedom from old liabilities.

Yet another example may be cited of the strange vagaries of justice, this instance being one in which civil rights, as between one citizen and another, depended on political opinions. Takao Heibei, a Socialist who came into some prominence in 1920 in connection with the trial of Professor Morito, went one morning to call on Yonemura, a lawyer, who was President of the Anti-Bolshevik Society. Takao was accompanied by two friends, and all were unarmed. After some words, Yonemura shot Takao dead. It took years to bring Yonemura to justice, and at last he was sentenced to a short term of imprisonment with "postponement of execution of sentence," thus escaping scot-free, while the two companions of Takao each got three months' hard labour—apparently for trespass. This judicial indifference to the life of a Socialist contrasted strongly with the solicitude shown for the lives even of criminals, a householder about this period being sentenced to three years' imprisonment for shooting a burglar.

The concentration of effort on the detection of political crimes had a deplorable effect on police efficiency, and there were many complaints of the miscarriage of justice. One man serving a life sentence for a crime which another convict confessed, declared that he had confessed because the police had promised him that if he did so he would be liberated. In another case two young men were kept a year under examination on a charge of theft of which they proved to be innocent. And so little confidence did the courts have in their own decisions that men condemned to death were kept for months, and even for years, in order that they might be persuaded to confess before execution. From time to time

Sakai and other Socialists who had been arrested in June 1923 came before the courts; more than two years after their arrest their trials were still proceeding, their resolution being proof against all blandishments used to induce them to confess.

In May 1925, less than two years after the great Kwanto earthquake, there was a convulsion in the Tajima province which was less violent, yet might have been almost equally disastrous had it occurred in a densely populated area. The town of Toyooka was destroyed, and also the hot-spring resort of Kinosaki, besides many villages. Fire destroyed what the earthquake left standing. This disaster, coming so soon after that of the Kwanto district, was the more disturbing because, while earth tremors in Tokyo and Yokohama were of almost daily occurrence, Tajima province was supposed to be free from this instability; yet here, in a moment, four hundred people were killed and four thousand houses destroyed in a quake of which the vibrations were alarming even at a hundred miles from the centre.

Constant troubles in China made Baron Shidehara's task of cultivating friendship one of peculiar difficulty, not least from the demands of his own countrymen. Strikes in Japanese cotton-mills in Tsingtau and Shanghai were the most salient features of the unrest which culminated on May 30, 1925, in a demonstration in Shanghai, when the police, under British officers, fired on the demonstrators. Japanese propagandists not very graciously seized the opportunity to divert as much as possible of the ill will from Japan to Britain. Mr. Tokutomi, editor of the *Kokumin*, a great scholar and historian, surpassed himself in his anti-British virulence, and he had many imitators. The "Shameen massacre" later in the summer made their work supererogatory, all Chinese resentment being visited on Britain. The boycott of British ships compelled some to engage Japanese crews, but these made no attempt to keep the situations thus offered to them. Indeed, they behaved in such a manner that one voyage was as much as any captain could endure with them. While the cry was all against British imperialism, and the Japanese naturally availed themselves of the opportunity to capture the trade which Britain lost by the boycott, it was equally natural that some should wish to enjoy the rewards of both policies at once. There were complaints that, whenever a Japanese steamer went ashore in Southern China it was looted by the piratical fishermen of that coast, and naval protection for Japanese trade was demanded.

Developments in Manchuria for a time overwhelmed the Shidehara policy. The Foreign Minister on December 4th admitted that the situation was disquieting, but declared that there was no immediate need to send troops; but the War Office took a hand and acted decisively. One of Marshal Chang Tso-lin's most trusted generals, Kuo Sung-lin, was bought over by the South and rebelled. The War Office issued a statement about the need of maintaining peace in Manchuria, and moved the Japanese troops in such a way that Kuo, who dare not fire a shot against them, was caught in a trap. His treachery had been singularly base. A defeated enemy in China is seldom harshly treated; but Kuo was taken and shot on December 24th. To point the moral and adorn the tale his wife also was shot and both bodies mutilated. It was reaffirmed that Japan's position was completely neutral, but Marshal Chang Tso-lin not long after, at a dinner at Port Arthur, thanked his Japanese friends for their assistance at a critical moment. Baron Shidehara, in the Diet, was sharply attacked for declaring that Japan had no desire to interfere with the independence of Manchuria, but refused to take up any other position. Five days after Kuo's execution General Hsu Shu-cheng (known as Little Hsu) was assassinated, in revenge for a murder that he had committed himself. Hsu had been the willing tool of Japanese expansionist intrigue, fleeing to the Japanese Legation when his treacheries to his country had jeopardised his life. His end was a fitting one, and was essential to the rehabilitation of Japan's reputation in China.

XXXIX

A STORMY CLOSE TO A SHORT ERA

As time went on the Cabinet quarrelled with and purged itself of the members not belonging to the Kenseikai, and its position became less stable, but it held its ground successfully. It drafted new legislation actively, especially such as was designed to prevent manhood suffrage from having a too disturbing effect. Besides the Peace Preservation Bill, it produced bills for governing the formation of trade unions, for the regulation of religions (with the intent that the propagation of religious dogma should be free only when it had the approval of the Home Office), for arbitration in labour disputes, for the control of organised gangs of roughs and bullies, for the control of the Press, and various other purposes. The navy put forward a big scheme for the "auxiliary vessels" which the Washington Conference had failed to limit—a project which added a certain absurdity to the Government propaganda for thrift, one of the manifestations of which was the appearance on countless door-posts of a little printed slip with four Chinese characters "Kin-ken Rik-ko," meaning "Frugality and Effort." It also emphasised the inadequacy of the provision made for the care of lepers, now an annually recurring demand. The Government gave the official estimate as 16,261, of whom the majority begged their bread in public places. By an extension of the existing homes, it said, accommodation for five thousand in all could be provided. The apparent exactness of the Government figures for the total number of lepers was delusive; more reliable estimates put the number at thirty thousand, and this figure was borne out by the number of conscripts annually rejected on the discovery of the disease at their enrolment examination.

Though strikes were no longer lightly undertaken, owing

to the hardness of the times, Labour politics went on developing. Some parties were local, such as the Kominto, or Citizen's Party, in Ashio and Central Japan, the centre being the copper-mines of the Furukawa firm—the scene of some determined struggles for better conditions; and the Kyushu Minkento, or Kyusho People's Party, the centre of which was the great Government ironworks at Yawata. In September 1925 there was a big meeting at the Central Public Hall, Osaka, with delegates from all the proletarian associations. In October four Russian Labour leaders visited Japan on the invitation of the Nippon Rodo Kumiai Hyogikai (Japan Labour Union Council), and the official fears of Bolshevism rose to a passionate height. It went for nothing that Mr. Tanaka was already in Moscow as Japanese Ambassador or that Mr. Kopp was similarly representing the Soviet Government in Tokyo. The visitors were surrounded by spies and were unable to utter a word to anybody except in the presence of two or three plain-clothes constabulary linguists. Perhaps this was not without its influence on the Government's decision when, on December 1st, a Proletarian Party, the Nomin Rodoto (Farmer-Labour Party) was inaugurated, with 140,000 members. The Government permitted the inauguration, but issued a mandate the same day ordering its dissolution. This order achieved the tactical advantage of splitting the party, but the more militant element went farther to the Left in consequence, and two parties were formed. It was on account of the proletarians' "platform" that the Nomin Rodoto was proscribed, and when the extremer elements formed their own party with an innocuous platform, they naturally came under suspicion and the system of espionage and the employment of *agents provocateurs* took deeper root.

On December 28th Viscount Kato, the Premier, died, at the age of sixty-seven, and the same day Viscount Miura, the political oracle, died also, at a much greater age. The two men were naturally contrasted, Kato, who had been Ambassador in London, was a product of modern Japan.

He was European in his ideas and even in his appearance, and his private life was strict and blameless by the highest Western standard. Miura, whose contrivance of the death of the Queen of Korea gave him so exalted a position, had the reputation of being an exceedingly religious man, contrasting with the philosophical scepticism of Kato; but his devotions were not found either by himself or his admirers to be inconsistent with an alcoholic conviviality or a senile passion for a pretty concubine. Perhaps they were at one in their ambitions for their country, but even here their methods were entirely different.

On Kato's death Mr. Wakatsuki became president of the Kenseikai Party and Premier, "Lion" Hamaguchi, who was in ill-health, becoming Home Minister. With the estrangement from the Seiyukai and the disappearance of Seiyukai Ministers, an agreement was come to with the Seiyuhonto, of which Mr. Tokonami was head. There was some talk of Tokonami entering the Cabinet, but he was disinclined to take any portfolio but that of Home Affairs, and his attitude towards the Kenseikai was correct rather than cordial.

A tremendous onslaught was made upon the Seiyukai at this time, General Tanaka, the new President, being openly charged with receiving enormous sums from Osaka millionaires for favours to come, and with malversations of secret service funds in connection with the Siberian campaign. The charges were never proved and they petered out, but were now and then revived. For a long time they were eclipsed by a much greater scandal. Among the 1,300 Socialists and other dangerous thinkers arrested immediately after the earthquake were a young Korean named Boku Retsu and his Japanese wife, Kaneko Fumi. That such people had been arrested was unknown until November 1925, over two years being occupied in their examination. They were tried *in camera* from February 26, 1926, till March 25th, when sentence of death was pronounced upon both of them. The nature of their crime was never disclosed, but was generally assumed to be high treason. The judge, Mr.

Tatematsu, who had conducted the preliminary trial, desiring a memento of so strange a case, visited the prison to get a photograph of the prisoners. The two were brought to one of the office rooms, and when the judge had the camera ready Fumi sat on the edge of Boku Retsu's chair and put her arm about his neck. Thus testifying that love still prevailed in the very shadow of the scaffold, they were photographed. Somehow a copy of the photograph got out and fell into the hands of the enemies of the Government. Horror and indignation were expressed to a degree that would have been excessive if the Government had betrayed the country into the hands of its enemies. The emotion was entirely hypocritical: it was part of the political game. The parties had little in the way of policy by which they recommended themselves to the electorate, and the Opposition generally attacked the Government only on such vague grounds as diplomatic weakness, extravagance, or slackness of official discipline. An actual case of such slackness was a godsend. This method of attack was preferred because it bound the Opposition to nothing if it succeeded. The photographing of a convict was not an everyday occurrence, and the Opposition ran no danger of being attacked on a similar charge. Judge Tatematsu resigned: the poor man had never supposed that he was doing wrong, and was greatly astonished at the storm he raised. Mr. Tokonami abandoned his working agreement and denounced the Government with the greatest vigour and severity. The affair lasted through the summer of 1926, and echoes were still heard of it until the end of the year. The Government refused to budge, and Saionji, the last of the Elder Statesmen, gave no sign. The storm died down at last. Its flashes had served to reveal the depths of unreality into which constitutional politics in Japan had sunk. Boku Retsu was not executed after all. The sentences of both were commuted to penal servitude for life, but Fumi contrived to hang herself in her cell. As the clamour of the Boku Retsu case died down, that regarding General Tanaka's alleged misuse of secret service money was revived. Both cases were finally overshadowed by the Matsushima brothels scandal, in which high officials were alleged to have enabled speculators to make money by giving them advance information about the Government's decision regarding the location of the new brothels. Mr. Minoura, a former Cabinet Minister, was deeply involved, and implicated the Premier himself, Mr. Wakatsuki, against whom he filed a complaint of perjury when he denied the implication.

In a year full of scandals it remains to record that the Japanese semi-official news agency, which had taken the place of Reuter, took a hand. It circulated a telegram purporting to be from one of its agents in China saying that the British-American Tobacco Co. and the Chartered Bank of India, Australia, and China were lending 50,000,000 *yen* to the North to aid it in its interminable civil war with the South. The *Mainichi*, of the million circulation, followed this up with an alleged telegram from one of its own correspondents to similar effect. The object was apparent. Japan was doing very well, both politically and commercially, out of the Chinese boycott of all things British, and the telegrams were fabrications intended to enhance the good effect. They succeeded. No rumours that could give any justification to the telegrams could be traced in the places of their alleged origin. The "Rengo" news agency promised to make an investigation, and remained thereafter silent. The *Mainichi* neither promised nor explained.

XL

THE TAISHO TENNO

TOWARDS the end of this year of sordid happenings the Emperor's health, precarious for seven years past, began to fail rapidly. In December it became apparent that he was on his death-bed, and the daily bulletins were scanned with anxious concern. The end came on Christmas Day, 1926.

Nothing lacked in the final honours rendered. The funeral was conducted with a stately magnificence, the interment taking place at a new site near the capital instead of at Momoyama, near Kyoto, in which district Japan's Emperors had been buried for so many centuries. His days had been marred by grave ill-health, and the forced seclusion was rather accentuated by the reverence paid to his illustrious father, the Emperor Meiji, whose memory became a patriotic cult of the most intense yet ubiquitous kind. When the Heir-Apparent, Prince Hirohito, became Regent, the most sedulous care was also taken to promote the idea of personal loyalty to him. Fate decreed that the Taisho Tenno should, while being Emperor of a Japan which had become third among the world's Powers, live a life almost as secluded as that of his ancestors, who were seldom seen by their subjects and whose very existence was hardly known to the world. Yet in this reign of fourteen years Japan witnessed changes no less remarkable than those seen in the previous reign. At its outset an entirely uneventful period seemed to lie before the country. It proved to be one of unprecedented activity, of undreamt-of prosperity, and of overwhelming misfortune. The chronicler of the period has to record many grave errors; but, while it is manifestly as impossible to forecast the new Emperor's reign as it was that of his father's, the brightest hopes arise from the blackest misfortunes. The new Emperor came to the Throne in a capital still bearing grievous traces of the destruction wrought three years before, but full of constructive energy and determination to attain to greater things. Many grave problems awaited solution at the outset of the new era. The only certainty was that they would all be tackled with energy and resolution.

INDEX

Abe, 41
Abe Iso, 57, 58
Adoption, 20
Agareff, 271
Akaike, General, 201-3, 270, 307
Akasaka Palace, 60, 298, 309
Akashi, General, 158
Alliance, Anglo-Japanese, 68, 71, 91, 123, 218-24
Amakasu, Captain, 300-1
Ando Masazumi, 251
Anesaki, Dr., 212
Antonoff, 267
Aoki, Dr., 211
Aoki Seichi, 329
Arahata, 233
Arishima Takero, 292-3
riyoshi Choichi, 236
Asano Wasaburo, 210-14
Asiatic Development Company, 99
Assassination, admiration for, 29, 41, 162, 248-54, 301
Awaya, 213

Balfour, Earl, 257
Banzai, General, 223
Barnardiston, General, 75
Bicycles, 51
Boku Retsu, 337-8
Borah, Senator, 255
British-American Tobacco Company, 66
Bushido, 72, 196, 279

California, 68, 102, 198, 220, 314
Chang Hsun, 40, 41, 86, 108
Chang Tso-lin, 89, 202, 275, 278, 287, 326-7, 334
Chang Tsung-hsiang, 98
Chicherin, 186, 262, 271, 273
Chientao, 32, 37, 159, 200-8
Chikamatsu, 46
Chinda, Viscount, 148

Chiushingura, 46
Choshu, 23
Clans, 23, 227
Colby, 220
Confucius, 62
Crown Prince, 225-9, 298, 305
Curzon, Marquis, 222
Czechs in Siberia, 129 *et seq.*, 178 *et seq.*, 264

Debuchi, 317
Deguchi Nao, 208
Deguchi Wanisaburo, 209-14
Den, Baron, 97, 118
Denikin, 270
Dietrichs, 273-7
Domae, 171
"Double Life," 113, 290
Drama, 46, 64, 147
Dyer, General, 205, 323

Eliot, Sir Charles, 139, 226
Emperor, Chinese (*see* Yuan Shih-kai)
Emperor, Coronation of, 82-9; breakdown in health, 176, 298; death, 340-1
Emperor, Korean, death of, 155
Empress-Dowager, death of, 43
Erimieff, 271
Esperanto, 214
Eta, 54, 151, 174, 254 (*see* Suiheisha)
Etsure, 321

Far Eastern Republic, 261-2, 271, 278
Feng Yu-hsiang, 326
Foreigners in Japan, 60, 318
Formosa, 52, 67, 68, 322
Forty-seven Ronin, 47, 249
Fujii, Rear-Admiral, 42, 48, 97
Fujimura, Baron, 199, 317

Fujishiro, Dr., 15 n.
Fukuda, General, 298
Fukuzawa, 61
Funatsu, 190, 315

Gaida, General, 134
Gary, Elbert, 102
Gempei wars, 23
Genro (or Elder Statesmen), 18–22, 29, 70, 92, 96, 260, 307, 338
Genroku Period, 63, 112
George V, King, 82, 164 n., 219
George, Lloyd, 153
Germany, war declared against, 71
Goto, 324
Goto, Viscount, 26, 39, 97, 132, 220, 241, 290, 303, 309
Graves, General, 179
Grey, Viscount, 20

Hamaguchi, 316, 318–20, 330, 337
Hanihara, 275, 314
Hany-eh-ping Company, 77
Hara, Major and Mrs., 276–7
Hara Sorejiro, 329
Hara Takashi, 79, 96–8, 120–1, 133, 195, 199, 226, 231, 243, 248–54, 281
Harding, President, 222, 256
Hasegawa, General, 97, 154, 157, 158, 201, 206
Hashimoto, 265
Hatano Akiko, 292–3
Hayakawa, 246
Hayashi, Baron, 98, 148, 190, 268
Higuchi, 274
Hioki Eki, 76, 80
Hiranuma, 243
Hirata, Viscount, 307
Horvath, General, 125, 138
Hosaka, Captain, 107
Hoshi Hajime, 217
Hsu, President, 223
Hsu Shu-cheng, 334
Hughes, C. E., 256–9
Hughes, William, 222

Ichiki Kitakuro, 330
Ichimatsu, 240
Inoué, 1st Marquis, 18, 19; 2nd Marquis, 80, 243, 259
Inukai, 26, 40, 80, 116, 123–4, 308, 316
Ishii (King of Bankrupts), 253
Ishii, Viscount, 92, 106–7, 161, 271, 273
Ishimitsu, General, 263
Ito Isaburo, 232–3
Ito Noe, 152–3, 301
Ito, Prince, 19
Ivanoff-Rinoff, 141
Iwamoto, 111

Janin, General, 142
Janson, 273
Joffe, 273–5, 290–2

Kagawa Toyohiko, 197, 236–8, 280, 284
Kajiwara, 193
Kalmikoff, 134–5, 139–41, 183, 196
Kamichika, 153, 194
Kamio, General, 74
Kaneko Fumi, 337
Kaneko, Viscount, 220
Kappel, 141, 196, 262
Karahan, 292, 322, 325
Katayama Sen, 57
Kato Sadakichi, Vice-Admiral, 73
Kato Tomosaburo, Admiral, 149, 223, 255, 283, 290, 294
Kato, Viscount, 70–1, 72, 76, 81, 91, 98, 177, 206, 222, 288, 308, 316–17, 330, 336–7
Katsura, Prince, 19, 22–30, 39, 97
Kawada Shiro, 122
Kawakami, 168, 291
Kelly and Walsh, raid on, 232
Kenseikai, 144, 195 et seq.
Keynes, J. M., 160 n.
Kiaochan, 71–4, 87
Kimura, Captain, 247
Kishii Seiichi, 242
Kishimoto Ryutaro, 144

INDEX

Kiuchi, 174
Kiyose, 206
Kiyoura, Viscount, 45, 127, 283, 305, 307
Kodama, 100
Kodera Kenkichi, 27, 92
Koga, Dr., 242–4
Koheikai, 189
Kokuminto, 26, 40, 195
Kokusuikai, 174, 230, 233, 252–3, 284–6
Kolchak, Admiral, 135–42, 177–8, 196, 264
Kopp, 336
Korean conspiracy, 31–38
Korean labourers, 299
Kotoku Denjiro, 57
Krasnoschekoff, Alexandra, 129, 184, 262
Krassin, 270
Kuge Peers, 19
Kuhara firm, 125
Kuo Sung-lin, 334
Kusunose, General, 31, 56
Kyochokai, 144, 165, 234, 239, 284

Lamont, T. W., 192–3, 198
Lansing, R., 107
Lebedeva, Nina, 185, 186
Lee, Lord, 222
Li Yuan-hung, 108
Lowell, Percival, 210 n.

McCune, Rev. G. S., 33, 34
Makino, Count, 148, 307
Manchuria, 68; extension of lease, 76, 78, 86, 94
Masumoto, 171–2
Matsudaira, 274–6
Matsui Sumako, 147
Matsukata Kojiro, 238
Matsukata, Prince, 19, 307
Matsumoto, Vice-Admiral, 46
Matsushima, 269, 272
Megata, Baron, 107
Meiji, Emperor, 16, 44, 82, 194
Merkuloff, 266–70, 273
Merlin, Martial, 325

Michaelovitch, Grand Duke George, 92
Midzumachi, Colonel, 205
Midzuno, Dr., 202, 283, 299, 307
Miki, 231
Minoura, 339
Miura, Viscount, 31, 98, 152, 307, 336–7
Mogi firm, 245
Monopolies, 67, 246, 279
Mori, Viscount, 29, 41, 45
Morito, 194, 332
Morphia, 86, 215–217
Motoda, 25
Motono, Viscount, 101, 123, 127, 132
Mowry, Rev. E., 157–8
Murasaki Shikibu, 50, 65
Murayama (Korea), 208
Murayama Ryohei, 136, 152
Murdoch, James, 15
Muto Sanji, 172

Nagase Hosuke, 107
Nakahashi, 279
Nakano, 243–4
Nakaoka Konichi, 249–51
Nakashoji, 199
Namba Daisuke, 305, 321
Neo-Shinto, 61, 209–214
Newspapers, 27, 59, 92, 107, 124, 205, 282, 302
Nichiren, 289
Nishihara loans, 99–102, 192, 319
Noda, 146
Nogi, General, 17, 18, 249

Oba Kaku, 107
Obata, 85, 148, 177, 190, 198, 223, 256, 263, 287
Ogawa, Dr., 329
Ogawa Umpei, 152
Oi, General, 262–5, 317
Oka, 243
Okada, 327–8
Okamura, Major, 205
Oki, Colonel, 204
Oki, Count, 151

Okuma, Marquis, 45, 72, 75, 87, 90, 95–6, 98, 163, 220, 224, 258–9
Okura, Baron, 97
Okura Hatsumi, 144
Omotokyo, 209–14
Oriental Colonization Company, 66
Oshikawa Norikichi, 143
Oshima, General, 132
Osugi Sakae, 57, 153, 194, 230, 300–1
Oura, Viscount, 80
Oyama, Prince, 21
Ozaki Yukio, 25, 27–9, 72, 75, 80, 84, 95, 101, 108, 124, 150, 168, 226, 231, 271, 329, 330

Petroff, 269

Red Cross, 187, 264
Regnault, 139
Reinsch, Paul S., 77, 119
Reuter, 78, 106, 208, 304, 339
Rikken Doshikai, 26, 42
Riots, 26–8
Rodo Sodomei, 251, 280, 285 (see Yuaikai)
Roninkai, 152, 217, 248–9, 317
Rozanoff, General, 180, 184
Russell, Hon. Bertrand, 237

Sakuma, General, 67
Saionji, Prince, 19–22, 25, 28, 148, 161–2, 260, 283, 307
Saito, Viscount, 23–25, 28, 46, 159, 200, 202, 204, 270
Sakai Toshihiko, 57, 194–5, 233, 332
Sakamoto, Baron, 265
Sakatani, Baron, 288, 317
Sasaki Toichiro, 242
Sasaki Yasugoro, 152
Sato Kojiro, General, 149
Satsuma, 23
Sei Shonagon, 66
Seiyukai, 27, 120, 195, 243

Semenoff, 130, 135, 138–142, 178, 196, 262–3
Sengoku, Dr., 327
Shaw, G. L., 206–8, 242, 281
Shibusawa, Viscount, 150, 234, 258
Shidehara, Baron, 197, 220, 316–17, 327, 333–4
Shima, 267
Shimada (Consul), 269
Shimada Saburo, 42, 66, 101, 124
Shimamura Hogetsu, 146
Shoda, 319
Shogun, 30
Siemens Schuckert, 35, 46
Stark, Admiral, 277
Stevens, Colonel John, 137
Sugimura Yotaro, 217
Suiheisha, 254
Sumitomo, Baron, 20
Sun Ping-hsi, 201
Sun Yat-sen, 40, 165, 287, 317
Suzuki Bunji, 114, 153, 236, 285
Suzuki firm, 69, 95, 116, 170, 319
Suzuki Fujiya, 279
Syndicate, Sextuple, 39–40, 103

Tachibana, General, 265–8
Taisho (meaning of), 36, 310
Takagi, 62
Takagi Masutaro, 155
Takahashi, 317
Takahashi, Viscount, 121, 167, 196, 279, 281, 285, 307, 316
Takao Heibei, 332
Takata firm, 97, 331–2
Takata Shinjiro, 144
Takayanagi, General, 180, 196, 263–5, 272, 274
Takekoshi Yosaburo, 95
Taketomi, 91
Tanaka (Ambassador), 336
Tanaka, Baron, 124, 132, 196–7, 265–6, 337–8
Tanaka Takao, Mrs., 172
Tatematsu, 338
Tazawa Gisuke, 284

INDEX

Tea Ceremony, 15, 63
Terauchi, Count, 31, 32, 38, 96–100, 115–19, 124, 127, 132, 201, 206 (*and see* Korean Conspiracy)
Thomas, Rev. J., 158
Tokodaiji, Count, 20
Tokonami, 61, 120, 173, 211, 228–9, 307, 337–8
Tokugawa, Marquis, 330
Tokugawa, Prince, 45, 221
Tokutomi, 47, 96, 288, 333
Tomidzu, Dr., 160
Toyama Mitsuru, 152
Treasures, Sacred, 82
Tripitzin, 182, 185, 186
Tsukada Kankaku, 107
Tsukamoto, 285
Tsumura, Dr., 113
Tuan Chi-jui, 101, 191
Turin, 269
Twenty-one Demands, 76–9, 87, 102, 105, 163, 193, 221, 258, 288

Uchida Ryohei, 152, 216–17
Uchida, Viscount, 124, 126, 161, 206, 220, 275, 283
Uehara, General, 21, 132, 276
Ungern, Baron, 141, 267
Universities, women at, 66
Utsunomiya, Rev., 194

Vanderlip, 198
Vickers & Company, 46, 47
Vologodsky, 138

Wada Toyoji, 234
Wakabayashi, 29

Wakatsuki, 316, 328–30, 337, 339
Wakayami, Dr., 265
Wales, Prince of, 282–3
Ward, Colonel John, 140 *n.*
Waseda University, 45
Wilson, President, 40, 102, 104, 154, 161, 163, 165, 192
Women in Universities, 66
Woods, Cyrus, 313–14

Yabuki, Baron, 317
Yamada, 249
Yamada, Colonel, 203
Yamagata, 1st Prince, 19, 70, 227, 260
Yamagata, 2nd Prince, 243
Yamamoto, 167
Yamamoto, Count, 29, 39, 42, 43, 44, 46, 97, 294, 305–6
Yamanashi, General, 276, 288
Yanagiwara, Lady, 44
Yashima Kajiko, 313
Yasuda Zenjiro, 248–9
Yasuoka, 243
Yi, Prince (*see* Emperor of Korea)
Y.M.C.A., 130–1, 154, 264, 272, 297
Yonemura, 332
Yoshino, Dr., 152
Yoshizawa, 322, 325
Young, Robert, 35
Yuaikai, 114, 153, 234–5, 237 (*see* Rodo Sodomei)
Yuan Shih-kai, 40, 42, 76, 85–89, 98, 103, 105
Yun Chi-ho, Baron, 35

Zeitlin, 270
Zen Philosophy, 15, 56, 98, 209

An environmentally friendly book printed and bound in England by www.printondemand-worldwide.com

PEFC Certified
This product is from sustainably managed forests and controlled sources
www.pefc.org
PEFC/16-33-415

MIX
Paper from responsible sources
FSC® C004959
www.fsc.org

This book is made entirely of chain-of-custody materials

#0173 - - C0 - 234/156/18 - PB